MARINADES

MARINADES

Dry Rubs, Pastes & Marinades for Poultry,
Meat, Seafood, Cheese & Vegetables

by Jim Tarantino

THE CROSSING PRESS, FREEDOM, CA 95019

Acknowledgments

People don't write a cookbooks by themselves. The writing of this one was truly a collaborative affair, and a contagious one at that. It started with friends and family who humored me when I arrived on their doorstep with zip-lock bags of wet food, and ended with those same folks returning the favor and flavor with their own recipes.

First, I want to thank my wife, Ellen, who really bore the brunt of this project. She was the eye of this hurricane that hit her kitchen incessantly, the first line of defense in shoring up faulty grammar and typos, and, at times, the last word on balancing the flavor of these recipes.

I want to thank my good friends who tasted, tested, and dropped recipes in my lap, such as Barbara Boswell, Nina Blum, Lisa Frank, Dunstan Harris, Jon Jividen, Holly Moore, Irene Rothschild, Dave and Stephanie Underwood, and Donna West, and my colleagues who cook for a living in the Delaware Valley and shared what they do best. And I want to thank Charlie Abdo and the staff at the North Star Bar, and Lynn Buono and the staff at Feast Your Eyes Catering, who took some of these recipes and made them fly during Philadelphia's Book and the Cook, as well as Judy Faye,

Project Coordinator, who always gave me free reign to throw the kind of party I wanted to during the event.

I'd like to thank cookbook author Elizabeth Rozin and food historian William Woys Weaver for their historical backup, as well as cookbook author Diana Kennedy for her much needed advice and encouragement.

I'd also like to thank my publisher, Elaine Gill, who gave me my ticket and the freedom and time to write the book, and Crossing Press sales manager Denny Hayes, who cheered this project from day one. Thanks also to Jane Marsh Dieckmann for the wonderful finishing touch and the indexing. And lastly I wish to thank my editor, Andrea Chesman, who besides putting up with my lightning strikes and computer viruses, brought my writing through this project gently and patiently.

While this book was being written, Ellen and I lost our mothers within two months of each other. They were our best fans and tipped us well too (with their compliments). They always had as much fun with our food as we did. This book goes out to the both of them.

Copyright © 1992 by Jim Tarantino
Cover design by David Charlsen
Photos courtesy of Digital Stock, photographer Joshua Ets-Hokin
Images © 1996 Photodisc Inc.
Interior art by Anne Marie Arnold
Printed in the U.S.A.
5th printing 1996

Library of Congress Cataloging-in-Publication Data
Tarantino, Jim.
    Marinades: dry rubs, pastes & marinades for poultry,
meat, seafood, cheese & vegetables / by Jim Tarantino.
        p. cm.
    Includes index.
    ISBN 0-89594-532-0 (cloth):—ISBN 0-89594-531-2 (paper)
    1. Marinades I. Title.
TX819.M26T37 1992   91-42574
641.7–dc20   CIP

CONTENTS

For Claire and Lila,

Thanks for the palates . . . they came in real handy!

1. About Marinades

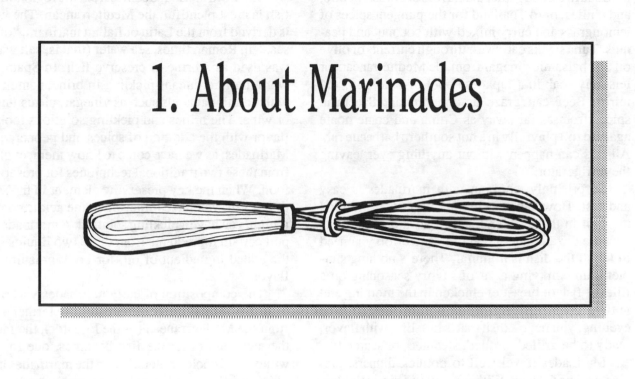

A cross continents, cultures, and cuisines, marinating is one of the most traditional and eclectic methods for adding flavor to food. A marinade is any liquid, paste, or rub that is applied to meats, fish, or vegetables to add flavor.

With a marinade, a chicken breast can travel to the Southwest and gather the flavors of citrus, cilantro, and chilies, or to Thailand for the pungent spices of lemongrass and curry mixed with coconut and peanuts. Tuna steaks can swim through currents of olive oil and balsamic vinegar from the Mediterranean, or leisurely soak in a Japanese pool of sake, soy, and mirin. Beef can graze among piquant Szechuan spices from as far away as China and come home again to roll playfully in a hot southern barbecue rub. All this can happen without anything ever leaving the refrigerator.

Surprisingly, cooking with marinades is easy and fast. How can a technique be fast, if the food must sit in the refrigerator for half a day? It's fast because the amount of real time and effort you need to finish the dish is minimal. There's nothing simpler than emptying a jar of savory seasoning on a fillet of fish or breast of chicken in the morning and letting your refrigerator do the cooking. Come evening, you have a dish that's bursting with flavor, ready to be grilled, broiled, steamed, or sauteed.

Marinades travel well to potluck dinners, picnics, and barbecues. With a couple of zip-lock plastic bags under your arm, filled with marinated salmon steaks or chicken wings, all you need is a hot grill or a warm saute pan, and you're ready to hold court. If you are spending a weekend at the shore or in the mountains, pack a couple of prepared marinades and add whatever fresh fish or meat is available at the local market. Marinated food is also perfect for boat galleys and RVs where cooking space and storage are at a premium.

Marinades can be a light and healthful alternative to heavy sauces filled with cream and butter. The calorie content of the dish is lower with no trade-off in flavor. Moreover, meat can be trimmed of more fat since the moisture (supplied by that fat) is returned to it by way of the nonsaturated oil in the marinade.

In the past, a marinade acted as a preservative, an antiseptic, and a tenderizer. Today we use marinades mostly to impart flavor.

The word marinade comes from the region where fish is most plentiful, the Mediterranean. The word is derived from the Latin or Italian marinara, "of the sea." In Roman times, sea water (that is, salt water) was used as a brine to preserve fish. In Spain, the word marimar means pickling in brine, sometimes with additional acids such as vinegar, citrus juices, or wine. The brines and pickling solutions took on flavor with the addition of spices and peppercorns. Marinades, as we have come to know them, evolved from these two traditional techniques for preserving food. When the key preserving element in the solution is salt, you have brine; when the acidic content is high, you have a pickling solution. A marinade can pull certain ingredients from these two liquids with the added ingredient of oil, for both moisture and flavor.

The composition of early marinades was often determined by a country's climate. The farther north from the Mediterranean (or the Equator), the fattier the meat and oilier the fish becomes, due to cold winters and cooler waters. There the marinades have a higher ratio of acid to oil in order to cut the richness of the fish or meat. The closer to the Equator, the leaner the meat becomes, and the marinade ingredient ratio is reversed: more oil is used in the marinade and sometimes more salt. Southern marinades tend to be spicier.

Marinades invaded Europe from every conceivable source. As populations migrated, they carried their food along with them. And that food had to be cured, brined, or marinated in order for it to travel well. The Mongol hordes gave north and central Europeans their first example of Chinese take-out food when they packed along crocks of marinated cabbage called kimchee (a spicy pickled cabbage that was soon to evolve into sauerkraut). The Vikings, as they toured the North Atlantic, noticed that herring traveled and smelled better when pickled, and therefore adapted the Mongolian cabbage pickling technique to herring.

Spicy brines arrived via the trade routes of the Middle East. Citrus marinades (known as escabeche) came up from the Moors in Africa into Spain. Those marinades were later taken to the Caribbean by the Spanish and used by African slaves to create a dish known as escouvitched fish.

When Christopher Columbus made his travels, eating was changed forever on both sides of the Atlantic. Spain got some chilies and in turn left the New World citrus. Citrus groves were planted by Spanish missionaries in Florida, California, and Mexico. We now have citrus and hot peppers in some Spanish marinated tapas and the seviche in the Yucatan Peninsula.

Even Asia felt the heat of New World explorations as the Portuguese peppered their trade routes with spicy chilies from South America. They went as far as India, China, and Southeast Asia, as well as ports of call around the horn of Africa.

In Asia, each country has its own distinctively flavored marinades. Garam masala and curry powder are the flavoring elements in Indian marinades. Thai marinades play off the sour flavors of lemongrass and lime, the heat of chili peppers, and the sweet balancing action of coconut or molasses. The Chinese used spicy marinades in the South and milder marinades in the North. Pockets of spice appeared in Hunan and Szechuan, while subtle spice blends appeared in some southern regions. The Japanese used simple ingredients that required a briefer marinating time.

Today's marinades mix cultures and cuisines in a culinary cross-pollination of flavors and seasonings. East-West marinades of Asian spices are blended with American chilies, Mediterranean olive oils, and Middle Eastern condiments in a new wave that redefines the way we create and think about flavor.

How Marinades Work

Before we talk about how marinades work, let's see how they don't work. First of all, marinades do not tenderize food. They soften or denature it. Tenderizing occurs in food when muscle tissue is separated, torn, or bruised. Tenderizing, for example, occurs when a cook pounds a chicken breast or a veal scallop with a kitchen mallet. Marinades soften or denature tissue with their acid ingredients. To explain it better, let's take a typical household kitchen sponge. When dry, it's like a lightweight brick. If you were to take that sponge and score its surface with a serrated kitchen knife, that texture appears soft, because you are breaking down or tenderizing the surface. Now add a few drops of water to the other side of the sponge and it becomes soft. Add a lot of liquid and it becomes mushy. The muscle structure of meat is like a sponge. Meat can be tenderized by bruising the surface, or softened by a marinade. It's the acid component in a marinade that triggers the enzymatic or softening reaction (not the presence of liquid); in fact, the marinade can also draw moisture *out*. Some marinades contain oil to replace the missing moisture and to add a little flavor.

Marinades do not penetrate deeply into muscle tissue. When a marinade hits the surface of meat or poultry, the muscle tissue softens and expands; in some cases this stops penetration. In most meat and poultry, surface penetration is minimal. The amount of penetration is determined by the grain of the meat, its texture, and temperature. Skin is a natural protective covering designed to keep the elements out. Dry rubs and pastes bite into the surface of meat and poultry (with skin on) better than baths or wet marinades because these interact chemically with the food's natural moisture and are absorbed more readily. I've found that I sometimes get better penetration using fish steaks rather than fillets because of the grain of the cut.

Even if surface penetration is minimal, food can still absorb tremendous amounts of flavor from marinades, more so than a sauce that finishes the dish at meal time. Take a raw steak and half a raw onion, place them together in a plastic bag, and leave them overnight in the refrigerator. The following morning that steak will smell of raw onion. The same happens if you use a stick of butter instead of the steak. Because food is porous, it will pick up the marinade's aromas and flavors while it's marinating. The flavor absorption is even greater during the cooking process when you're using a marinade as a basting liquid.

Marinades are made up of three parts with three specific flavor roles. The first is acid, such as wine, vinegar, citrus juice, or yogurt, acting as the softener. That softening actually speeds up the cooking process. But there's a price to pay for that process: moisture is lost. The way to put some of that moisture back is to add oil to the marinade. Though oil is primarily a moisturizer, it is also a flavor element.

Finally, there are the aromatics that give the marinade its aroma and flavor. They can be anything from fresh or dry herbs to spices, liqueurs, onions, scallions, and shallots.

As the acid in a marinade softens the meat, moisture goes back into it by way of the oil with a collection of aromatics tagging along for the ride.

Temperature is a deciding factor on how quickly a food will absorb a marinade. The lower the temperature, the slower the chemical reactions that occur. It's a known fact that cold will tighten up the muscle tissue a bit. This explains why marinating at room temperature is faster than marinating in the refrigerator. But it's riskier. When marinating food on a counter in a warm kitchen, you run the risk of

spoilage and bacteria growth, even when the food is submerged. My advice is to take your time and marinate it in the fridge.

A marinade is not an antiseptic. It lacks the acid concentration of a pickling solution. The acid in the marinade may kill certain strains of bacteria over long periods of time—from several hours or up to a couple of days. But that kind of time spread is chancy. Most of the marinating in Europe and Colonial America before the coming of refrigeration was done in cool, dark places, such as root cellars, not in warm kitchens.

The degree to which food is covered also influences a marinade's effectiveness. The greater the coverage, the faster the marinating process. However, marinating a large cut of meat requires quite a bit of marinade. Therefore, I recommend marinating in a tightly sealed plastic bag with the air squeezed out, thus reducing the amount of marinade needed to do the job.

Tips & Techniques

Making Marinades

Making marinades is easy. You can assemble most of the marinade recipes in this book in a few minutes. But the order and the method in which you combine ingredients are important. What you want is a stable marinade that has correct distribution of oil, acid, and aromatics. A successful marinade should be an emulsion, with particles and fluids merged.

When making a marinade, you have to deal with two elements, oil and water. By water I'm referring to the acidic liquid, wine, vinegar, citrus juice, or fruit juice, the primary content of which is water. Oil and water simply do not mix; oil floats on water. An unemulsified marinade will have oil coating the food with acidic and aromatic elements floating around it. Here's what's needed to bring the two together. Whisking your oil a little bit at a time into the water will break down the oil into tiny droplets that will remain suspended or emulsified. Shaking a marinade will produce a similar effect, as the agitation between the two liquids works to emulsify as well. A blender can also be used. It is better than a food processor because its container is narrow.

An emulsified marinade will not be thick like mayonnaise. It will be a cloudy liquid. A marinade's emulsion is temporary. When the oil content of the marinade is less than 20 percent, the emulsion can break down in a matter of hours. Should you make a marinade for use the following day, store it in a glass jar which you can shake. There's not much risk of a marinade breaking down while it is in the refrigerator. First, the surface of meat and poultry contain some fat or oils that act as emulsifying agents. Second, the cold temperature in a refrigerator increases oil's viscosity.

Equipment

When it comes to equipment, I can count on a single hand the number of pieces you need to start marinating. What is imperative is that every surface a marinade contacts must be nonreactive metal; that is, there can be no aluminum foil, pots, utensils, or containers which will interact with the marinade's acid. You'll have aluminum and acid interacting instead of flavor penetration.

The single appliance that I would have a hard time parting with is a blender. A blender will grind spices, chop shallots, garlic, and ginger, and emulsify the oil in marinades in just one pass. You also need an inexpensive grater for citrus peel and ginger, a glass or wooden reamer for citrus, steel measuring spoons, and glass measuring cups. Marinades are user friendly and easy on your budget.

Traditionally, marinating containers were earthen crocks that would sit covered in a root cellar. Today we don't have root cellars or crocks; we have to rely on our refrigerators and other containers. Glass or ceramics are good as marinating containers. Pyrex baking dishes are perfect for marinating cuts of food that are no more than one-inch thick. Deep ceramic bakeware and mixing bowls work as well, but beware of ceramics. They may contain lead-based paints or glazes. As pretty as they are, I wouldn't recommend serving acid-based food in them, let alone marinating something for several hours in one of them. The plain, old garden variety ceramic mixing bowls (glazed without lead) found at your local hardware store work just fine. Terra cotta containers are too porous to be used for marinating. They absorb flavors, odors, and food color like a sponge. Above all, be sure that the containers are free of cracks, as these are breeding spots for bacteria.

Overall, my first preference for marinating containers is glass. Pyrex dishes are good, but what I really find handy are old wide-mouth peanut butter jars. They're wide enough to handle a couple of salmon steaks, a pound of shrimp, or a couple of chicken breasts. I lay the jars on their side in the refrigerator and they're great for turning food. And from an ecological standpoint, they're recyclable.

Avoid soft plastic or rubber containers that pick up odors and can be easily stained. My favorite marinating containers are one-gallon zip-lock plastic bags, which can hold up to one pound of food and two to three cups of marinade. I suggest that you use them only once. For bigger cuts of meat, such as briskets, roasts, and whole turkey breasts, I use large plastic oven-roasting bags. These bags travel better and, since they're disposable, you never have to worry about washing them or remembering to bring them back from a potluck dinner.

On Marinating Times

The tighter the food tissue, the longer the marinating time. Fish with its loose soft tissue can absorb a marinade faster than a beef brisket, which is generally considered a tough or dense cut of meat. Most of the marinade recipes in this book can be used interchangeably with meat, chicken, or fish, but consider the texture of the dish before you begin.

Do not leave food in its marinade beyond its recommended time. Overmarinated food will cook unevenly. You can tell when food is overmarinated just by looking at it before you start to cook. Fish will become slightly opaque; salmon lightens to a light pink, and tuna turns a light gray, just as fish in a seviche turns opaque. Chicken breasts will turn white and beef light gray. When that happens, pat the food dry and strain out the marinade's solids. Rub the solids lightly onto the food surface, wrap in plastic wrap, and refrigerate until you're ready to cook. For ideas on how long to bathe your favorite food, see the chapters on vegetables, fish, poultry, and meat.

Don't Reuse Marinades

When marinating raw meats, such as chicken or turkey, some blood will naturally seep into the marinade, and there is a risk of salmonella bacteria. The danger is great. Don't use that same marinade again on another batch of meat. Also, fresh aromatic veggies, such as onions, shallots, or scallions will become limp after a few days in the refrigerator. Herbs and spices will usually adhere to the meat, enroute to the grill or skillet, thus thinning out a good deal of the marinade's aromatic element. Finally, the alkalis present in some ingredients, such as peppercorns, will break down in the acid found in wine, vinegars, or citrus and will cause them to lose some of their bite. It just isn't sensible to reuse marinades. You can make up a quantity of your favorite marinade ahead of time, but add the fresh ingredients and dry aromatics the day you use it.

Basting

After removing your food from the marinade, you may want to use the leftover marinade as a basting liquid. You will need to heat it first. You can cook it in a microwave for about three minutes at full power or bring it to a low boil and then remove it from the heat. Not only do you avoid the fire-hose effect, that is, cold liquid on a hot surface, but you kill bacteria. The worst thing you can do is to brush a lukewarm marinade over a grilled chicken breast and then serve. It simply transfers bacteria from the marinade to the basting brush to the chicken to the plate and ultimately to your guests. When basting on a grill, brush sparingly. Don't pour, as oil in any form is a fuel and, when dropped on hot coals, it will cause flare ups and smoky food.

Sauces

To use a marinade as a sauce, strain the marinade and gently warm it over a low heat, stirring constantly. The more oil you have in a marinade, the more likely it will separate during a high heat reduction or pan deglazing. A marinade with an oil content of 25 percent or more will throw off oil much the same way stock will throw off its fat content, but it is harder to skim off the oil in a marinade. Marinades are fairly thin so they need to be combined with a demiglaze or reduced poultry or veal stock to give them some density and additional flavor. I use two parts stock to one part marinade. Adding butter to emulsify the marinade is a possibility, but then you lose the option of a lowfat meal.

Most of the fish marinades make wonderful light sauces with no additional ingredients. Before serving, you may want to add one to two tablespoons of citrus juices, one to two tablespoons of fresh herbs (preferably of the same kind you used in the recipe), and a few turns from your peppermill, as the citric acid, herbs, and pepper will have burned off during the cooking.

Cooking Marinated Foods

Some of my friends regard cooking as a form of alchemy, complete with sorcerers (chefs), incantations (recipes), and secret ingredients. Thank goodness there's more common sense than mystery in preparing food. With a few exceptions, most of the recipes that follow can be prepared by sauteing, stir-frying, broiling, braising, steaming, or smoking and grilling. I've added a chart at the back of this section with suggested recipes to help you match marinades and techniques.

No recipe can detail the different heating properties of a cast iron skillet compared to a copper saute pan. The use of an electric or gas oven, the freshness of ingredients, your own palate, and the mood you're in while measuring and cooking can alter a finished dish. Trust your senses; they're your most important kitchen tools. The first thing to do when cooking marinated food is to let it sit at room temperature for about 30 minutes (no longer for poultry) before you begin to cook. If you remove the food from the marinade, it will come to room temperature more quickly. This will also enable the food to cook more evenly so that you'll avoid raw or cold centers that could still harbor bacteria. The proper internal temperature for cooked food varies with each food group. Check the specific food chapters for safe internal temperatures and approximate cooking times.

Sauteing, Frying, and Stir-Frying. In sauteing the food is cooked quickly in a lightly oiled saute pan or frying pan over direct heat. Oil is used to keep the food from sticking to the surface of the pan. You'll need to shake some marinade off your food before sauteing. If your food is dripping wet with marinade when you drop it in a hot saute pan, you may set off your smoke alarm with the steam.

The terms sauteing and panfrying are often used interchangeably, but one of the basic differences is the amount of fat used and the temperature. With panfrying, fat is used as a cooking medium and a good part of the food is submerged in the fat or oil and cooked at a higher temperature than with sauteing. The oil temperature should be at least 350°F so the oil will not penetrate the food and give it a greasy feel in the mouth.

Stir-frying is an Asian gift to western kitchens. Usually peanut oil is used as a heating medium, sometimes combined with chili or oriental sesame oil to give the dish deeper flavor. A well-seasoned wok is worth its weight in spices for this method because its curved sides are perfect for tossing small cuts of food. Smaller cuts of food are essential for even heating. The advantage of stir-frying marinated food is speed. It's faster than sauteing in a flat-bottom pan.

The wok can also be used to poach seafood like shrimp or scallops quickly in a marinade. You can turn your poached food the same way you turn your stir-fried ingredients.

Oven Broiling and Roasting. I use oven broiling as an indoor substitute for outdoor grilling. Granted the flavor from a broiler is not even close to grilling, but you do get a surprising amount of the marinade's flavor. Oven broiling differs from roasting in that you use smaller cuts of food with shorter cooking times. With oven broiling you can use your marinade as a baste for added flavor.

Oven roasting is primarily a slow, dry-cooking process. Roasting produces a dark crusty exterior with a moist interior. Since this is a dry-cooking process, basting your cut of food with your marinade simultaneously adds flavor as well as needed moisture. Another tip for adding moisture is something I first learned when roasting a Thanksgiving turkey. I placed a pan of ice cubes on the floor of the oven for instant steam, which gives added moisture for a wonderful, succulent turkey, with perfect crisp golden crackling.

Braising. With braising, the marinade becomes the cooking medium to steam flavor into a cut of food. Braising is really low simmering or wet roasting in a tightly covered pot after the meat is lightly browned. Tougher cuts of beef, pork, or veal are preferred for braising. Poultry can be braised, but not for the same length of time.

The braising liquid or marinade should come about halfway up the side of the cut that you are using. You may have to double your marinade recipe or add additional wine or stock. Also, since braising is a moist way of cooking, you'll need less oil in the marinade, which will break down during the cooking process anyway.

Steaming. Steaming is one of the best ways to infuse fish with the flavors of your marinade. You can steam fish in a vegetable steamer or small cake rack in a large covered pot or dutch oven. One of my favorite methods of steaming for both flavor and table presentation is in parchment paper or banana leaves, which are available frozen in Asian and Spanish grocery stores. I place vegetables and aromatics in the center of the parcel, soak it with marinade, place the cut of fish on top, seal, and steam. The advantage of using banana leaves is that they impart a wonderful flavor. They also can be steamed on the grill for additional flavor. See the recipe for Tamarind-Marinated Pompano Steamed in Banana Leaves in Chapter 7.

Smoking and Grilling. Marinades are practically synonymous with grilling. It's not coals, charcoal, or butane that power most grills, but marinades. I like to think that marinades were the flavorful spark that ignited the grill explosion. I also think that smoking and grilling are the best ways to cook marinated food.

The process of smoking or grilling food may be pretty straightforward, but there is a radical, delightful change of flavor when you use an outside grill instead of your kitchen broiler. It's a real pleasure to experiment with seasoned smoke as an added flavor ingredient. However, ultimately you have to taste the food first, and the smoke second.

Outdoor gas grills, unless you add soaked wood chips or chunks, are more neutral in imparting flavor than charcoal grills. But the advantage is an instant heat source. Charcoal grills will give you more flavor and will burn hotter, reaching surface temperatures of up to 700°F if you are using lump hardwood charcoal, which is perfect for grilling a good steak.

Precise cooking times and temperatures for outdoor cooking are about as easy to forecast as the weather. In fact, you're dealing with as many variables as the weather: the amount of moisture in the coals, the thickness of meat, and so on. And unless it's a gas grill, no two fires will burn as hot or as long. So how do you determine when the coals are ready or not? The tried-and-true hand test really works. First, wait until the fire dies down and your coals are ash gray. Hold your hand an inch above the rack in your grill. For a hot fire, with coals glowing with a red edge, three to four seconds is about all you can stand. A moderate fire, without the red edge, allows you to hold out your hand for six to eight seconds before you react. Shellfish, small cuts of firm fish, small cuts of skinless poultry, and only the most tender cuts of lamb, pork, veal, or beef can handle a hot fire. The larger the cut, the longer your cooking time, and the lower the temperature. With a large cut, you may want to consider smoking or cooking over low indirect heat like a southern pit barbecue (see the Smokehouse method) or over a smaller fire. The same idea applies to cooking indoors. Use high-heat broiling or sauteing for small cuts and slow oven roasting for larger cuts.

I don't have a verdict on wood chips versus wood chunks (or logs), but I'll tell you what my nose thinks. I get more flavor from the chunks and logs than I do from packaged smoking chips. There is no way of knowing if a bag of chips is all mesquite or hickory or if it has a little filler added. Think of the surge of popularity of smoking chips in the last few years and then think of the last time you drove past a mesquite or hickory farm. In fact, when a cooking magazine did a taste test on mesquite chips a few years back, they complained about the lack of flavor intensity. I took the test one step further, and I found that an equal weight of mesquite wood chunks packs a lot more flavor than the same amount of commercial wood chips. And yes, wood chunks can be soaked. One thing to note, however, is that placing a piece of chicken or beef over a hot grill with wood chips for 10 minutes or so will give you merely hints of a smoked flavor. For a more seasoned smoke flavor, indirect cooking or cold smoking is the way to go.

Hickory, mesquite, and oak are aromatic hardwoods. Because of their density, these woods will burn hotter and smoke longer than some fruit woods, and they will throw off more aroma than charcoal briquettes and lump hardwood charcoal. They take longer to come up to their heat peaks, but they do hang in a lot longer once they get there. So when timing dinner for your guests, double up your fire-up times when cooking with hardwoods.

Which wood to use and when? My two favorite barbecue pits in Philadelphia go either way. Dwight's in West Philadelphia prefers hickory for their short ribs, while Mama Rosa's in North Philadelphia is strictly a mesquite user. I like them both. I love a hickory-smoked turkey breast marinated and basted with a sweet plum marinade. Then again, I couldn't imagine beef brisket without a spicy rub and a slow smoke over mesquite. Perhaps it's a flavor I associate with bacon or ham, but hickory seems to have the most pronounced flavor of the three. Mesquite burns the hottest of the seasoned woods with heat up to 900°F but can vary wildly in scent from a sweet to a slightly bitter aroma. Each batch can be different, so try a little first, then stand downwind, sniff, and test. Oak has a smoother and more neutral flavor. Dried herbs and grapevine trimmings are so subtle that I prefer to get those flavors by adding fresh herbs to the marinade.

Cutting down trees just for smoking woods has an environmental impact according to cookbook author Diana Kennedy. "Mesquite grows in arid areas and actually provides shade to cattle, as well as being a traditional food source in the form of mesquite meal (from the pods) for Native Americans." She suggests using fruit woods, such as apple or cherry (wood trimmings only) from your own area as an alternative to cutting down trees just to smoke food.

Smokehouse Method

When most people think of preparing smoked food, they think of salty brines plus days in a smokehouse. You can bypass the brine by using your favorite marinade and reduce the time with the following technique.

With a kettle grill (or any covered grill) and a wok you can get that real smokehouse flavor at home. The advantage is that your meat and poultry will retain much more moisture, and they can be seasoned with the smoky aromas of hickory or mesquite. Here's how to start.

What you'll need is a kettle (Weber) grill, a Chinese wok with a lid, but without wooden handles, and a charcoal chimney that will enable you to load the grill with smoking coals. The chimney is available in most cookware stores and some hardware stores. It's inexpensive and worth its weight in gold. You'll need some trimmings of hickory, mesquite, alderwood, or any of the fruit woods. The trimmings should be soaked in water for at least 30 minutes before you add them.

Remove the top grill or grate from the kettle and place the wok in the middle of the bottom charcoal grate. Cover the wok with its lid and add the coals around the outside of the wok. Here's where the charcoal chimney really earns its keep. It's easier and faster to start your coals in the chimney and pour them around the covered wok than to get them lit in the grill at this point. Remove the lid from the wok and fill the wok about 2/3 full with your basting liquid. You can really be creative by adding any leftover marinades, apple cider (if you're smoking a pork loin or turkey), orange juice for duck, red wine for beef, etc. When the charcoal is ash gray add the wet smoking woods, replace the top grill, and position your meat or fish directly over the wok. Cover the grill with its lid and follow the instructions for indirect cooking times with your covered grill for various types meat and fish. This method is called "indirect" because the food is never placed directly over its heat source.

Finally, a safety tip: When you remove your succulent, marinated creation from the grill or smoker, don't put it back in the container in which you marinated it because bacteria are still present. Either clean the dish thoroughly and keep it warm in the oven until serving time, or simply get another dish. Protect yourself.

Matching Techniques and Recipes		
Technique	Group	Recipe
Sauteing	Fish and Shellfish Poultry Meat	Soft-Shell Crabs with Thai Coconut Marinade Sauteed Duck Breast with Pomegranate-Cognac Marinade Cognac-Marinated Veal Chops
Frying	Fish and Shellfish Poultry	Pecan-Breaded Catfish with Mustard-Bourbon Marinade Thai Fried Chicken
Stir-Frying	Vegetables Poultry Meat	Stir-Fried Carrots in a Cinnamon Marinade Five Spice Chicken Stir-Fry Oriental Beef and Broccoli Stir-Fry
Oven Broiling	Fish and Shellfish Poultry Meat	Cider-Marinated Salmon Grilled Fillets Thai Marinated Chicken with a Cashew Sauce Tenderloins with Wild Mushroom Marinade
Roasting	Poultry Meat	Roast Chicken with Creole Mustard-Bourbon Marinade Marinated Roast Rack of Lamb
Braising	Vegetables Fish and Shellfish Meat	Braised Chanterelles Braised Shad with White Wine Marinade Braised Beef with Provençal Red Wine Marinade
Steaming	Fish and Shellfish	Salmon Steamed in a Japanese Marinade Tamarind-Marinated Pompano Steamed in Banana Leaves
Smoke and Grilling		Just about all of the recipes

2. Stocking
the Pantry

There's a good chance that most of the ingredients for making marinades are sitting in your pantry, or in the back of your refrigerator. Like most cooks, I use the front six inches of my refrigerator, while all those honey-apricot mustards, blackberry vinegars, and jalapeño jellies live in a retirement community for condiments in the back. For me, marinades are the perfect way to do some tasty and imaginative refrigerator housekeeping.

You can easily classify the basic marinade ingredients according to shelf life—ingredients are either fresh or they are stable staples. Fresh ingredients can be acidic as in fresh oranges, lemons, and limes or aromatics such as fresh herbs, shallots, or ginger. Most ingredients with a limited shelf life fall into that group, including opened oils. Natural fresh foods are not suspended in time, but are always undergoing enzymatic changes. Oil, once opened, interacts with air and begins a slow decomposition process; at that point you need to store it in the refrigerator as you would a fresh ingredient.

Stable staples are vinegars, liqueurs, dried herbs and spices, mustards, condiments, and sweeteners, such as molasses and honey. Within this group are oriental condiments, such as hoisin, oyster, soy, and fish sauces. Also in this group are dried chilies, dried fruit, and even sun-dried tomatoes. However nothing lasts indefinitely. Kitchen heat is the primary cause for flavor loss of stable staples, and even dry ingredients lose their quality over time. The ideal temperature for storing these ingredients is around 60°F. These ingredients will maintain their flavor for longer stretches if properly stored; and they're easy to keep on hand as a foundation to build on with fresh ingredients.

In substituting stable staples for fresh ingredients, remember that not only is there a taste difference but also a flavor intensity. Be judicious with dry aromatics, and generous with fresh. I like a three to one ratio of fresh versus dry aromatics for some of the more piquant and pungent spice aromatics and a two to one ratio for most substitutes.

Marinades are easy to make on a moment's notice as long as you keep the basic formula in mind: Acid + Oil + Aromatics = Flavor. There is also one rule of thumb that applies to your choice of ingredients, that is, flavor in—flavor out. If it doesn't have flavor before you put it in a marinade, it's not going to add any flavor to the food coming out of it. Go for the finest, freshest, quality ingredients you can find. It makes all the difference.

Acids

Acid helps stimulate your taste buds. Most foods contain a certain amount of naturally generated acid, but the amount is really too little to use in a marinade. If the ingredients you are combining are particularly sweet, or if the recipe has a high oil content, acid will help bring the marinade into balance with a little bit of tang. The acid in a marinade can come from vinegar, wine, fruit juice, or dairy products. The chief advantage of vinegars, wines, and champagne over fresh juice and dairy products is their longevity. Vinegar holds its bite a little longer in the cooking process than wine, champagne, or fruit juice. Marinades that contain fruit juice instead of vinegar are smoother, with generally less pucker on the sides of one's mouth.

Vinegar, wine, and fruit juice can be combined within a marinade to balance the sharpness. Lemon juice and grated lemon zest pair wonderfully with balsamic vinegar to form the basis of Mediterranean-style marinades. A light berry-flavored Beaujolais wine with orange juice and grated zest can give hints of Sangria to a red wine marinade. Sauternes combined with lime juice and aromatic ginger gives a wonderful flavor to grilled shrimp.

Citrus

Citrus is rich in vitamin C. The higher the acidic level of citrus, the more difficult it is to drink it straight. The easier it is to swallow, the lower the acid level. Conversely, the more pucker behind the juice, as in lemon or lime, the more bite to the marinade. Peak-season citrus fruit tends to be heavier, which means a higher and sweeter juice content. When buying freshly squeezed citrus juices in soft plastic containers, transfer them to glass bottles or jars and refrigerate them to extend their shelf life. Lemon juice will interact with soft plastic and shouldn't be frozen in it. The recipes that follow will always call for freshly squeezed juice. Bottled lemon or lime juice are not good substitutes. Both lemons and limes have about the same acid content when ripe. Too much lemon or lime juice will discolor dark meat over long marinating stretches and should be avoided. Use red wine instead.

High-acid citrus juices can denature or soften food faster than some wines but they lose their bite during the cooking process. I like to keep some fresh lemon or lime juice on the side to add at the last minute to bring up the tang before I serve the dish.

Lemons. Lemons impart a neutral flavor in a marinade. You can feel their presence, but not necessarily their flavor (which comes from the grated zest). They're grown year-round and are at their peak in mid-summer with thin-skinned, juicy fruit. Choose lemons with smooth, brightly colored skins without tints of green, which indicate that they were picked before their time. An average lemon yields three to four tablespoons of juice and about two teaspoons of grated zest. They last for about two weeks wrapped in plastic in the fridge.

Limes. Limes are used extensively in the marinades of Asia, the Southwest, and the Caribbean. Limes impart a tropical flavor, and their juice and zest have a more pronounced flavor than lemons.

Although limes are available year-round, off-season limes in late winter and early spring tend to be pulpy, juiceless, and expensive. Peak season limes from May to August are dark green and filled with juice that can freeze well for up to six months. An average-size lime yields about two to three tablespoons of juice and about one teaspoon of grated zest. They last about two weeks wrapped in plastic in the fridge.

Juice Oranges, Tangerines, and Grapefruit. These low-acid citrus fruits make up in flavor what they lack in bite. They may need to be supplemented with either lemons or limes in order to activate a marinade. Juice oranges are the citrus of choice among the orange family, yielding about one-quarter to one-third cup juice and about two tablespoons of grated peel. The zest is the most flavorful and the juice is the sweetest. Tangerines can be delightful in most orange-based or lemon-based marinades. The tropical combination of grapefruit and orange juice can give a marinade a savory sourness.

Vinegars

Vinegars have been around almost as long as wine. Vinegar has been used throughout history as a preserving agent and for medicinal purposes. Next to salt, it's one of the oldest condiments. The acidic level of vinegar is measured by percentage on the label, from 4 to 5 percent being mild to 7 percent being a bit sharper.

Shelf life for flavored fruit or herb vinegars is three to four months; wine and rice vinegars, and balsamic vinegars hold on to their flavor for a good deal longer. Most vinegars hold their tang for about a year, but not necessarily their flavor.

Distilled white vinegar, which is extracted from a grain alcohol mixture, is rather harsh in the mouth and without much taste. It should be avoided in marinades.

Cider Vinegar. Made from fermented apple cider, cider vinegar is probably the most popular domestic vinegar. Cider vinegar plays a supportive role in marinades; it needs other flavors around it. Cider vinegar becomes sweeter when cooked and is ideal in marinated dishes that are going to be smoked or roasted over long periods of time. Its flavor is too strong for delicate fish, working better in full-bodied marinades for poultry, pork, or beef.

Fruit and Herbal Vinegars. I use commercial fruit and herbal vinegars mainly in marinades that have fruit or herbs as their predominant flavor. These vinegars combine best with nut oils. I've successfully substituted raspberry vinegar in place of sherry or sherry vinegar in Asian marinades having a peanut oil base. However, these vinegars will clash with fruity, extra virgin olive oil.

Herbal vinegars stand a better chance of combining with olive and grapeseed oils. These vinegars can be made at home; see Chapter 3 for some easy recipes.

Balsamic Vinegar. Imported from Italy, balsamic vinegar is made from white Trebbino grapes boiled down to a caramelized syrup. It has as much acid as other vinegars, but it is the aging process in oak boards that smoothes the edge off this vinegar and gives it its color. The delicate sweetness is combined with just enough tartness and body. It can be used on red snapper as well as strawberries. Balsamic vinegar is graded by age: the longer it's in the cask, the better the quality and higher the price.

True balsamic vinegar comes from the region of Modena. Beware of inferior grades without that provenance. Balsamic vinegar pairs well with Dijon-style mustard. I add a tablespoon or two if the mustard is too dominant in a marinade. There are no substitutes for balsamic vinegar's flavor, but a good-quality sherry vinegar shouldn't throw your marinade recipe out of balance if used sparingly.

Wine Vinegars. Good-quality wine vinegars are really made from drinkable wines, not good wines that have turned. Vinegar making is as a much a controlled process as wine making. The more a wine vinegar is aged the less harsh it feels in the mouth. In other words, age equals smoothness.

The acidity of most of the imported red wine vinegars can be pretty high. The trick behind determining quality is simple. It should have some red wine character behind it. That is, you can determine the taste of wine behind the sharpness. Some red wine vinegars will have berry or fruity flavors, while others can be woody and earthy. As with white wine vinegar, you're looking for taste over tang. Imported red wine vinegars have more depth and less harshness in spite of their higher acidic levels than their domestic counterparts. Red wine vinegar can be used to make raspberry or blueberry vinegar. They are the vinegar of choice for beef marinades and are great for deglazing a skillet.

White wine vinegar and champagne vinegar can be made from either red or white wine. They can be either domestic or imported. There have been some chardonnay vinegars produced on the West Coast, which leads me to believe that eventually we may even see wine vinegar varietals on the condiment shelves of gourmet stores. I use white wine vinegar in a marinade when I'm looking for a neutral acid. White wine vinegars take well to herbal infusions.

Sherry Vinegar. Imported sherry vinegar from Spain can be exquisite, with a nutty aroma and a hint of brandy. Like balsamic vinegar, sherry vinegar is aged in wooden casks. It is flexible enough in flavor to be used in Asian marinades and is excellent paired with nut oils in marinades.

Rice Wine Vinegar. Oriental rigeloine vinegar has less bite than its western cousin, white wine vinegar. It has a lower acidic level, making it a bit a softer in the mouth. Rice wine is used in Asian marinades to counteract soy sauce and oriental sesame oil. It cuts some of the oil's nuttiness, which can easily overpower a dish. Rice wine vinegar is good for marinating delicate fish.

Wines

Is it really necessary to use the wine that you'll be serving as part of the marinade? No, but it's essential that it's a wine that you are able and willing to drink. Don't marinate with commercial cooking wines. There are lots of sensibly priced and tasteful alternatives. And don't use opened wine that has been sitting in your refrigerator for a week. If you're not willing to serve it in a glass, don't soak good food in it.

Red Wine. Young full-bodied red wines, such as Rhônes, Chateauneuf du Papes, Riojas, and Chianti Reservas, make great marinades. They don't have to be expensive, just young. A light-bodied wine like Beaujolais brings berry-like flavors to marinades and is soft enough to make excellent red wine marinades for fish.

White Wines. Dry white wines such as Sauvignon Blancs and inexpensive Vinhoe Verdes from Spain work best in savory marinades. Instead of rice wine vinegar in Asian marinades, light wines such as a dry Reisling work particularly well. Unless the marinade features Chardonnay as a principal flavor, this wine gets lost in the shuffle of aromatics and oil. Avoid blush wines and white zinfandels; they can give your marinade a soda pop flavor. Champagne is all but useless in marinades. The evanescent quality fizzles out way before the cooking process starts. Champagne that has good flavor also commands a good price. Save it for your guests.

Surprising enough, the white wine that I've found packs the most amount of acid is Sauternes. A good Sauternes has to have a good acid balance to offset its sweetness. I accidentally cooked a breast of pheasant while recipe testing by simply leaving it in a Sauternes marinade for less than two hours. For an interesting variation in Asian marinades, substitute Sauternes for rice wine vinegar. You'll discover that Sauternes pairs wonderfully with freshly grated ginger.

Fortified Wines. Sherry's nutty flavor pairs nicely with nut and sesame oils. It is one of the more flexible fortified wines and very useful in marinades. It's good in Asian and Mediterranean marinades. Port brings a bit more fruit to a marinade than sherry. Madeira and Marsala play more of aromatic role in marinades. Their strength can be domineering, so use them judiciously.

Rice Wine. Chinese rice wine or Shaoxing (shao xing) wine is closer to a dry sherry (which is an acceptable substitute) than dry white wine. Chinese rice wine is the basis of Chinese rice wine vinegar. Don't confuse Chinese rice wine with Japanese sake or mirin. They are dramatically different in flavor.

Mirin. Slightly syrupy rice wine, mirin is vital to Japanese cooking. It acts as a balancing factor against the saltiness of soy sauce and the acidity of rice wine vinegar. There are two types of mirin, the most preferable being hon-mirin, which is naturally brewed. Aji-mirin contains additives, such as salt or soy sauce (which is added to avoid U.S. liquor taxes). Mirin has a low acid content and shouldn't be used on its own as an acidic element. Because it is sweeter than rice wine, it should not be as a substitute.

Sake. Sake, one of the foundations in Japanese cuisine, can also be used as an acidic element in marinades. It acts as a balancing element, counteracting the saltiness of soy and reducing fishy odors. I use sake as a replacement for white wine and rice wine vinegar with wonderful results.

Dairy Products

Dairy products simultaneously provide moisture and acid in a marinade, but they definitely need a strong shot of robust aromatics to bring them up to flavor.

Yogurt. The lactic acid in yogurt works relatively the same way as citrus acid. The advantage of yogurt is that it also provides moisture. Yogurt finds its way into marinades on both shores of the Mediterranean and India. Recipes call for plain yogurt. My very favorite is the freshly made laban found in Middle East grocery stores. It has a high level of tartness but unfortunately a brief shelf life.

Buttermilk. Because of its lactic acid, buttermilk makes a tasty marinade base for freshwater fish. It carries more flavor than whole milk with less fat.

Oils

Oil's primary role in marinades is to add moisture. It also helps to replace some of the moisture in meat that the acid draws out.

Oil can have either a neutral or an assertive role in flavoring a marinade. Oils such as sunflower, grapeseed, and canola are neutral in flavor; they also can be used as a basis for making your own infusion oils (see Chapter 3). Nut oils, infusion oils (such as herb or chili oils), extra virgin olive oils, and oriental sesame oil play an assertive flavor role in marinades. Too much of a strong oil may offset a marinade's flavor and make it taste flat.

Grades of olive oil can differ radically in flavor and viscosity. Top-of-the-line oils are usually extracted by what is called the cold-pressed method, where neither heat, water, nor chemicals are used in the extraction. Their chief advantage is taste, but cold-pressed oils have a shorter life span in the pantry than heat-extracted oils. When you are buying oil, note that oils in plastic bottles turn rancid more quickly than those in glass bottles. Canned oils (some of the imported nut and olive oils) should be transferred to dry sterilized glass jars or bottles immediately after opening and then stored in a cool place away from sunlight. Opened oil, if left in the can, will pick up a bitter metallic taste as oxidation sets in and also will turn rancid faster.

Oils are fragile in their chemical balance and the same guidelines that apply to storing wine also apply to storing premium oils. Oil will last longer and taste better in a cool, dry, dark place. Heat and light are the main enemies of oil. Avoid keeping oil near your kitchen stove or any other warm areas, such as window sills or countertops close to heating ducts or vents. Most opened oils will last for six months if kept refrigerated. Keep the heat factor in mind when purchasing oil as well. An oil that's shelved near a sun-lit store window may look good on display but won't taste so good in your marinade.

The best way to judge the quality of an oil is to taste it when you first open the bottle. That's when the taste is at its peak. The taste will serve as an important point of reference when you go back and check the oil from time to time. As soon as you pop off the cap, sniff. A premium nut oil will smell of fresh roasted nuts, an extra-virgin olive oil will reek of fragrant fruity olives. If the oil smells like stale potato chips, the oil is rancid. (Note it's not a stale potato chip that smells rancid, but the vegetable oil that coats it.) Next take a piece of bread and dip it into the oil, which should be at room temperature, and taste. Quality oils will taste clean. If there is a bit of an unpleasant aftertaste, it's a pretty good indication that the oil was stored improperly. Next, consider flavor. If the particular oil is a nut oil, you should be able to distinguish the difference between a walnut oil from hazelnut oil on the first try.

One basic benefit to weight watchers using marinades is cutting away high-cholesterol animal fat and replacing it with healthier cholesterol-free vegetable oil.

From time to time, you'll see the words "no cholesterol" on oil bottles, but don't be conned. The fact is that most oils are cholesterol free. Cholesterol is found in such animal products as meat and dairy foods, and in coconut and palm oils. These two oils cause as much a ruckus in your arteries as a cup of heavy cream. For healty eating, mono-unsaturated oils such as olive and canola are the most desirable oils to consume.

The following is a list of oils that you will encounter in the recipes here. It's okay to substitute one oil for another in a marinade recipe. But try to understand the role in the marinade that the oil is playing for flavor and moisture. A full-bodied, fruity olive oil may be out of balance when substituted for peanut oil in a spicy Thai marinade; the best choice may be one of the more neutral oils. You should avoid a generic vegetable oil. Usually this blend of oil contains additives and less-desirable and calorie-packed oils, such as coconut, palm, or cottonseed. Since grades vary from brand to brand, you're really gambling on flavor. After all, adding flavor, not diluting it, is what cooking is mostly about.

Avocado Oil.
Avocado oil has a distinct flavor. Use it for adding moisture. I often substitute avocado oil for olive oil in seafood marinades to give a Southwest flavor. Opened oil keeps in the refrigerator for five to six months.

Canola Oil.
Canola oil is neutral in flavor and lower in saturated fats than any other oil. It is used primarily for adding moisture. When preparing infusion oils, canola is a blank canvas awaiting paint.

Chili Oils.
Chili oils are really aromatics and need to be used sparingly. A basic rule of thumb is "flavor over flame." You should be able to taste the chili as well as feel it. There are as many chili oils as there are chilies and they can easily be made at home.

Grapeseed Oil.
Grapeseed oil has a neutral flavor. Use for adding moisture to meats. Its neutral flavor does not get in the way of the subtle flavorings that I'm trying to balance in marinades. Keep it cool, dry, and in the dark, and it will keep well for a good six months.

Peanut Oil.
Peanut oil has a distinct flavor and is used for adding moisture. While most domestic brands are great for deep-frying, they lack peanut flavor. Asian peanut oil found in oriental food markets and Loriva Peanut Oil, a domestic brand, are cold-pressed, actually tasting like roasted peanuts; these are great for oriental marinades. Store peanut oil in the fridge after opening.

Almond, Hazelnut, and Walnut Oils.
Almond, hazelnut, and walnut oils have assertive flavors and are used for adding moisture. They also add flavor and help bind the marinade. They are best used with vegetable marinades. Use them sparingly with seafood marinades. These oils may be expensive and have a much shorter storage life after opening, two to three months. Canned nut oils should be transferred to sterile jars or bottles and stored in the refrigerator.

Olive Oils. Olive oils are used for adding flavor and moisture. While there is nothing better than a good-quality, extra-virgin olive oil drizzled over a slice of garden-fresh tomato, it may be too heavy and fruity for some marinades. Generally, the deeper the color, the more intense the fruity flavor. For marinated fish, vegetables, or white meat poultry use light-bodied virgin or pure olive oil. It will give you hints of olive without interfering with the rest of the ingredients.

Oriental Sesame Oil. Oriental sesame oil, like chili oil, has an a strong aromatic role. It's used sparingly and in conjunction with other oils in Asian-style marinades. Dark brown and fragrant, it is pressed from roasted sesame seeds. The better premium grades are cold-pressed. Because of its low smoking point, it shouldn't be used for sauteing or frying. Light sesame oil found in health food stores is an expensive substitute for canola or grapeseed oil. It is not used to flavor food.

Safflower Oil. Safflower oil is a neutral-tasting oil that is particularly good for adding moisture. It has a high smoking point, but it deteriorates quickly once opened.

Sunflower Oil. Sunflower oil is neutral in flavor, but the cold-pressed varieties do have some nuttiness. A good-quality sunflower oil can be used as a substitute for a light, domestic peanut oil.

Fat Profile of Marinating Oils

This will tell you at a glance the fat content of most oils that are used to add moisture in marinades. Remember, all vegetable oils are cholesterol free. The first column deals with saturated fats. The higher the percentage, the more grief it can cause you. A high percentage of mono-unsaturates in the second column is optimum. The poly-unsaturates in the third column should be no higher than 30 to 35 percent. Vegetable oil, which is a generic term for blended oils, is not listed because its fat content can vary widely. Note: The figures below can vary from season to season as well as region to region by 5 to 10 percent.

	%Saturated Fat	%Mono-unsaturated Fat	%Poly-unsaturated Fat
Avocado Oil	10.0	80.0	10.0
Butter*	66.1	29.8	4.1
Canola Oil	6.8	55.5	33.3
Coconut Oil*	86.5	5.8	1.8
Corn Oil	12.7	24.2	58.7
Grapeseed Oil	6.0	55.0	20.0
Olive Oil	13.5	73.7	8.4
Palm Oil*	49.3	37.0	9.3
Peanut Oil	16.9	46.2	8.4
Oriental Sesame Oil**	15.2	40.3	43.4
Safflower Oil	9.1	12.1	74.5
Sunflower Oil	10.3	19.5	65.7
Walnut Oil	9.0	27.2	63.6

Source: U.S. Department of Agriculture.
*Not used in this book—I wanted to give you a frame of reference regarding oils high in saturated fats.
**Basically an aromatic, used only in small quantities.

Aromatics

Aromatics—herbs, spices, and other flavorings—are like a perfume in marinades. Needless to say, too much perfume can overwhelm a marinade throwing it out of balance.

Fresh Herbs and Aromatics

Garlic, Onions, Scallions, and Shallots. These pungent lilies provide bouquet when added raw to a marinade. They become much sweeter when cooked at high heat, providing a counter to the marinade's acid content. The more finely chopped these aromatics are, the more quickly their flavor emerges during the cooking process. So, a good rule of thumb is the finer the chop, the finer the flavor.

When buying garlic, onions, and shallots, the harder they feel, the better the flavor. If they are soft or sprouting green tails, they are spoiled. The green shoots in scallions should be firm. Onions and shallots generally last for two to three weeks in a cool, dark pantry; refrigerated they can last up to a couple of months but they give off their aroma to other refrigerated food. Chopped onions will last for about two to three days refrigerated. Scallions will last about a week refrigerated.

Fresh Ginger and Galangal. Ginger is one of the cornerstones of Asian cuisine. In cooking it's used as widely as garlic in the cuisines of North Africa, Mexico, the Caribbean, and China. Although available year-round, ginger is seasonal (it peaks in midsummer) and can vary in flavor according to its age. Larger and heavier ginger has the most pronounced flavor with a mild degree of heat. Fresh ginger has a smooth unwrinkled surface. Although you can freeze it, it's pointless to do so because it's so readily available and inexpensive.

Galangal, also known as ka or laos, is Thailand's ginger substitute. It looks like a pinkish-gold ginger root with rings. The flavor is that of a spicy ginger with a bit of afterburn. It combines well with lemongrass in spicy dishes. It can be purchased frozen in Asian grocery stores or through one of the mail order sources in the appendix. Leftover galangal can be used in infusion oils or vinegars.

Herbs. Herbs, such as basil, mint, parsley, and cilantro, can help make a marinade's bouquet. Usually, they are at their peak within five minutes of cooking and then they fade rapidly. These herbs are especially tasty when you're using a marinade as a baste while grilling. When you are using your marinade as part of a sauce reduction, strain out the solid aromatics and add fresh herbs to the pan at the last minute during deglazing to emphasize their flavor.

Pungent fresh herbs, such as rosemary, sage, thyme, or tarragon, should be used sparingly unless the flavor of the marinade is built around them.

Fresh Lemon, Lime, and Orange Zest. If you are going to add fresh citrus juice, add the flavor with it—freshly grated zest is really where the flavor is. Lemon juice is pretty neutral in flavor so, in order to get that breezy burst of lemony taste, go for the zest. Each recipe in this book, when calling for a specific amount of fresh citrus juice, will most likely include grated zest. Be careful not to grate into the white pith, the bitter layer between the skin and the segment.

Kaffir Leaves. Kaffir leaves or lime leaves are usually used in Thai soups and have a very pronounced perfume that adds a cool, marvelous flavor to marinated shrimp or fish. They need to be heated to release the wonderful aroma from the oil on the surface of the leaves. They are available in Asian grocery stores and can be frozen. Kaffir leaves are a signature ingredient in Southeast Asian cuisine; there are no substitutes.

Lemongrass. Lemongrass, which looks like a stalk of petrified scallion, is found in most Asian groceries. Lemongrass is to Southeast Asian marinades what garlic is to Mediterranean marinades. It's a signature aromatic that gives lemony, perfume-like flavor to Thai cuisine. Store the base in a glass of water to keep it from going too dry. Only the bulb—the first 6 inches—is used.

Dried Herbs and Spices

Most spices, be they sweet or savory, benefit from toasting or cooking, which activates their flavors. Opened jars of spices will lose their flavor in about a year, some even sooner. I suggest that you put dates on the labels showing when spices were first opened or purchased.

Toasting whole spices releases their aromatic oils. So you can gain extra flavor by buying spices whole and toasting them in a dry, nonstick or cast iron frying pan. Cumin, coriander, and cardamom will improve with roasting in a nonstick frying pan; fenugreek and achiote require it.

To roast whole spices, heat a frying pan for about two minutes over medium heat. Add the spices and stir constantly. For the first couple of minutes the color will be unchanged. Then the seeds suddenly will begin to brown. At this point, stirring is crucial. If the spices are not stirred, they will burn. Continue stirring over heat until the spices become light brown. Remove them from the pan immediately.

Cool them in a jar or bowl before grinding. Cooking times depend on the amount of spice, the size of the pan (large is best), and whether or not the spice is in the form of flat seeds (cumin) or round seeds (coriander).

Place the spices in the jar of a coffee grinder, spice mill, or blender and grind to a soft powder. (You can grind spices coarsely between two sheets of wax paper with a rolling pin or wine bottle in a pinch.) Some chefs prefer the mortar and pestle over the blender or grinder because the heat releases too much of the spices' oils, thus speeding up decomposition and flavor loss. After grinding, store in airtight containers in a cool, dry place. I suggest you invest in an inexpensive spice grinder, as spices naturally throw off aromatic oils and will leave some of that flavor behind in your coffee mill. I keep two grinders in my kitchen, one for sweet and one for savory spices.

How well you store your dried herbs and spices will ultimately affect their flavor and life span. I know cooks who like to keep their spices within arm's reach of the stove. But it's more flavor drain than gain. Heat will break down the essential oils contained in a spice and create a medicinal aftertaste, or destroy the flavor completely. Any area in the kitchen where an appliance throws off heat and light (even the refrigerator) will undermine the flavor of your spice rack.

Herbs and spices throughout history have had not only culinary value but medicinal value as well. Old-time apothecaries were filled with opaque jars of herbs and teas. Those opaque jars are perfect storage containers for dried aromatics. Any drug store will be glad to sell you opaque medicine bottles (with tight-fitting caps) that are perfect for labeling, dating, and storing your spices in the refrigerator. And if you buy your spices loose or in bulk, there is no better way of protecting your investment.

Herbes de Provence. Herbes de Provence (also called Herbes Provençales) is probably my favorite dry herb mix. I use a pinch of it with a dried wild mushroom in stock reductions. It has a wonderful summery flavor that explodes in a marinade. Herbes de Provence can be purchased from specialty or gourmet food markets, or mixed at home. Herbes de Provence needs to be lightly crushed before adding to a marinade or seasoning base. There is no substitute.

Achiote. Achiote (also called Annatto) has a slightly musky flavor and is used in Caribbean and Mexican marinades. It's sometimes sold in jars as annatto seeds or in some Spanish grocery stores as annatto paste. Look for a brick red color as opposed to dark brown, which indicates the achiote has passed its prime. Achiote requires heat to bring out its flavor.

Chinese Five Spice Powder. Chinese five spice powder can contain more than five different spices. Basically, it's made up of star anise, cloves, peppercorns, ground ginger, and cinnamon. While it has some kick, five spice powder is a sweet spice mix. Japanese seven spice powder, shichimi, is not the same as five spice powder—the two are not interchangeable.

Curry Powder. Curry powder is found in the cuisines of both the East and West Indies. Indian curries are different from the curries of the West Indies, which have various degrees of spice and heat. Commercial curry powders contain anywhere from six to eight ingredients as opposed to rempehs and garam masala that can have up to twenty-five ingredients. Use curry sparingly in marinades as this aromatic can easily overpower a dish. Over time, the flavor of curry powder will age and break down unevenly. Some of the spices in the powder will taste more assertive, while others will taste flat. Date and store curry powders in tightly covered glass jars in the refrigerator or in a cool, dark place. They will retain their flavor for at least three months.

Salt and Pepper. Salt and pepper are pretty basic stuff, one would think, but these two elements can make all the difference in flavor. Use additive-free kosher salt, which is a coarse sea salt that dissolves well in marinades and contains a fair amount of flavor. Salt indeed brings out flavor in food. The question is how much is needed. The term "salt to taste" in a marinade recipe can be anywhere from 1/2 teaspoon to a full tablespoon depending on your personal preference, the type of food you're marinating, and the volume of the marinade. But remember salt will pull out moisture in food, so use sparingly or compensate by adding a little additional oil for moisture.

Peppercorns, whether white, black, or pink, should always be freshly cracked for their flavor to peak. An old-fashioned peppermill, a blender, or even a rolling pin over a cutting board will do the trick. Cracked pepper has a flavor life of a week. Preground pepper has as much flavor as gray sawdust and should not find its way into any of your marinades. Soft green peppercorns are often packed in brine and are often left whole or pureed.

Wasabi Powder. Wasabi powder, also known as Japanese horseradish powder, is mixed with liquid to produce a paste that accompanies most Japanese dishes. I like to use this powder in marinades to give a floral or herbal heat, as opposed to the more vegetal-tasting heat of chilies.

Chilies—Fresh, Dried, and Powdered

These add spicy excitement to marinades. Before you start to wake up the sleeping palates of your guests, make sure you check their heat tolerance ahead of time. One would think that a cool, green serrano or Thai bird chili packs a lot less burn than a fiery red one. It's just the opposite. A chili sweetens as it ripens from green to red and becomes milder. That's something to keep in mind while buying Thai curry paste. The red pastes are milder than the green ones.

The smaller the chili, the hotter it is. The small, pumpkin-shaped chili called the habañero or Scotch bonnet is truly one of the world's hottest edible chilies.

A chili's heat is rated by something called the Scoville Scale, which is based on the number of grams of water it takes to extinguish (or cancel) the heat of a single gram of chili. Basically it would take a bucket of water to douse a jalapeño rated at 2500 Scoville units, compared to a half-filled swimming pool for the habañero at 200,000 Scoville units. If you're not used to chili heat, start with the milder chilies and work your way up. I've had some success in freezing fresh chilies. They are softer when defrosted but the bite is still there.

Fresh Chilies

Jalapeño and Serrano Chilies. Jalapeño chilies are training wheels when it comes to heat. Seeded and in small portions, these represent the best place to begin when you are starting to turn up the heat in your marinade. Serrano chilies are smaller and hotter with a more pronounced flavor than jalapeños.

Thai Bird Chilies. Thai bird chilies are tinier than serrano chilies. They get their name because birds feed on them and help spread the seeds by their migratory habits. These skinny chilies are about one and a half to two inches long. The red and green chilies are the basis of Thai chili pastes, the red being less incendiary then the hotter green ones. When you leave in the seeds, you get a high impact heat. Removing the seeds calms things down a bit.

Habañero or Scotch Bonnet Chilies. Habañero or Scotch bonnet chilies have a wonderful sweet flavor but you have to pay a price to get it—their searing heat. They are the basis of most Caribbean marinades. Jalapeños or serranos may be substituted for Scotch bonnets, but their flavor and effect are radically different. Domestic green habañeros are no hotter than the riper orange-colored ones. Habañeros are available dried—they can be ground and added to rubs.

Dried Chilies

Ancho and Guajillo Chilies. Ancho chili is really a dried poblano chili, while a Guajillo is a mild chili. Both need to be reconstituted before they find their way into an adobo sauce or marinade. They can be ground into chili powder or combined with other spices to form a rub. These chilies are available from some of the mail order sources in the appendix.

Chipotle. Chipotle chili is my favorite dried chili. Chipotles are actually ripe jalapeños that have been smoked and either dried or canned in adobo sauce. If dried, they can be ground into a spice mix, or reconstituted by soaking in boiling water for about thirty minutes. Canned and packed in adobo sauce, they can be pureed and added to marinade. They combine superbly with orange zest and orange juice.

Asian Dried or Dry Oriental Chilies. Asian dried or dry oriental chilies are generally dried Thai bird chilies. They are found in Szechuan, Indian, and even Caribbean cuisines. They are about one and a half to two inches long and should be seeded before using. You can reconstitute them much the same way you would a chipotle, or they can be crumbled into a marinade or ground into a rub. The tinier the dried chili the hotter its flame.

Red Pepper Flakes.

Red pepper flakes are actually chili seeds that have been dried. Use red pepper flakes when you want an occasional burst of heat in your marinade instead of having the fire permeate it. Anytime I seed a hot fresh chili like a serrano, jalapeño, or Thai bird, I leave the seeds to dry overnight in my gas oven to give me an ongoing supply of flakes.

Powdered Chilies

Cayenne. Cayenne is the furnace behind Cajun cuisine. This brick red powder has a flavor that dips within three months, but its heat works long after that. I store it in opaque medicine bottles in the freezer to keep its flavor alive. Cayenne is usually combined with milder dry chilies to bring up the heat in pastes and rubs. When purchasing avoid the label red pepper. This could be any combination of pepper, sugar, or other ingredients.

Paprika. Paprika is made from dry chili. It ranges in heat from sweet to hot. Sweet paprika is used more for coloring and garnishing, but hot Hungarian paprika is what you want to use for marinades.

Chili Powder. Commercial chili powder is really a spicy mystery dust. There's no know way of knowing what goes into it. Your best bet is to purchase chili powder from Spanish grocery stores or make your own (see Chipotle Seasoning in Chapter 3).

Condiments

Anchovies. Anchovies are tiny fish fillets which are salt cured and packed in olive oil. An anchovy or two brings a light hint of salt and savory depth to seafood marinades. Anchovies are used much the same way as nam pla (fish sauce) is used in Southeast Asian cuisines. Anchovies last almost indefinitely in the refrigerator.

Capers. Capers are an essential accent in Mediterranean-style cuisines. Capers may purchased pickled or packed in a salt brine, in which case you should rinse them before using. For quality, go for the small nonpareils capers from southern France. Capers, fresh lemon, parsley, and extra-virgin olive oil make one of the most flavorful marinade combinations imaginable.

Coconut Milk and Toasted Coconut. Canned coconut milk, found in Asian, Indian, and Hispanic grocery stores, is my substitute for fresh coconut milk. Slamming a fresh coconut around with a hammer is fine if you're having a particularly bad day and want to vent some frustration. Otherwise, scraping the coconut meat away from the shell, shredding it, and pouring boiling water on it is a lot of work. Canned coconut milk, preferably a Thai brand called Chaokoh, brought to a simmer with one-quarter cup of toasted, unsweetened dried coconut is my way to go. It's easy to prepare and it tastes good when wrapped around other ingredients in a marinade. I've listed coconut milk in the aromatic section because it assumes a flavor role. It lacks the acidity of citrus or vinegar and doesn't do much to add moisture to food.

Hoisin, Oyster, and Plum Sauces. Hoisin, oyster, and plum sauces used in marinades give a distinct oriental signature to dishes. These sauces are thicker and more concentrated than other Asian condiments.

Slightly more spicy than the other two sauces, hoisin is a sweet, reddish brown sauce, containing garlic, soybeans, five spice powder, chili, and other ingredients. Once opened, it stores indefinitely in the refrigerator.

Oyster sauce is the most savory of the oriental sauces. It's actually a reduction of soy sauce, oysters, and brine. Although thicker and richer than nuoc cham from Vietnam and nam pla from Thailand, it introduces a rich, dark, slightly sweet flavor into oriental stir-fries. Oyster sauce should not be used as a substitute for nam pla or fish sauce. Once opened, it stores indefinitely in the refrigerator.

Plum sauce is the sweetest of the three condiments. For marinating purposes, plum sauce needs to be thinned out and balanced with other oriental spices, vinegar, and oil to work in a marinade. I like to use the combination of chili oil and plum sauce in a marinade, which can set off flavors like a string of Chinese firecrackers.

Soy Sauce.
Light and dark soy sauce are named for flavor and color, not for sodium content. Japanese soy sauce is lighter in color, less salty, and a bit sweeter than Chinese. However, to confuse matters even more, light Japanese soy sauces are saltier than dark Japanese soy sauce, while the light Chinese soy sauces are less salty than dark Chinese soy sauces. If the marinade is Japanese, do not substitute a dark Chinese soy sauce or it will throw the dish out of balance. I like using light Japanese soy sauce (like Kikkoman) as a base for Asian dipping sauces and light Japanese marinades, vegetables, fish, shellfish, and white meat poultry. Dark Japanese soy sauce stands up better to duck and beef. Buy soy sauce in the smallest glass bottles you can find. Once opened, refrigerate covered, for two to three months, as the

flavor dips and the saltiness becomes more concentrated over time. Unless you're used to working with different types of soy, it's best to stick with what's readily accessible. Kikkoman is widely available and workable in all the recipes calling for light soy sauces.

Tamari, sold in health food and Asian grocery stores, has a stronger flavor than dark soy sauce. You can substitute it for soy, but keep its stronger flavor in mind and cut back your quantity.

Hot Sauces.
Flavor over flame is my rule for choosing hot sauces. Since the heat in most hot sauces fades in a marinade and burns off during cooking, you need to taste the chilies as well as feel them for a hot sauce to earn its keep. A good hot sauce should have hints of vegetable behind it. My favorites are locally grown ones that are available through the mail (see mail order sources). These combine chili with fruit or they are made from a specific chili varietal.

Mustards.
Dijon-style, moutarde, Creole, and powdered mustards truly run the range in piquancy. Dijon-style mustard packs more flavor per tablespoon than most mustards and can easily overpower a marinade if not used judiciously. It should be balanced with something sweet, like sherry or balsamic vinegar. Coarse-grain mustards are wonderful for texture. They have a little sweetness behind their tang. Prepared mustards last about a year refrigerated, fancy blended mustards with fruit, herbs, or other seasonings lose their zest in a third to half that time.

I treat mustard powder purely as a spice instead of a condiment. Powdered mustard can hold its bite for a least a year.

Nam Pla or Nuoc Mam. The fish sauce named nam pla in Thailand goes by the name of nuoc mam in Vietnam. It is a fermented fish sauce, which is an essential ingredient in Thai and Vietnamese marinades. It's less salty than soy sauce and has a more savory depth. You'll find fish sauce available in Asian grocery stores. It has a six month refrigerated shelf life.

Tamarind Juice. Tamarind is found in cuisines of the Caribbean, India, and Southeast Asia. Purchase the paste. Use a four to one ratio of boiling water to paste and press the pulp through a strainer. Discard the pulp and use the resulting sour liquid.

Worcestershire. Worcestershire sauce is described as western soy. That's not so far from the truth. Worcestershire was originally an Indian sauce consisting of, beside other Asian ingredients, soy sauce, garlic, tamarind, and lime. It gives a musky, piquant flavor to beef and pork marinades.

Sweeteners

Sweeteners are sometimes used to counter high acid marinades or to extend the marinade as a tasty glaze on the grill. I prefer sweeteners that have more flavor than granulated sugar. All sweeteners will caramelize over high heat (you want this action) or burn over high heat if broiled or grilled too long. Sweeteners in marinades are best used sparingly on thinner cuts of chicken or pork chops.

Molasses. Unsulphured molasses is really a sugar by-product. It's the syrupy substance that remains after white crystal sugar has been removed. It's also one of the most flavorful and savory sweeteners,

with slight hints of smokiness, which makes it perfect for marinades.

Pomegranate Molasses. Pomegranate molasses, which is available in Middle Eastern grocery stores, has a unique combination of tart and sweet. I like using this in marinades for rich poultry, like duck or goose, or as a sweet substitute for honey or molasses.

Dark Brown Sugar. Dark brown sugar carries tinges of molasses and is one of the more volatile of the sweeteners. It will caramelize quickly, even at low temperatures. Mixed into a rub, it enables the spices to cling to the meat. Dark brown sugar has a more pronounced flavor than light brown.

Maple Syrup and Honey. Maple syrup and honey are included in this group because they are sweeteners in a natural form. They can be used interchangeably with interesting results. Each has a pronounced flavor print and will change the taste of the marinade. I like pairing maple syrup with bourbon, and honey with a splash of cognac in some of my marinades.

Indonesian Sweet Soya Sauce or Ketjap Manis. This is a thick, sweet, savory sauce that tastes like a combination of molasses and soy sauce. I've used it in place of molasses in barbecue sauce with excellent results. Ketjap (from which we get the word ketchup) may be spelled as "kecap" on some labels. To make your own, combine two tablespoons molasses and one tablespoon dark Chinese soy sauce.

Jams, Jellies, and Marmalades. These have grown up quite a bit since I was spreading them on sandwiches with peanut butter. They are now both sweet and savory. I use herbal jams and jellies to counteract vinegar or other acids in marinades. Fruit jellies prop up fruit marinades and work with the other ingredients to create some wonderful savory glazes for the grill. I combine orange marmalade with Caribbean spices to create a bitter orange marinade for roast pork.

Liqueurs and Liquors. I've listed liqueurs and liquors, such as cassis, brandy, cognac, and rum in the sweetener section, because they can play that role in marinades. Cassis and rum will caramelize over high heat and can form a glaze on marinated chicken breasts. Heat causes the flavor to fade on liqueurs; keep them cool.

3. Flavored Vinegars, Infusion Oils, Spice and Herb Mixtures

I would like to subtitle this chapter "Secret Ingredients" because these intensely flavored mixtures will light up a marinade's flavor like neon. Making your own flavored vinegars, infused oils, and herb and spice mixes gives marinades that additional touch without overpowering other ingredients.

Make up a small collection of oils or vinegars at one pass. It takes just as much time to set up four or five flavored vinegars as it does one. I make flavored mixtures right around the end of season when I'm wondering what to do with all the good stuff from my garden. Once made, you will have a pantry full of flavor-infused vinegars, oils, and spices that can be pulled together in a moment's notice for a quick marinade before you start your busy day. At the day's end, you're ready to relax over a wonderful, easily prepared dinner.

Flavored Vinegars

Flavored vinegars add an extra burst of flavor to marinades. Replacing rice wine vinegar in an Asian marinade with either Orange or Raspberry Vinegar gives a zesty tang of sweet and tart to the spicy ingredients. You can build combination vinegars pairing the sweet with the hot, the savory with the spicy, and the piquant with the floral. While flavored vinegars, such as rosemary, fennel, or raspberry, may seem to be the latest culinary fad, you may be surprised to learn that they were a pretty big hit back in the Middle Ages too.

To make flavored vinegars, you need a quality red or white wine vinegar. When selecting wine vinegars, check the acidity level which is usually anywhere from 4 percent to 7 percent. This is much like proof in alcohol, that is—5 percent is equal to about 50 proof, or for our purposes, 50 percent vinegar diluted with 50 percent water. The acidity you want is at least 5 percent, preferably 7 percent. The higher acidic level will preserve your fruit and herbs. If fruit is pureed, it will dilute lower-strength vinegars. High-acid vinegars also hold up better over time, and they can hold their own during the cooking process.

Joel Assouline, proprietor of Assouline & Ting, a Philadelphia-based specialty food purveyor, makes more than 30 varieties of flavored vinegars on the premises. Joel ages his vinegars in wood casks, which we both agree smoothes the bite but not the tang. In lieu of stacking wooden casks in your garage, sterilized wine bottles are the next best thing. If you really like to make flavored vinegars, especially if you plan on using them for gifts, wooden barrels, available from wine- or beer-making suppliers, may be worth the investment. The recipes for flavored vinegars for the berry, herb, honey, and peppercorn vinegars are from Assouline & Ting.

Not all vinegars require aging. A few I call my "overnight sensations," because that's all the time you need to infuse them. These have pulled me out of a tight spot when I needed a last-minute ingredient for a recipe and didn't have the extra minutes to run out shopping for it. Store-bought specialty vinegars are fine in a pinch, but there is nothing like the real thing that you infuse yourself.

Berry Vinegar

Berry vinegars are wonderful for marinades used with duck or quail. I also like the way berry vinegars hold up in sauce reductions.

4 to 5 cups fresh berries, cleaned (raspberries, blueberries, or strawberries)
1 quart red or white wine vinegar (preferably 7 percent strength)
1/4 cup sugar

Lightly mash berries in a nonreactive bowl. Do not puree in a blender. Steel blades break the seeds and make the vinegar bitter. If necessary, use the plastic dough blade of a food processor. Combine the ingredients in a sterilized glass jar, and seal with plastic wrap and rubber bands. Or combine the ingredients in a nonreactive double boiler and bring to a quick simmer for added flavor strength. Cool and place in a sterilized jar, seal with plastic wrap and rubber bands. Let the vinegar infuse for 10 days to 2 weeks in a cool, dark place. Strain through cheesecloth and discard the solids. Heat the vinegar over medium heat and simmer for 3 to 5 minutes. Cool to room temperature. Funnel the vinegar into sterilized bottles, add whole fresh berries (optional), and seal. Fresh fruit vinegars maintain their strength for 3 to 4 months refrigerated.

Yield: 1 quart

Variations

Red Currant Vinegar. Substitute fresh currants for the berries.
Cranberry Vinegar. Substitute cooked cranberries for the berries.

Herb Vinegar

White wine vinegar is good for delicate herbs, red wine for punchier herbs. Herb vinegars are the easiest of the flavored vinegars to make.

1 quart white or red wine vinegar
1 to 2 cups fresh herbs (tarragon, rosemary, or basil)

Pour the vinegar over the herbs in a sterilized glass jar. Seal with plastic wrap and a rubber band. Store in a cool, dark place for a month. Fresh herb vinegars should never be exposed to direct sunlight. Plants react chemically to direct sunlight.

Herb vinegars maintain their strength for 4 to 6 months. Store in a cool, dark place.

Yield: 1 quart

Honey Herb Vinegar

Honey infusion vinegars are wonderful replacements for balsamic vinegar. The honey plays to the same taste buds as the balsamic vinegar.

1/4 to 1/3 cup honey
1 quart white or red vinegar
1/4 cup dried herbs (mint, lavender, or Herbes de Provence)

Heat the honey and vinegar together and simmer for 3 to 5 minutes to dissolve the honey. Cool to room temperature. Pour the honey vinegar mixture over the herbs in a sterilized glass jar. Seal with plastic wrap and a rubber band. Store in a cool, dark place for a month. Herbal vinegars maintain their strength for 4 to 6 months. Store in a cool, dark place.

Yield: 1 quart

Pink Peppercorn Vinegar

Pink peppercorn vinegar is particularly delightful with a citrus-based marinade. In the variations that follow, the Coriander-Cumin Vinegar revitalizes Asian, Southwest, and Caribbean marinades. I use Vanilla Vinegar for marinating shrimp or scallops.

1 quart white wine vinegar
3 to 4 tablespoons pink or green peppercorns

Bring the vinegar to gentle simmer in a nonreactive pot. Add the peppercorns. Gently simmer over low heat for 8 to 10 minutes. Cool to room temperature and strain. The vinegar is ready to use. It will maintain strength for 4 months.

Yield: 1 quart

Variations

Coriander-Cumin Vinegar. Substitute 2 tablespoons toasted cumin seeds and 2 tablespoons toasted coriander seeds for the peppercorns and proceed with the recipe as above.

Vanilla Vinegar. Substitute 2 vanilla beans, split, for the peppercorns. After cooling the infused vinegar, seed the vanilla bean with the tip of a sharp paring knife and add scrapings to the vinegar. The vinegar is ready to use. It will maintain strength for 4 months.

Yield: 1 quart

Quick Ginger-Lemongrass Vinegar

1 quart rice wine vinegar
2 stalks lemongrass, chopped, bulb only, outer leaves removed
1/4 cup freshly grated ginger root

Combine the vinegar, lemongrass, and ginger in a nonreactive pot. Simmer over low heat for 30 minutes, then leave overnight. The longer it sits, the stronger the flavor. Pour into sterilized glass jars and seal with plastic wrap and rubber bands. Store in a cool, dark place. The vinegar will hold its strength for 3 to 4 months.

Yield: 1 quart

Quick Orange Chipotle Vinegar

1 quart white wine vinegar
Julienned peel of 2 large juice oranges, white pith removed
3 to 4 dried chipotle peppers

Bring the vinegar to gentle simmer in a nonreactive pot. Add the peel and peppers. Gently simmer over low heat until the chipotles are reconstituted, about 8 to 10 minutes. Cool to room temperature, and let it stand overnight. At this point you can either strain the vinegar or let it steep for additional heat. Pour into sterilized glass jars and seal with plastic wrap and rubber bands. Store in a cool, dark place. The vinegar will hold its strength for 3 to 4 months.

Yield: 1 quart

Quick Lime Chili Vinegar

1 quart white wine vinegar
Julienned peel of 4 medium limes, white pith
  removed
8 to 10 serrano chilies or 2 to 4 habañero chili
  peppers
8 to 10 sprigs cilantro

Bring the vinegar to a gentle simmer in a
nonreactive pot. Add the peel and peppers. Gently
simmer over low heat for 8 to 10 minutes. Cool to
room temperature and strain, or leave the chilies in
for a more volcanic vinegar. Pour into sterilized
glass jars. Add the sprigs of cilantro for garnish and
seal with plastic wrap and rubber bands. Store in a
cool, dark place. The vinegar will hold its strength
for 3 to 4 months.

Yield: 1 quart

Quick Fruit Vinegar

Here's a quick way to make flavored fruit vinegars
when your recipe calls for only a small portion.
Reduce to 1/3 of its original volume over low heat:
Cassis (for black currant red wine vinegar), Cointreau
(for orange white wine vinegar), Framboise (for
raspberry red wine vinegar), Peach Brandy, Poire
William, etc. Combine 1 part reduced liqueur to 1
part white wine or red wine vinegar. Add more
reduced liqueur or vinegar to taste. The reduced
liqueur intensifies the flavor of the vinegar.

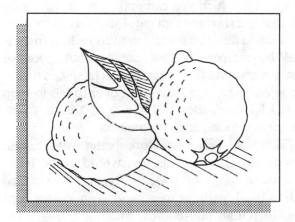

Infusion Oils

While working on my last cookbook, *Sorbets!*, I began to realize the possibilities of infusing sugar syrups with fresh and dried herbs, ginger, and flower petals. Then I discovered infusion oils. Infusion oils—redolent with herbs, peppers, and spices—can perfume food with exotic and savory flavors ranging from Asian spices to Mediterranean capers, herbs, and peppers. Infusion oils are nothing new. Olio canto, an olive oil infused with basil and garlic, is an Italian staple. The Chinese have been using chili-infused oils in their cuisine for centuries. Some of the best applications of infusion oils can be found in *Simple Cuisine* (Prentice Hall, 1990) by Jean George Vongerichten.

Infusion oils in marinades add extra flavor. One other advantage of keeping infusions oils on hand is the speed in which you can make up a marinade by just adding a flavored vinegar. Infusion oils are easy to make and they last several months in the refrigerator. When recipes call for a couple of tablespoons of exotic or esoteric fresh ingredients to spice a dish, I like to add whatever I have left over to oils to keep around for marinades. All you need are glass jars, refrigerator room, and imagination.

There are oils that work better with certain ingredients. Olive oil, as you would guess, lends itself to steeping with Mediterranean ingredients, such as basil, garlic, capers, and even roasted peppers. In Italian households, making and cooking with infused oils has been a long-standing tradition. Initially, infused oils were made from second pressings of olive oils to bolster flavor. Nowadays, there's nothing finer than infusing extra-virgin olive oil with freshly picked herbs. But you don't need to buy an expensive olive oil; some of the more expensive oils may be so fruity that the flavor of the infusion is more of a distraction than an addition.

Grapeseed oil, which is more neutral, is the oil I like to use for steeping fresh herbs such as sage or tarragon. Light peanut oil holds up better than any of the other nut oils (which tend to turn rancid) so it can be heated for forced infusions with ingredients such as dried chilies or robust Asian spices such as lemon grass, galangal, or kaffir leaves. Canola oil is another neutral oil that can be used for heated forced infusions with cinnamon, curry, dried chipotles, and wild mushroom powders.

Infusions can be done in two basic ways: steeping and heating. Steeping requires time to allow the flavors to develop, while heated infusion oils are ready to use fairly quickly.

The following set of recipes should give you some basic ideas on how to make infusion oils as well as where to use them. Herb-infused olive oils can be substituted throughout the book wherever a recipe calls for olive oil. Or for a simple marinade in minutes, simply mix 2 parts infused oil with 1 part balsamic or sherry vinegar.

Olio Rosmarino (Rosemary-Infused Oil)

This is great with marinades for beef or lamb.

2 cups extra-virgin olive oil
1/4 cup chopped fresh rosemary, plus 2 to 3 sprigs
 for garnishing

Combine the ingredients in a sterile glass jar or wine bottle and seal with plastic wrap and rubber bands. Store in a cool, dark place for 10 to 14 days, or up to 1 month. Strain the oil and return to sterilized glass jars or bottles with the sprigs of rosemary. Seal with plastic wrap and rubber bands. Keep for several months in a refrigerator.

Yield: 2 cups

Olio Canto
(Basil-Garlic-Infused Olive Oil)

Wonderful with seafood and chicken.

12 small garlic cloves, peeled and skewered on bamboo skewers
2 cups extra-virgin olive oil
1/4 to 1/3 cup fresh basil leaves, bruised in a mortar and pestle or coarsely chopped

Combine the ingredients in a sterile glass jar or wine bottle and seal with plastic wrap and rubber bands. Store in a cool, dark place for 10 to 14 days, or up to 1 month. Strain the oil and return to sterilized glass jars or bottles. Seal with plastic wrap and rubber bands. Keep for several months in a cool, dark place or refrigerated.

Yield: 2 cups

Basil-Caper Oil

Perfect for marinating tuna or swordfish steaks for the grill.

2 cups extra-virgin olive oil
1/4 to 1/3 cup fresh basil leaves, bruised in a mortar and pestle or coarsely chopped
2 to 3 tablespoons capers

Combine the ingredients in a sterile glass jar or wine bottle and seal with plastic wrap and rubber bands. Store in a cool, dark place for 10 to 14 days, or up to 1 month. Strain the oil and return to sterilized glass jars or bottles. Seal with plastic wrap and rubber bands. Keep for several months in a cool, dark place or refrigerated.

Yield: 2 cups

Oil Herbes de Provence

You can splash this oil on goat cheese, marinate haricots verts, drizzle on tomatoes, and nap salmon fillets on their way to the grill. Combine the oil with a little balsamic or sherry vinegar, and you have an instant marinade.

1/2 cup extra-virgin olive oil
1 1/2 cups grapeseed oil
3 to 4 garlic cloves
2 shallots, quartered
1 teaspoon fresh cracked black peppercorns
1 tablespoon dried parsley
2 tablespoons Herbes de Provence (see page 37)

Combine the olive oil and grapeseed oil in a small nonreactive saucepan. With a garlic press and strainer, press the garlic and shallots to extract their juice only. Discard the solids. Add the garlic-shallot juice, peppercorns, and Herbes de Provence to the oils. Simmer over low heat for 10 minutes, cool to room temperature. Strain the oil, pour into a glass jar, and refrigerate. This will keep for up to 3 months.

Yield: 2 cups

Orange Chipotle Oil

Orange peel and dried chipotle chili infuse this oil with a smoky citrus flavor that enlivens Mexican and Southwestern-style marinades. The dried orange peel gives the oil a savory intensity, but you can use fresh zest in a pinch. You'll also find that the oil is perfect for Yucatecan-style recipes.

3 to 4 dried chipotle chili peppers
3 tablespoons dried orange peel (see page 39)
2 cups canola oil

In a spice mill, grind together the chilies and orange peel. Combine the chipotle-orange mix with the canola oil in a clean glass jar and infuse for 2 to 3 days, shaking the jar occasionally. Filter the oil through a paper coffee filter into a clean glass jar. Store in the refrigerator for up to 6 months.

Yield: 2 cups

Niçoise Oil

Niçoise oil works wonders on fish. A few splashes of Niçoise Oil with balsamic vinegar and fresh parsley are all you need to infuse tuna with the taste of the Mediterranean.

1 1/2 cups virgin or pure olive oil
12 Niçoise olives
1/2 teaspoon dried thyme
1/2 teaspoon dried marjoram
1 tablespoon Herbes de Provence (see page 37)
10 coarsely cracked black peppercorns
1 bay leaf

Warm the olive oil over a low flame. Add the olives, thyme, marjoram, Herbes de Provence, and black pepper. Remove from the heat. Pour into a clean glass jar. Allow the oil to steep for 2 days in the refrigerator before using. Store the oil in the refrigerator for up to 1 month.

Yield: 1 1/2 cups

Curried Hazelnut Oil

The combination of curry with hazelnuts creates an oil that crackles with highly charged flavor. If you like, just add 2 tablespoons of chopped, toasted hazelnuts to the curried oil and you will have the perfect coating for grilled shrimp.

2 tablespoons curry powder
1 tablespoon boiling water
2 cups hazelnut oil

Stir together the curry and water to form a paste. Combine the curry paste and the hazelnut oil in a clean jar and infuse for 2 to 3 days, shaking the jar occasionally. Filter the oil through a paper coffee filter. Store in an airtight jar in the refrigerator for up to 1 month.

Yield: 2 cups

Wild Mushroom Oil

This oil captures the muskiness of wild forest mushrooms. This is the way I extend expensive dried wild mushrooms like porcinis, cèpes, morels, or chanterelles. I like to use the oil in meat marinades. In fact, by just adding Madeira and a little red wine vinegar to morel oil, you've got the perfect marinade for beef tournedos.

3 to 4 dried wild mushrooms, about 1/4 cup loosely packed
1 tablespoon heated Madeira wine
2 cups canola oil

Grind the mushrooms to a fine powder in a food mill or blender; you should have about 2 tablespoons. Mix the powder with the Madeira and form a paste. Add the mushroom paste to a sterile jar and pour in the oil. Shake vigorously and set aside for 2 days, shaking the contents periodically. Strain the oil through a paper coffee filter. The oil will keep for 3 to 4 months refrigerated.

Yield: 2 cups

Chili Oil

The chili oil that you make at home is going to be ten times more flavorful than any oil you buy. Since we're talking dried chilies here, you can substitute any of the following in the recipe: dried chipotles, dried habañeros, or dried Asian chilies. You can use this oil in place of tabasco or chili sauce.

1 cup cold-pressed light peanut oil
2 tablespoon dried chili flakes or 4 dried Asian chilies, crumbled

Heat the peanut oil over medium heat for several minutes. Add the crumbled dried chilies and immediately remove from the heat. Cool to room temperature. Place the oil in a sterile jar and let it sit for 24 to 48 hours. Then strain the oil or leave the chilies in for your own version of refrigerator lava; the more it sits the hotter it gets. Refrigerated, it lasts indefinitely.

Yield: 1 cup

Annatto Oil

1/2 cup light peanut oil
1 tablespoon annatto (achiote) seeds

Heat the oil until a smoky haze appears. Remove from the heat and add the seeds. Let the seeds steep until the oil cools to room temperature (1 to 2 hours). Then strain the oil and discard the seeds.

Yield: 1/2 cup

Infusion Oil Substitutes in Marinades

Infusion oils make great marinades with the addition of a little citrus or infused vinegars. Here are some tasty ways of substituting these oils in some of the marinades throughout the book. This is only a sampling of flavor possibilities. Each one of these oils could easily find its way into dozens of recipes.

Oil	**Recipe**
Olio Rosmarino	Lemon-Peppercorn Marinade, 164
	Lebanese Yogurt Marinade, 160
	Beef or Lamb Marinade for Kabobs, 46
Basil-Garlic Oil	Basil Balsamic Vinegar Marinade, 111
	Lemon-Sorrel Marinade, 59
	Marinated Swordfish Kabobs, 142
Basil-Caper Oil	Lemon-Caper Marinade, 60
	Basic Fish Marinade, 43
	Mediterranean Marinade, 144
Oil Herbes de Provence	Basic Beef Marinade, 44
	Port Marinade, 45
	Marinated Roast Rack of Lamb, 193
Orange Chili Oil	Orange-Ginger Glaze, 75
	Bitter Orange Marinade, 76
	Yucatecan Citrus Marinade, 68
Niçoise Oil	Herbes de Provence Marinade, 104
	Tapenade Marinade, 61
	Provençal Red Wine Marinade, 184
Curried Hazelnut Oil	Sherry-Hazelnut Marinade, 107
	Curry Marinade, 55
	Tequila-Almond Marinade, 131
Wild Mushroom Oil	Basic Beef Marinade, 44
	Grilled Marinated Lamb Salad, 189

Seasonings and Spice Mixes

In the past, herbs and spices were the currency (the money) that people traded with. Continents were discovered, trade routes established, and wars fought over herbs and spices. The following recipes are combinations of seasonings that are both traditional and contemporary. These are foundation recipes that are best used in small portions as aromatics. The flavors of these spices will be concentrated, and it's pretty difficult to strain them out of a marinade once they've been shaken in.

Herbes de Provence and garam masala are signature seasonings from two very different cuisines. Herbes de Provence is a dried herb mix from the cuisine of Southern France. Garam masala from India is a sweet and spicy mix that is as pungent as the Herbes de Provence is subtle. The chipotle seasoning that follows is the seasoning I use when a recipe calls for generic chili powder. The citrus dust recipes are what I like to use to give some of my marinades a little accent.

When preparing spice mixes, use whole spices wherever possible. I pack my seasonings in medicine jars, date and label them, and put them in the freezer for future marinades.

Herbes de Provence

Herbes de Provence is my favorite wintertime seasoning. I use a pinch of it along with a dried wild mushroom to give a woodsy taste to my stocks, soups, and sauces. Sprinkle a teaspoon on chicken and add a splash of olive oil with some salt and pepper, and you have a ready-made rub that typifies the cooking of Provençal France.

4 to 5 tablespoons dried marjoram
4 to 5 tablespoons dried thyme
4 to 5 tablespoons dried summer savory
4 to 5 crumbled bay leaves
2 tablespoons dried basil
2 tablespoons dried oregano
1 tablespoon dried rosemary
1 teaspoon crumbled sage
1 teaspoon dried lavender

Combine the ingredients in a small bowl. Store in a cool spot in an opaque jar or bottle for about 1 year.

Yield: 1 cup

Garam Masala

Garam masala is an Indian sweet spice used in curries and marinades. When it's cooking, it fills the kitchen with a sweet, exotic fragrance. There are as many mixes of garam masala as there are regions in India. This is an easy mix to try on your own. A teaspoon of homemade garam masala does wonders when added to store-bought curry powders or stirred into plain yogurt for a marinade.

3 tablespoons cardamom pods
1 inch cinnamon stick
2 teaspoons fenugreek seeds
1 tablespoon whole cumin seeds
1 tablespoon whole coriander seeds
2 teaspoons ground turmeric
1 tablespoon freshly ground black pepper
1/2 teaspoon whole cloves

Break open the cardamom pods, discard the skins, and reserve the seeds. Break the cinnamon stick into small pieces between sheets of waxed paper, using a rolling pin or kitchen mallet. Heat a dry skillet for about 2 minutes over medium heat. Combine the cardamom, cinnamon, fenugreek, cumin, and coriander and toast in the hot skillet until the seeds turn golden brown.

Cool the spices and combine with the turmeric, pepper, and cloves in a spice mill or blender. Grind to a fine powder. Store the mix in a jar (and remember to date it). It will keep, tightly covered in the refrigerator, for up to 3 months.

Yield: 1/3 cup

Chipotle Seasoning

This seasoning will definitely give commercial Cajun spice mixes a run for the money. I add a tablespoon or two to Caribbean and Southwestern-style marinades, as well as to Cajun dishes, to give the flavors a little punch. Dried chipotle pepper with the two chili powders gives this mix its depth. The chili powders and chipotle peppers are available at Hispanic grocery stores, as well as specialty food stores. See the mail order listings for additional sources.

2 tablespoons ancho chili powder
2 tablespoons New Mexican chili powder
1 inch cinnamon stick
2 teaspoons cumin seeds
1 tablespoon dried Mexican oregano
1 tablespoon kosher or sea salt
3 to 4 dried chipotle peppers
Dried peel from 2 juice oranges (see page 39)

Combine all the ingredients in a spice mill or blender and grind to a coarse powder. Store in an airtight jar. This will keep its potency in the freezer for 3 to 4 months.

Yield: 1/3 cup

Citrus Dust

Necessity may be the mother of invention, but I really think that serendipity is its father. I stumbled onto this recipe for citrus dust purely by accident when I made a chocolate dessert recipe (in the cookbook *Fantasy Chocolate Delights*), which called for ground dried orange peel with cardamom, and I added cumin by mistake. Orange-cumin dust has been one of my favorite staples ever since. Any time a recipe calls for cumin, I use Orange-Cumin Dust. It works wonders in Southwestern-style recipes, oriental cuisine, and even curries.

Citrus dust is 3 to 4 parts oven-dried citrus peel and 1 part spice. The flavors we identify most as orange, lemon, lime, grapefruit, and tangerine come from the oils in the peel. The surface of the citrus should be shiny and fragrant, indicating a good oil presence. Dull, dry surfaces will taste dull when dried. Use whole spices instead of ground. Although it may seem to take a lot of fresh peel to give you dried peel, it is quite concentrated. It literally permeates dishes with citrus fragrance, so use sparingly. When a recipe calls for citrus juice, save the peels. A rind is a terrible thing to waste.

To prepare dried citrus peel, score the surface lightly with a paring knife and carefully pull the peel off the fruit. Lay the peel skin down on a hard surface and, with a small serrated knife, remove the bitter white pith that coats it. You're done when you no longer see white pith, only peel. Peel can be dried overnight in a gas oven by the pilot light, at 150° F in a warm electric oven, or on a rack in a warm, dry spot in a couple of days.

Yields are approximate because citrus varies in size from region to region and season to season. These recipes are easy to correct as you mix them, and you can replenish them with more spice or citrus peel as time goes by. To prepare citrus dust, use a spice grinder or blender to grind together any of the following combinations into a fine powder. Here's a collection of some of the citrus dust I keep in my pantry.

Orange-Cumin Dust

Use with barbecue rubs for ribs or beef. A combination of this dust and paprika is excellent on grilled chicken breasts.

1 teaspoon whole cumin seeds
Dried peel of 3 to 4 juice oranges (see this page)

Yield: 2 tablespoons

Orange-Chipotle Dust

Add to Southwest or Mexican marinades or rubs. Great for Texas beef brisket.

1 dried chipotle pepper
Dried peel of 3 to 4 juice oranges (see this page)

Yield: 2 tablespoons

Lemon-Sage Dust

Use this to perk up seafood marinades.

1 teaspoon dried sage
Dried peel of 6 to 8 medium lemons (see this page)

Yield: 2 1/2 tablespoons

Lemon-Cinnamon Dust

This gives Moroccan and North African flavors to seafood and Mediterranean-style marinades.

1 stick of cinnamon, broken up
Dried peel of 6 to 8 medium lemons (see page 39)

Yield: 2 1/2 tablespoons

Lime-Pequin Pepper Dust

Add to Southwestern or Mexican marinades or rubs.

1 tablespoon dried pequin peppers (or dried Asian pepper)
Dried peel of 6 to 8 medium limes (see page 39)

Yield: 2 1/2 tablespoons

Grapefruit-Brown Sugar Dust

This combination tastes like a sweet spice and is wonderful on grilled papaya or mango, splashed with a little rum.

1 tablespoon dark brown sugar
Dried peel of 1 pink grapefruit (see page 39)

Yield: 2 1/2 tablespoons

Tangerine-Coriander Dust

I sprinkle this on salmon steaks before they hit the grill.

1 tablespoon toasted coriander seeds
Dried peel of 5 to 6 tangerines (see page 39)

Yield: 2 1/2 tablespoons

Lime Salt

This traditional Caribbean staple is simple to prepare and doesn't require dry peel.

1 tablespoon kosher salt
1 dried red chili pepper, seeds removed, crushed
Grated zest of 1 lime

Combine the salt, dried pepper, and lime zest. Place in an oven to dry overnight. Use as a salt substitute in Caribbean rubs and marinades.

Yield: 2 tablespoons

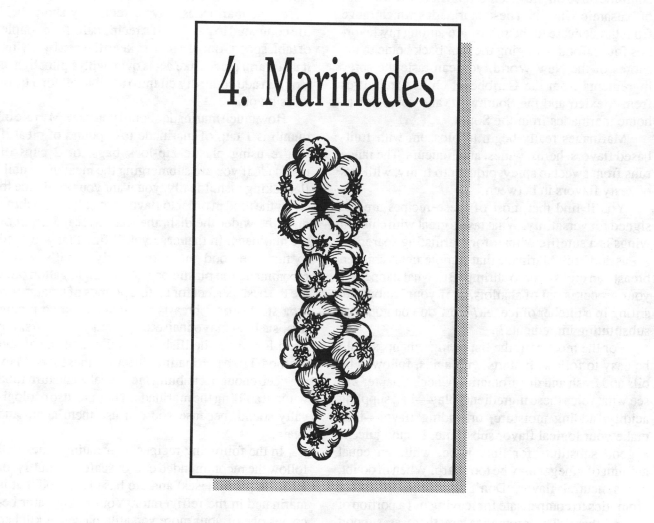

4. Marinades

With this section we do some culinary traveling. First we go to Asia, from Indonesia to Northern China and Korea. In between you'll find spicy samples from Southeast Asia and India, along with the exquisite flavorings of Japan. Next we stop at the shores of the Mediterranean where we combine olive oil, fresh lemon and herbs, and dashes of balsamic vinegar. These marinades which range from the delicate to the robust are among my favorites for seafood. Bringing the tour back home to the shores of the New World, you can taste the spicy ingredients from the Caribbean, chilies and citrus from Mexico and the Southwest, and some down-home marinades from the South.

Marinades really begin to blossom with fruit-based flavors, herbs, wines, and liqueurs. The range runs from sweet to spicy, piquant to fruity, with lots of zesty flavors in between.

You'll find that most of these recipes are designed for versatility. What tastes great with chicken wings is a surefire winner for marinating spareribs. A Passion Fruit Marinade that complements chicken breast can cross over to shrimp. But what happens if your grocer is out of shallots, or if your lemons are sitting in a pitcher of ice tea? How do you go about substituting ingredients?

For the most part, the list of ingredients should be easy to follow. It starts with acids, followed by oils and fresh and dry aromatics. Check Chapter 2 to see what roles these ingredients play—i.e., suppling acidity, adding moisture, or adding flavor—then make your logical flavor substitute. Lemon juice is a good substitute for lime juice, while an equal amount of vinegar may be too sharp. When in doubt, use a neutral flavor. Don't double up on other aromatics to compensate for leaving out a portion of one of them. The aromatics are there as support flavors. Doubling up on a strong spice like cumin may throw the marinade out of balance. If you have qualms about substituting an herb or a spice, put a little bit of your marinade aside, sprinkle in a pinch and taste.

I've tried to keep the recipes user-friendly. With fresh ingredients such as lemon, lime, or orange juice, I'll specify a whole fruit, not half a fruit and similarly whole jalapeños and onions. The measurements are guidelines. Fresh herbs, unless you're growing your own, pose a problem. Fresh cilantro leaves, which you'll use in few Asian and Southwest-style marinades, have a relatively short shelf life compared to parsley. If a recipe calls for a couple of tablespoons out of a bunch, keep the rest by drying it in a warm place (like a gas oven with a pilot light). You can add some dry cilantro to olive oil for a tasty infusion oil.

How much marinade should you use? My rule of thumb is 1 cup of marinade to 1 pound of meat if you're using plastic zip-lock bags, or 2 cups of marinade if you are submerging the meat in a small, flat baking dish. Ideally, you want your marinade to cover the food in order to flavor it evenly. In a baking dish, the wider the dish, the shallower the depth of the marinade. In that case you'll find that you need to turn the food more frequently. That's why I recommend the plastic bags. The single gallon ones are the best, perfect for up to 2 pounds of meat, a few tuna steaks, or 2 breasts of chicken. Large mouth jars, such as mayonnaise or peanut butter jars, are good for some shellfish or small cuts of meat and seafood. I like marinating shrimp in these jars. They are deep enough, enabling me to shake and turn food without spilling the marinade. They are also ecologically sound, because you can use them again and again.

In the following recipes, marinating times will follow the recommended cuts of seafood, poultry, or meat (in parentheses) and are based on food that is marinated in the refrigerator. Your refrigerator becomes one of your more versatile pieces of kitchen equipment. This style of cooking thrives on neglect. You don't have to watch a marinade cook. Begin your marinade in the morning, go off to work, take a long drive, or catch up on some reading. Relax—your refrigerator is doing the work.

Here's an easy rule of thumb for marinating times: Fish needs the least amount of time, followed by chicken, then meat. The firmer the texture, the longer the soak. You can marinate fish or chicken in the refrigerator overnight or up to a couple of days by adding the acid portion of your recipe during the last few hours. Perhaps you will spot a recipe for chicken that you feel would be great with grouper or monkfish. It should be fine but do check out the amount of acid in the recipe. The acid level for seafood should be lower than it is for chicken. If the acidic level is more than 25 percent—when the vinegar or citrus exceeds 25 percent of the total liquid volume—reduce the marinating times.

How long should one wait to marinate food after you've finished making a marinade? Actually you can start marinating food immediately. Or you can leave a marinade refrigerated overnight to let the flavors meld. Marinades can last for 4 to 5 days before they start to break down and the aromatics lose their strength. You may need to refresh the marinade's flavor with additional aromatics and citrus the day you start marinating your food.

See Appendix II, Marinades at a Glance, for some handy charts on marinating times with your favorite cut of food.

Basic Fish Marinade

This is the recipe I recommend for folks who want an easy seafood marinade. I tell my guests that I chose this recipe because I'm not sure of their preferences. However, I really use it because it's so simple and good. You can't go wrong with white wine, olive oil, and fresh herbs.

1 1/2 cups dry white wine or 1 cup dry vermouth
1/2 cup fresh lemon juice
1 tablespoon lemon zest (or lime zest, if using cilantro)
1/4 to 1/2 teaspoon tabasco
1/2 cup olive oil
3 garlic cloves, minced or pressed
3 to 4 tablespoons chopped fresh herbs, such as parsley, mint, cilantro leaves, or basil
1 teaspoon dried oregano
1 teaspoon chopped fresh rosemary
Kosher salt and fresh cracked black peppercorns, to taste

Combine the wine, lemon juice, zest, and tabasco in a nonreactive mixing bowl. Whisk in the oil a little at a time. Add the garlic and herbs.

Yield: 2 1/2 cups

Recommended cuts: Either fresh-water or ocean fish (steaks or fillets), shellfish (2 to 4 hours)

Basic Chicken Marinade

This combination of citrus, mustard, and herbs, is one of my favorite year-round recipes for chicken breasts. This marinade is perfect for the grill or the skillet.

1/2 cup fresh orange juice
1/4 cup fresh lemon juice
1 teaspoon Dijon-style mustard
1 teaspoon worcestershire
1/4 cup canola oil
2 to 3 garlic cloves, minced or pressed
1/4 cup chopped fresh parsley
1 teaspoon dried oregano
Kosher salt and fresh cracked black peppercorns,
   to taste

Combine the orange juice, lemon juice, mustard, and worcestershire in a nonreactive mixing bowl. Whisk in the oil a little at a time. Add the garlic, parsley, oregano, salt, and pepper.

Yield: 1 1/2 cups

Recommended cuts: Chicken breasts (3 to 4 hours), chicken wings (4 to 6 hours)

Basic Beef Marinade

This all-around basic marinade works well with round steak, flank steak, and London broil. Marinate the beef at least overnight but not longer than 2 days, or the marinade will overpower the meat. You can intensify the flavor of this marinade by bringing it to a simmer for about an hour, cooling it, and then adding it to the beef.

1/4 cup sherry vinegar or red wine vinegar
1/2 cup dry red wine
2 tablespoons soy sauce
1 tablespoon worcestershire
1 teaspoon sugar
1/2 cup pure olive oil
2 garlic cloves, sliced
Coarsely ground black pepper, to taste
2 tablespoons chopped fresh parsley
2 tablespoons chopped fresh herbs (any combination of rosemary, tarragon, and thyme)

Combine the vinegar, red wine, soy sauce, worcestershire, and sugar in a nonreactive mixing bowl. Whisk in the olive oil a little at a time. Add the pepper, parsley, and herbs.

Yield: 2 cups

Recommended cuts: Beef and venison steaks and kabobs (6 to 8 hours), roasts and flank steak (10 to 12 hours)

Port Marinade for Game Fowl

Nut oils work especially well with fortified wines in marinades. Chef Kevin von Klaus of West Philadelphia's White Dog Cafe balances the sweetness of port and raspberry vinegar with walnut oil. Marinate wild (or domestic) duck, pheasant, guinea hen, or quail in the refrigerator overnight in this marinade. It is great for any roasted or sauteed game bird.

1/2 cup raspberry vinegar
1 cup ruby port
1/4 cup walnut oil
1/4 cup chopped shallots
3 whole cloves
3 bay leaves, crumbled
1 tablespoon freshly cracked black peppercorns
1 tablespoon coriander seeds, lightly toasted and crushed
1 tablespoon allspice berries, crushed
1 tablespoon juniper berries, crushed

Combine the vinegar and port in a nonreactive mixing bowl. Whisk in the oil a little at a time. Add the shallots, cloves, bay leaves, peppercorns, coriander, allspice, and juniper berries.

Yield: 2 cups

Recommended cuts: Duck (8 hours to overnight); guinea hens, quail, and pheasant (4 to 6 hours)

Asian Marinade

This is a great all-purpose marinade brimming with Asian flavors for chicken or beef. The hoisin sauce replaces the chili in some Thai marinades, and the star anise and five spice powder pick up where the lemongrass leaves off. This marinade works in oriental stir-fries and in marinating skirt and flank steak for the grill.

1/2 cup lime juice
1/4 cup soy sauce
2 tablespoons hoisin sauce
1 tablespoon honey or molasses
1/3 cup Asian or cold-pressed domestic peanut oil
2 tablespoons oriental sesame oil
1 to 2 star anise, ground or crushed
1 teaspoon five spice powder
1 to 2 tablespoons grated fresh ginger root
3 garlic cloves, minced or pressed
3 to 4 tablespoons chopped fresh cilantro leaves
1/4 cup chopped scallions, white part removed

Combine the lime, soy, hoisin, and honey in a nonreactive mixing bowl. Whisk in the oils a little at a time. Add the anise, five spice powder, ginger, garlic, cilantro, and scallions.

Yield: 1 1/2 to 2 cups

Recommended cuts: Chicken breasts (3 to 4 hours); beef and pork tenderloins (6 to 8 hours), kabobs (6 to 8 hours), flank steak (overnight)

Korean Beef Marinade

This robust Korean marinade is perfect for marinating beef, pork loin, or chicken for the grill. The marinade combines the nutty sesame flavors with just enough spice to set it apart from other Asian marinades.

1/4 cup toasted sesame seeds
1 tablespoon oriental sesame oil
1/4 cup rice wine vinegar
2 to 3 tablespoons soy sauce
1/2 cup Asian or domestic cold-pressed peanut oil
2 tablespoons brown sugar
2 to 3 garlic cloves, minced or pressed
2 to 3 tablespoons chopped scallions
1 teaspoon freshly ground pepper
2 Asian dried red chilies, crumbled (seeds removed, optional)

In a spice mill or blender, grind the toasted sesame seeds to a fine powder. In a food processor (or the same blender), add the oriental sesame oil, rice wine vinegar, and soy sauce and puree to a smooth paste. Stir in the oil a little at a time. Add the sugar, garlic, scallions, pepper, and chilies.

Yield: 2 cups

Recommended cuts: Chicken breasts (3 to 4 hours); beef and pork tenderloins (6 to 8 hours), kabobs (6 to 8 hours)

Thai Marinade

Thai marinades combine tart citrus with multiple levels of fire and spice. They can be used on shrimp, chicken, pork, and beef. This marinade can be the starting point for satays, or it can work its wizardry for oriental-style kabobs, with skewers of marinated vegetables, chicken, or shrimp.

2 to 3 tablespoons nam pla (fish sauce)
1/4 cup fresh lime juice (2 to 3 limes)
1/2 cup oriental sesame oil
1 large stalk lemongrass, chopped
1/4 to 1/2 teaspoon crushed dry red Asian pepper
2 tablespoons crushed roasted peanuts
3 garlic cloves, minced or pressed
1/4 cup chopped fresh cilantro leaves
1 tablespoon brown sugar

Combine the fish sauce and lime juice in a nonreactive mixing bowl. Whisk in the oil a little at time. Add the lemongrass, chili pepper, peanuts, garlic, cilantro, and brown sugar.

Yield: 1 to 1 1/2 cups

Recommended cuts: Shrimp (2 to 3 hours); chicken breasts (3 to 4 hours); beef and pork tenderloins (6 to 8 hours), kabobs (6 to 8 hours)

Thai Basil Marinade

Whether you marinate vegetables for stir-fry, shrimp for the grill, or chicken breasts for the broiler, this versatile marinade is a culinary passport to Southeast Asia.

3 tablespoons nam pla (fish sauce)
1 tablespoon sweet soya sauce (ketjap manis) or 2 teaspoons molasses and 1 teaspoon dark Chinese soy sauce
1/2 cup dry white wine or oriental rice wine
1/4 up Asian or domestic cold-pressed peanut oil
1/4 cup chopped fresh basil
2 to 3 tablespoons chopped fresh mint
3 to 4 garlic cloves, minced or pressed
2 tablespoons chopped fresh ginger root
3 shallots, chopped
2 tablespoons chopped fresh lemongrass

Combine the nam pla, soya sauce, and wine in a nonreactive mixing bowl. Whisk in the oil a little at a time. Add the basil, mint, garlic, ginger, shallots, and lemongrass. This marinade will keep in an airtight jar in the refrigerator for 4 to 5 days.

Yield: 2 cups

Recommended cuts: Vegetables (3 to 4 hours); shrimp (2 to 4 hours); chicken breasts (4 to 6 hours)

Thai Curry Marinade

Kaffir or lime leaves throw off a very aromatic perfume along with fresh galangal, ginger's spicier cousin, which are the two signature ingredients in this recipe. Tying it all together are the flavors of coconut and Thai red curry paste. The marinade can work well on shrimp or beef. All of the ingredients can be found in most Asian grocery stores and in the mail order sources in the Appendix.

12-ounce can Asian coconut milk, (preferably Chaokoh brand)
4-ounce can Thai red curry paste
1 stalk lemongrass, finely chopped (about 1/4 cup)
6 kaffir (lime) leaves, chopped into very thin shreds
1 inch square fresh galangal, diced
1/4 cup chopped fresh cilantro leaves
1/4 cup fresh lime juice, (2 to 3 limes)
2 tablespoons nam pla (fish sauce)
1 tablespoon sweet soya sauce (ketjap manis) or 2 teaspoons molasses and 1 teaspoon dark Chinese soy sauce

Combine the coconut milk, curry paste, lemongrass and kaffir leaves in a small saucepan and simmer over low heat for 20 minutes. Cool to room temperature and stir in the galangal, cilantro, lime juice, nam pla, and soya sauce.

Yield: 2 1/2 cups

Recommended cuts: Shrimp (2 to 4 hours); chicken breasts (4 to 6 hours); beef (overnight)

Vietnamese Peanut Marinade

Vietnamese cuisine can take the same herbs and spices of spicy Thai marinades and turn the heat into a delicate savory fragrance. To make a delectable dipping sauce, warm the leftover marinade to a gentle simmer and serve warm.

1 cup Tamarind Juice (see page 25)
1/3 cup rice wine vinegar
3 tablespoons peanut butter (preferably natural and chunky)
1 stalk lemongrass, finely chopped (about 1/4 cup)
2 to 3 garlic cloves, minced or pressed
1/4 cup fresh mint, chopped
1 tablespoon nam pla (fish sauce)
1 tablespoon dark brown sugar
1/2 teaspoon ground turmeric

In a blender or food processor, combine the tamarind, vinegar, peanut butter, lemongrass, garlic, mint, nam pla, sugar, and turmeric. Puree until all the ingredients are blended.

Yield: 2 cups

Recommended cuts: Shrimp (3 to 4 hours); chicken breasts (4 to 6 hours); tofu (overnight)

Cilantro Marinade

This light Southeast Asian-style marinade works well on either grilled shrimp or chicken breasts, also on stir-fried vegetables, such as snow peas or carrots.

2 tablespoons light soy sauce
3 tablespoons rice wine vinegar
3 tablespoons fresh lime juice
1 tablespoon fresh lime zest
1 tablespoon oriental sesame oil
3 tablespoons Asian or domestic cold-pressed peanut oil
1 tablespoon brown sugar
1/2 teaspoon ground coriander
1/2 cup chopped fresh cilantro leaves

Combine the soy sauce, vinegar, lime juice, and zest in a nonreactive mixing bowl. Whisk in the oils a little at a time. Add the brown sugar, coriander, and cilantro.

Yield: 1 cup

Recommended cuts: Vegetables (3 to 4 hours); shrimp (2 to 4 hours); chicken breasts (4 to 6 hours)

Asian Tamarind Marinade

This has all the flavor complexity of a Southeast Asian marinade without the heat. The sour flavor of tamarind with the citrus kaffir leaves is a great combination with the roasted coconut and fresh cilantro. This is one of my all-time favorite seafood marinades. I never seem to run out of things to use it on.

1 1/2 cups Tamarind Juice (see page 25)
4 large kaffir (lime) leaves, cut into narrow strips
1/4 cup fresh lime juice
1 tablespoon light soy sauce
1/4 cup Asian or cold-pressed domestic peanut oil
3 tablespoons chopped shallots
4 garlic cloves, minced or pressed
1 tablespoon diced fresh ginger root
1 tablespoon brown sugar
1/4 cup toasted dried coconut, unsweetened
1/2 cup chopped fresh cilantro leaves

Combine the tamarind and kaffir leaves in a nonreactive saucepan and simmer over low heat until the kaffir leaves soften. Remove the tamarind mix from the heat and cool to room temperature. Combine the tamarind-kaffir mix with the remaining ingredients.

Yield: 2 cups

Recommended cuts: Shrimp and scallops (2 to 4 hours), fish fillets (3 to 4 hours)

Indonesian Honey Chili Marinade

The sweet and hot flavors of Malaysia combine nicely in glaze for chicken wings, quail, and barbecued spare ribs. The recipe calls for a sweet Thai soya sauce called ketjap manis, which tastes like a combination of molasses and soy sauce.

1/4 cup honey
3 to 4 tablespoon ketjap manis (or 2 tablespoons molasses and 1 tablespoon dark Chinese soy sauce)
1/4 cup fresh lemon juice
1 tablespoon rice wine vinegar
2 tablespoons Tamarind Juice (see page 25)
1/2 cup Asian or cold-pressed domestic peanut oil
3 to 4 Thai bird peppers, seeded and diced
1 to 2 tablespoons fresh ginger root, minced

Combine the honey, sweet soya sauce, lemon juice, vinegar, and tamarind in a nonreactive mixing bowl. Whisk in the oil a little at a time. Add the chilies and ginger.

Yield: 1 1/2 to 2 cups

Recommended cuts: Chicken wings (6 to 8 hours), quail (8 hours to overnight); ribs (8 hours to overnight)

Malaysian Marinade

This simple marinade is perfect for scallops of pork tenderloin. Since the tenderloin is the most delicate and flavorful part of the pork loin, you don't want a marinade that is too assertive. The marinade is versatile enough to match well with chicken or shrimp.

2 tablespoons sweet soya sauce (ketjap manis) or honey
3 tablespoons fresh lime juice
1 teaspoon grated lime zest
1/4 cup light soy sauce
1/4 cup Asian or cold-pressed domestic peanut oil
2 tablespoons grated fresh ginger root
3 tablespoons chopped shallots
1/2 teaspoon ground cumin
1/2 teaspoon ground coriander seeds
1/4 cup chopped fresh cilantro leaves

Combine the soya sauce, lime juice, lime zest, and soy sauce in a nonreactive mixing bowl. Whisk in the oil a little at a time. Add the ginger, shallots, cumin, coriander, and fresh cilantro.

Yield: 1 cup

Recommended cuts: Shrimp (3 to 4 hours); chicken breasts (4 to 6 hours); pork scallops (3 to 4 hours)

Szechuan Sesame Marinade

This marinade is China's answer to a Thai peanut sauce. I use this as a base for the Szechuan Chicken Salad. The recipe is excellent for marinating chicken or shrimp for the grill or the wok.

1 tablespoon sherry wine vinegar
1 tablespoon rice vinegar
1/4 cup Asian sesame paste (not tahini)
1/2 cup oriental sesame oil
1 teaspoon Hot Chili Oil (see page 35)
1/4 cup tightly packed chopped fresh cilantro leaves
3 garlic cloves, minced
1 inch fresh ginger root, minced

Combine the vinegars, sesame paste, oriental sesame oil, and chili oil in a blender or food processor. Pour into a nonreactive bowl and add the cilantro, garlic, and ginger.

Yield: 1 1/2 cups

Recommended cuts: Shrimp (3 to 4 hours); chicken breasts (4 to 6 hours)

Spicy Garlic Oriental Marinade

This marinade combines garlic and oriental spices with just a bit of heat from cayenne pepper. Marinate chicken wings in this, and watch them take off.

1/2 cup rice wine vinegar
1/2 cup low-sodium soy sauce
1/4 cup Asian or cold-pressed domestic peanut oil
6 to 7 garlic cloves, minced or pressed
1 tablespoon ground cayenne pepper
2 teaspoons ground ginger
2 tablespoons dark brown sugar

Combine the vinegar and soy sauce in a nonreactive mixing bowl. Whisk in the oils, a little at at time. Add the remaining ingredients and combine. This marinade will keep in an airtight jar in the refrigerator for 1 week.

Yield: 1 1/2 cups

Recommended cuts: Chicken wings (6 to 8 hours); ribs (8 hours to overnight)

Orange-Sesame Marinade

This marinade works with both grilled and stir-fried chicken. The hot chili oil gives a Szechuan bite to the marinade, but you can easily omit it for a less incendiary journey to the Orient.

1/4 cup soy sauce
3 tablespoons red wine vinegar
1 tablespoon honey
1/2 cup fresh orange juice
2 tablespoons grated orange zest
1/4 cup Asian or cold-pressed domestic peanut oil
3 tablespoons oriental sesame oil
1 tablespoon Hot Chili Oil (see page 35)
2 garlic cloves, minced
1 tablespoon fresh ginger root, minced
1 teaspoon toasted sesame seeds

Combine the soy sauce, vinegar, honey, orange juice, and orange zest in a nonreactive mixing bowl. Whisk in the oils, a little at a time. Add the garlic, ginger, and sesame seeds.

Yield: 1 1/2 cups

Recommended cuts: Shrimp (3 to 4 hours); chicken breasts (4 to 6 hours)

Ginger Marinade

This is a very versatile marinade. You can use it with chicken and pork chops, but it's even better with shrimp or tuna. You can make up a quantity ahead of time and add the chopped cilantro and scallions on the day you want to use it.

1/3 cup minced fresh ginger root
1/4 cup light soy sauce
1/4 cup dry sherry
1/4 cup fresh lime juice (about 2 limes)
1 tablespoon dark brown sugar
1/2 cup safflower oil
2 to 3 tablespoons chopped fresh cilantro leaves
1/4 cup sliced scallions, white part only (about 1
  bunch)

Combine the fresh ginger, soy sauce, sherry, lime juice, and brown sugar in a nonreactive mixing bowl. Whisk in the oil a little at a time. Add the cilantro and scallions.

Yield: About 2 cups

Recommended cuts: Shrimp (3 to 4 hours); chicken breasts (4 to 6 hours); pork scallops (3 to 4 hours)

Variations

Chili-Ginger Marinade. Add 1 teaspoon of Hot Chili Oil (see page 35).
Ginger-Mint Marinade. Replace the fresh cilantro with fresh mint.

Sake Marinade

A little bit of this Japanese marinade goes a long way on chicken breasts or wings. Another advantage is that you need to marinate your chicken breast for only 1 to 2 hours. Make a second portion and use it as a dipping sauce.

1/3 cup sake
3 tablespoons mirin
1/4 cup dark soy sauce
1/4 cup dry white or rice wine
2 tablespoons brown sugar

Combine the sake, mirin, soy sauce, wine, and brown sugar in a nonreactive mixing bowl. The marinade will keep in an airtight jar in the refrigerator for up to 2 weeks.

Yield: 1 1/4 cups

Recommended cuts: Shrimp (1 to 2 hours); chicken breasts (1 to 2 hours), wings (6 to 8 hours); ribs (6 to 8 hours)

Sesame-Rice Wine Marinade

This light marinade has more taste than calories, working well with tuna, monkfish, mahi-mahi or chicken breasts. The addition of toasted sesame seeds gives the marinade added crunch and flavor.

**1/4 cup Chinese rice wine (do not substitute sake
  or mirin)**
3 tablespoons fresh lime juice (about 1 lime)
1 teaspoon grated lime zest
2/3 cup safflower oil
1 teaspoon oriental sesame oil
1/2 teaspoon toasted sesame seeds
1 tablespoon minced fresh ginger root

Combine the rice wine, lime juice, and zest in a nonreactive mixing bowl. Whisk in the oils a little at a time. Add the sesame seeds and ginger.

Yield: 1 1/2 cups

Recommended cuts: Fish steaks, 1 inch to 1 1/2 inches thick (2 to 3 hours); chicken breasts (4 to 6 hours)

Miso Marinade

Miso, a Japanese staple found in everything from dressings to soups, is the basis of this marinade. I like to add it to oriental marinades instead of soy sauce because of its distinctive flavor. Should you want to make the flavor of the marinade hotter, add a teaspoon of wasabi powder (Japanese horseradish) to the mix. The miso marinade works particularly well with salmon steaks, which can be briefly marinated and then broiled or grilled.

**2 tablespoons light miso (available at specialty
  food or health food stores)**
1/4 cup rice wine vinegar
1/4 cup mirin
1/2 cup sake
1 teaspoon five spice powder
1/4 cup finely diced chives

Blend all the ingredients in a blender or whisk together in a nonreactive bowl until thoroughly blended.

Yield: 1 cup

Recommended cuts: Tuna or salmon steaks (1 to 2 hours)

Oriental Plum Sauce Marinade

This is becoming a stock item in my refrigerator, especially during the warm weather grilling months. The spicy, fragrant marinade will cling to spare ribs and chicken wings, creating a brilliant red glaze.

2/3 cup plum or duck sauce
2 teaspoons hoisin sauce
2 tablespoons dry sherry
1 tablespoon low-sodium soy sauce
1 teaspoon oriental sesame oil
2 tablespoons Asian or domestic cold-pressed
   peanut oil
1 tablespoon grated fresh ginger root
2 garlic cloves, minced or pressed
1/4 cup chopped fresh cilantro leaves
1/2 teaspoon crushed dried red chili pepper

Combine the plum sauce, hoisin, sherry, and soy sauce in a nonreactive mixing bowl. Whisk in the oils a little at a time. Add the ginger, garlic, cilantro, and chili pepper.

Yield: 2 cups

Recommended cuts: Chicken breasts (4 to 6 hours), wings (6 to 8 hours); spare ribs (8 hours to overnight)

Honey-Hoisin Marinade

This sweet and spicy marinade works as a savory glaze for oriental spare ribs and chicken wings. Have your butcher crack the spareribs into small pieces to give meat better flavor absorption.

1/4 cup low-sodium soy sauce
2 tablespoons hoisin sauce
1/3 cup oriental or dark honey
1/4 cup tomato sauce
2 tablespoons dry sherry
2 tablespoons rice wine vinegar
2 garlic cloves, minced or pressed
2 tablespoons grated fresh ginger root
2 small dried red chilies, crumbled (seeds removed for less heat)
1 teaspoon five spice powder

Combine all the ingredients in a nonreactive bowl or blender.

Yield: 2 1/2 cups

Recommended cuts: Chicken wings (6 to 8 hours); spare ribs (8 hours to overnight)

Teriyaki/Yakitori Marinade

One basic difference between teriyaki and yakitori is that yakitori uses the ingredients as a marinade, while teriyaki works as a glaze. These marinades need only an hour or so to work their magic on chicken breasts and fish. Or you can thread meat or fish on skewers with bell pepper, pearl onions, and mushrooms. Grill or oven broil chicken, fish, or beef. The leftover marinade can be heated until boiling and then used as a dipping sauce.

1/2 cup sake
1/4 cup mirin
1/2 cup low-sodium soy sauce
2 tablespoons rock sugar (or 1 1/2 tablespoons
    granulated white sugar)
1 tablespoon crystallized ginger

Combine all the ingredients in a nonreactive mixing bowl.

Yield: 1 1/2 cups

Recommended cuts: Shrimp (3 to 4 hours); chicken breasts (4 to 6 hours); beef steaks (2 to 3 hours), kabobs (3 to 4 hours); pork scallops (3 to 4 hours)

Note: For quick marinating, cut chicken into 1-inch pieces and marinade for 30 minutes up to one hour.

Curry Marinade

The sweet heat of curry comes rolling across your mouth, hitting every corner of your taste buds. Every time I make this I find something new to put it over— shrimp, chicken wings, spare ribs, tofu, etc.

4 tablespoons curry powder
1 teaspoon cinnamon
2 tablespoons dry sherry
1/4 cup fresh lime juice
1/4 cup fresh lemon juice
1/3 cup Asian or domestic cold-pressed peanut oil
2 to 3 tablespoons chopped shallots
1/4 cup chopped fresh cilantro leaves
2 dry red chilies, crumbled (remove seeds for less
    heat)
1 tablespoon dark brown sugar

In a blender or food processor, combine the curry and cinnamon with the sherry and citrus juices. With the motor running, drizzle in the oil a little at a time. Stir in the shallots, cilantro, chilies, and brown sugar.

Yield: 1 1/4 cups

Recommended cuts: Tofu (overnight); shrimp (2 to 3 hours); chicken wings (6 to 8 hours); spare ribs (8 hours to overnight)

Sake-Mustard Marinade

The mustard adds an interesting depth to this Japanese-style marinade. The marinade is flexible enough to handle poultry, seafood, and vegetables.

1/3 cup sake
3 tablespoons rice wine vinegar
2 tablespoons mirin
1 tablespoon Dijon-style mustard
1/3 cup Asian or domestic cold-pressed peanut oil
1 tablespoon minced shallots
2 to 3 garlic cloves, minced or pressed
1 tablespoon brown sugar

Combine the sake, rice wine vinegar, mirin, and mustard in a nonreactive mixing bowl. Whisk in the peanut oil a little at a time. Add the shallots, garlic, and brown sugar. This marinade will keep in an airtight jar in the refrigerator for 1 week.

Yield: 1 3/4 cups

Recommended cuts: Broccoli or cauliflower (2 to 4 hours); shrimp or scallops (2 to 4 hours); chicken breasts (2 to 3 hours), wings (6 to 8 hours)

Variation

Sake Wasabi Marinade. Substitute 1 tablespoon wasabi powder dissolved in 1 tablespoon of boiling water for the Dijon-style mustard. Proceed with the recipe above.

Lemongrass Marinade

Chef Lynn Buono, of Feast Your Eyes Catering in Philadelphia, says that this is her stock marinade for grilling soft-shell crabs and shrimp in the shell. The flavor centers around the lemony spice of lemongrass.

2 stalks lemongrass, white part only
1 cup olive oil
2 garlic cloves, minced or pressed
1/4 cup soy sauce
1 tablespoon nam pla (fish sauce)
2 tablespoons fresh lime juice (about 1 medium lime)
1 jalapeño chili pepper, chopped (for less heat, remove seeds)
2 tablespoons chopped fresh cilantro leaves

Smash the lemongrass with a mallet or a rolling pin and chop into small pieces.

Heat the olive oil, add the lemongrass and garlic, and cook for about 30 seconds. Cool the mix to room temperature and add the soy sauce, nam pla, lime juice, jalapeño, and coriander. This makes enough to marinate 1 pound of unpeeled shrimp or 8 soft-shell crabs. Lynn suggests that you do not marinate the shellfish longer than 3 to 6 hours, or the fish will become too salty.

Yield: 1 1/2 cups

Recommended cuts: Shrimp (2 to 3 hours), soft-shell crabs (3 to 4 hours)

Tahini Marinade

Tahini, the sesame seed paste of the Middle East, complements the toasted flavor of sesame oil of the Orient. This seafood marinade is particularly good for tuna, red snapper, and swordfish.

3 tablespoons tahini
1 tablespoon oriental sesame oil
1/4 cup fresh lemon juice
1 tablespoon grated lemon zest
1 teaspoon soy sauce
1 tablespoon honey
1/4 cup olive oil
1-inch square fresh ginger root, minced
3 to 4 garlic cloves, minced or pressed
1/4 cup chopped fresh parsley

Combine the tahini, oriental sesame oil, lemon juice, lemon zest, soy sauce, and honey in a nonreactive mixing bowl. Whisk in the oil a little at a time. Add the ginger, garlic, and chopped parsley.

Yield: 1 1/2 cups

Recommended cuts: Fish steaks or fillets (2 to 4 hours)

Lemon Sesame Seed Marinade

The exotic flavors of the Middle East come brimming to the surface of this marinade. The fenugreek and cumin give the marinade its savor, while the lemon and olive oil of the Mediterranean brighten the flavor. Marinate red snapper fillets with this and serve over a bed of couscous.

1/3 cup fresh lemon juice
1 tablespoon grated lemon zest
2/3 cup olive oil
2 teaspoons fenugreek seeds
1 tablespoon sesame seeds
1 teaspoon ground cumin
1/4 teaspoon kosher salt
1/2 teaspoon coarsely cracked white peppercorns
3 garlic cloves, minced or pressed
1/4 cup chopped fresh parsley

Combine the lemon juice and zest in a nonreactive mixing bowl. Whisk in the oil a little at a time. Toast the fenugreek seeds in nonstick frying pan with a lid until they pop. Shake the frying pan constantly to avoid burning. Grind the toasted seeds in a blender or spice mill.

Toast the sesame seeds until they turn golden brown (about 3 to 4 minutes), shake the frying pan constantly to avoid burning. Add the fenugreek, sesame seeds, cumin, salt, pepper, garlic, and parsley to the rest of the marinade.

Yield: 1 1/2 cups

Recommended cuts: Any seafood (1 to 2 hours)

Herbes de Provence Marinade

The southern coast of France known as Provence combines the flavors of the French countryside with the Mediterranean. Some say the regional cooking follows traditional Italian cuisine, but the summery flavor of Herbes de Provence gives the region and this marinade its signature.

1/4 cup fresh lemon juice
1 tablespoon grated lemon zest
1/4 cup dry white wine (preferably French)
2 tablespoons sherry vinegar
1/4 cup olive oil
1/4 cup grapeseed oil
2 tablespoons Herbes de Provence (see page 37)
3 garlic cloves, minced or pressed
1 tablespoon fresh rosemary
1 tablespoon cracked black peppercorns
Kosher or sea salt, to taste

Combine the lemon juice, zest, wine, and vinegar in a nonreactive mixing bowl. Whisk in the oils a little at a time. Add the Herbes de Provence, garlic, rosemary, cracked pepper, and salt. The marinade will keep in an airtight jar in the refrigerator for about 1 week.

Yield: 2 cups

Recommended cuts: Fillets of tuna, grouper, or haddock (2 to 3 hours)

Basic Italian Marinade

This delicious marinade is a culinary catalog of some of Italy's distinct flavors. You'll find variations on this Italian-style marinade good on either vegetables or chicken. This also happens to be one of my favorite fish marinades.

1/3 cup balsamic vinegar
1/4 cup fresh lemon juice
2/3 cup extra-virgin olive oil
4 to 5 garlic cloves, minced or pressed
2 anchovies, mashed with a fork into a paste
1 teaspoon capers, drained
2 to 3 scallions, white part only, finely chopped
1/4 cup chopped fresh flat-leaf parsley
1 to 2 tablespoons freshly cracked black peppercorns
Kosher or sea salt, to taste

Combine the balsamic vinegar and lemon juice in a nonreactive mixing bowl. Whisk in the oil a little at a time. Add the garlic, anchovies, capers, scallions, parsley, pepper, and salt.

Yield: 1 1/2 cups

Recommended cuts: Seafood (2 to 4 hours); chicken breasts (2 to 4 hours)

Basil Marinade

This easy marinade is perfect for grilling fish in the summer. You also may find yourself drizzling it over mozzarella cheese and fresh tomatoes. The Sambucca in the recipe adds a wisp of licorice that really perks up the basil and lemon.

3 tablespoons balsamic vinegar
1/4 cup fresh lemon juice
1 tablespoon fresh lemon zest
1 tablespoon Sambucca (or other licorice or anise
    liqueur)
1/2 cup olive oil
1/3 cup finely chopped basil leaves, tightly packed
3 garlic cloves, minced or pressed
1 tablespoon chopped shallots
Salt and freshly cracked pepper, to taste

Combine the vinegar, lemon juice and zest, and Sambucca in a nonreactive mixing bowl. Whisk in the oil a little at a time. Add the basil, garlic, shallots, and salt and pepper.

Yield: 1 cup

Recommended cuts: Firm-textured seafood, such as tuna, swordfish, and mahi-mahi (3 to 4 hours)

Lemon-Sorrel Marinade

The combination of lemon, sour sorrel, and extra-virgin olive oil makes this marinade perfect for broiled seafood and steamed vegetables. The vinegar plays a dual role by adding just a little bit of sweetness to the tang of this lemony and savory marinade.

1 teaspoon coarse-grained brown mustard
1/3 cup fresh lemon juice
1 tablespoon grated lemon zest
3 tablespoons sherry or balsamic vinegar
1/3 cup extra-virgin olive oil
1/4 cup chopped fresh sorrel leaves
1 teaspoon fresh thyme
1 teaspoon coarsely cracked black peppercorns
1 teaspoon coarsely cracked white peppercorns
Kosher or sea salt, to taste

Combine the mustard, lemon juice and zest, and vinegar in a nonreactive mixing bowl. Whisk in the oil a little at a time. Add the sorrel, thyme, pepper, and salt.

Yield: 1 1/2 cups

Recommended cuts: Haricots verts, white or green asparagus (4 to 6 hours); seafood, such as tuna steaks and mahi-mahi (2 to 3 hours)

Lemon-Caper Marinade

Many Italian households celebrate the Feast of the Seven Fishes on Christmas Eve by preparing the traditional seven seafood dishes. This distinctly Mediterranean marinade with lemon and savory capers is the perfect way to feast on fish no matter what the occasion.

1/3 cup fresh lemon juice (2 medium lemons)
1 1/2 tablespoons grated lemon zest
1 teaspoon Dijon-style mustard
1/2 cup olive oil
3 tablespoons medium capers, rinsed
3 garlic cloves, minced or pressed
2 tablespoons chopped shallots
2 tablespoons chopped fresh flat-leaf parsley
Kosher salt and crushed black peppercorns, to taste

Combine the lemon juice, zest, and mustard in a nonreactive mixing bowl. Whisk in the olive oil a little at a time. Add the capers, garlic, shallots, parsley, salt and pepper. This marinade will keep in an airtight jar in the refrigerator for up to 1 week.

Yield: 1 1/2 cups

Recommended cuts: Seafood, such as red snapper, halibut, or grouper fillets (2 to 3 hours)

Lemon Mint Marinade

This is a minted marinade with tart bursts of lemon. Try drizzling it over grilled chicken or lamb kabobs, and then pack the meat into a toasted pita bread.

1/4 cup dry white wine
1/3 cup fresh lemon juice
2 tablespoons grated lemon zest
1/2 cup olive oil
1/4 cup chopped fresh mint
3 tablespoons chopped shallots
1 tablespoon fresh rosemary
1 teaspoon dried oregano
Kosher salt and cracked peppercorns, to taste

Combine the wine, lemon juice, and zest in a nonreactive mixing bowl. Whisk in the olive oil a little at a time. Add the mint, shallots, rosemary, oregano, and salt and pepper.

Yield: 2 cups

Recommended cuts: Chicken breasts (2 to 4 hours), kabobs (3 to 4 hours); lamb kabobs (4 to 6 hours)

Tapenade Marinade

This marinade is an olive lover's delight. Combining the flavors of Niçoise olives with fruity olive oil and capers, it coats grilled tuna steaks with a shiny glaze.

1 cup pitted Niçoise or brine cured black olives
8 anchovy fillets
2 to 3 tablespoons nonpareil capers
1/4 cup balsamic vinegar
1/3 cup fresh lemon juice
1 tablespoon Dijon-style mustard
1 tablespoon cognac or brandy
1 cup extra-virgin olive oil
2 garlic cloves, minced or pressed
1 teaspoon dried oregano
1/4 cup assorted fresh herbs (parsley, fresh thyme, sage, etc.)

In a food processor, puree the olives, anchovies, capers, vinegar, lemon juice, mustard, and cognac. With the motor running, add the olive oil in a slow, steady stream. Stop the processor, add the garlic, oregano, and herbs and pulse the mixture until it is evenly blended.

Yield: 2 1/2 cups

Recommended cuts: Tuna or swordfish steaks (2 to 4 hours)

Balsamic-Herbal Marinade

What appears to be a tart marinade becomes zesty and fruity on the grill. This may become your standard seafood marinade. It is also good over fresh tomatoes and slices of mozzarella or goat cheese, making this marinade all the more versatile.

1/2 cup balsamic vinegar
1/4 cup fresh lemon juice
1 tablespoon grated lemon zest
2/3 cup extra-virgin olive oil
2 garlic cloves, minced or pressed
1/4 cup chopped flat-leaf parsley
3 to 4 tablespoons fresh basil, shredded
1 teaspoon dried oregano
Kosher salt and coarsely cracked black peppercorns, to taste

Combine the vinegar, lemon juice, and zest in a nonreactive mixing bowl. Whisk in the oil a little at a time. Add the garlic, parsley, basil, oregano, and salt and pepper. The marinade will keep for about 1 week in the refrigerator.

Yield: 2 cups

Recommended cuts: Mozzarella or goat cheese (up to 1 week); any seafood (1 to 3 hours); chicken breasts (2 to 4 hours)

Tomato-Basil Marinade

Garden-fresh tomatoes and sweet basil are a great summertime combination. The balsamic vinegar and extra-virgin olive oil are clues to the marinade's Italian origin. By substituting sherry vinegar and hazelnut oil, you can have a delightful variation. This marinade is simple to prepare and simply delicious. It could double as a chunky pico de gallo, perfect with red snapper, tuna, and swordfish steaks.

1/3 cup chopped fresh basil leaves
4 to 5 medium tomatoes, peeled, seeded, and
  coarsely chopped
1/3 cup extra-virgin olive oil
1/4 cup balsamic vinegar
1/3 cup chopped scallions
3 garlic cloves, minced or pressed
Kosher salt and cracked black peppercorns,
  to taste

Combine all the ingredients in a nonreactive mixing bowl.

Yield: 1 1/2 cups

Recommended cuts: Fish steaks (2 to 4 hours)

Spicy Tomato Marinade

When the bounty of summer-ripened tomatoes hits the produce stands in August, this marinade is the perfect choice for swordfish or tuna steaks. You can use either the slightly tart yellow tomatoes, or the sometimes sweeter red tomatoes, or both of them in the same marinade. Gently warm the leftover marinade for a sauce.

1/4 cup fresh lime or lemon juice
1/2 cup olive oil
4 firm, ripe yellow or red tomatoes, peeled,
  seeded, and diced
1/2 cup finely diced white onion
4 to 5 garlic cloves, minced or pressed
1/2 cup chopped fresh cilantro leaves
3 serrano chilies, seeded and diced
1 tablespoon dark brown sugar
Kosher salt and cracked black peppercorns,
  to taste

Whisk together the lime juice and oil. Combine the remaining ingredients with the lime juice and oil in a food processor and pulse to a coarse texture. Do not puree, as the marinade should have some texture.

Yield: 2 1/2 cups

Recommended cuts: Fish steaks (2 to 4 hours)

Laurel and Lemon Marinade

Chef Kevin von Klaus of West Philadelphia's White Dog Cafe combines the aromatic and peppery perfume of bay leaves with lemon and dry vermouth. While most marinades add flavor, this marinade adds color as well, with the red and yellow slices of onion and lemon. Try to get the more flavorful imported Turkish laurel (bay) leaves with serrated edges, as opposed to the California leaves, which are longer and narrower and have smooth edges.

1/2 cup dry vermouth
1 cup olive oil
2 medium lemons, thinly sliced
1 red onion, thinly sliced
6 laurel leaves, broken
1 tablespoon freshly cracked black peppercorns

Place the vermouth in a nonreactive mixing bowl. Whisk in the oil a little at a time. Add the lemons, onion, garlic, laurel leaves, and pepper. This marinade is good for grilling or broiling.

Yield: 2 cups

Recommended cuts: Shellfish, such as squid, scallops, or shrimp (1 to 2 hours); fish steaks (2 to 3 hours)

Mustard-Dill Marinade

Mustard-Dill Marinade is a natural for salmon, tuna, or swordfish steaks. The richly flavored Dijon-style mustard along with the slightly sweet moutarde is tempered by the cool dill. This marinade can do double duty as a sauce.

1 cup dry white wine
2 tablespoons Dijon-style mustard
3 tablespoons moutarde (or any sweet coarse-
    grained mustard)
3 tablespoons fresh lemon juice
1 tablespoon fresh lime juice
2 tablespoons grapeseed oil
1/4 cup chopped fresh dill
1 teaspoon green peppercorns, drained
1 tablespoon grated lemon zest
Kosher salt, to taste

Combine the white wine, mustards, lemon juice, and lime juice in a nonreactive mixing bowl. Whisk in the oil a tablespoon at a time. Add the dill, peppercorns, lemon zest, and salt.

Yield: 2 cups

Recommended cuts: Salmon, tuna, or swordfish steaks (2 to 4 hours)

South Carolina Mustard Marinade

This easy-to-prepare marinade can be also used as a basting or barbecue sauce for grilled chicken or pork tenderloins. Mustard- and vinegar-based barbecue sauces are popular on chicken in South Carolina, and one taste of this will show you why.

1/2 cup cider vinegar
2 tablespoons Dijon-style mustard
1 tablespoon pure maple syrup or honey
2 teaspoons worcestershire
1/2 teaspoon tabasco
1/3 cup safflower oil
2 tablespoons chopped fresh herbs (tarragon, rosemary, thyme, etc.)
1 tablespoon diced shallot (about 1/2 shallot)

Combine the vinegar, mustard, maple syrup, worcestershire, and tabasco in a nonreactive mixing bowl. Whisk in the oil a little at a time. Add the herbs and shallot.

Yield: 2 cups

Recommended cuts: Chicken breasts (2 to 4 hours), wings (6 to 8 hours); pork chops (3 to 4 hours), spare ribs (8 hours or overnight)

Mustard-Soy Marinade

This is my favorite in-a-hurry marinade when I need something fast, simple, and tasty.

1/3 cup coarse-grained brown mustard
1/4 cup rice wine vinegar
1/2 cup light soy sauce
1 teaspoon tabasco
1 tablespoon dark brown sugar

Combine the mustard, vinegar, soy sauce, tabasco, and brown sugar in a nonreactive mixing bowl. The marinade will keep in a tightly covered jar in the refrigerator for up to 1 week.

Yield: 1 cup

Recommended cuts: Salmon steaks (1 to 2 hours); chicken breasts (2 to 4 hours), wings (6 to 8 hours); pork chops (3 to 4 hours), spare ribs (8 hours or overnight)

Variation

Dijon Mustard-Sherry Marinade. Substitute Dijon-style mustard for the brown mustard and dry sherry for the rice wine vinegar. Proceed with the recipe above.

Mustard-Ginger Marinade

Mustard and ginger lead the parade, followed by sweet tinges of honey and sherry wine vinegar, complementing the nuttiness of the walnut oil. It is one of those marinades that you can make before you go shopping, and whatever you return with will work wonderfully with it.

1/3 cup sherry wine vinegar
1 tablespoon coarse-grained mustard
1 tablespoon honey
2 tablespoons soy sauce
1/3 cup walnut oil
2 tablespoons grated fresh ginger root
2 to 3 garlic cloves, minced or pressed
1 to 2 tablespoons chopped shallots
Kosher salt and pepper, to taste

Combine the vinegar, mustard, honey, and soy sauce in a nonreactive mixing bowl. Whisk in the oil a little at a time. Add the ginger, garlic, shallots, and salt and pepper.

Yield: 1 1/2 cups

Recommended cuts: Salmon steaks (2 to 3 hours); chicken breasts (2 to 4 hours), wings (6 to 8 hours); lamb kabobs (4 to 6 hours); pork chops (3 to 4 hours), spare ribs (8 hours or overnight)

Southwest Chili Corn Marinade

If I were to try putting all the flavors I associate with Southwest cuisine into one marinade, it would be this one. My friend Barbara Boswell has already done it for me. Her marinade has the right amount of heat from the habañeros without overpowering the rest of the ingredients.

1 cup fresh corn kernels (preferably white)
1 tablespoon concentrated tomato paste (from tube)
2 tablespoons molasses
2 tablespoons fresh lemon juice
1 cup corn oil
2 habañeros chilies, seeded and diced
2 tablespoons chopped fresh cilantro leaves
2 tablespoons scallions, white part only
1/3 cup chopped green pepper

Combine the corn kernels, tomato, molasses, and lemon juice in a food processor or blender, and puree to a smooth paste. With the motor running, drizzle in the oil. Fold in the habañeros, cilantro, scallions, and green pepper.

Yield: 2 1/2 cups

Recommended cuts: Tuna or swordfish steaks (2 to 4 hours); chicken breasts (2 to 4 hours)

Honey Ancho Marinade

I wanted a marinade for chicken breasts that would capture the flavor of ancho chilies in an adobo marinade but wouldn't be as heavy. This recipe is the result of my experiments, and it has joined my inner circle of marinades for chicken wings and spare ribs. The secret ingredient in the recipe is the honey; it gives the meat a nice glaze and balances the flavor of the anchos (which are actually dried poblano chilies).

6 dried ancho chili peppers, seeded
1/2 cup fresh orange juice
2 to 3 tablespoons grated orange zest
1/4 cup fresh lime juice
1/3 cup honey
1/3 cup Orange Chipotle Oil (see page 34 or
   substitute cold-pressed peanut oil)
1/4 cup diced white onions
3 garlic cloves, minced or pressed
1/3 cup chopped fresh cilantro leaves

To prepare the ancho chilies, tear them into large pieces. Heat a dry skillet or a comal (a Mexican griddle used for cooking tortillas) to medium heat and press the anchos with the back of the spoon and heat until they plump up and soften; do not let them crisp or burn. Place the anchos in bowl and pour 2 cups of boiling water over them. Cover with a small plate to keep them submerged and let soak for 20 to 30 minutes.

To make the marinade, drain the chilies (discard the fluid) and combine with the orange juice, zest, lime juice, and honey in a food processor or blender; puree until smooth. With the motor running, drizzle in the oil a little at a time. Add the onions, garlic, and cilantro.

Yield: 2 cups

Recommended cuts: Chicken breasts (2 to 4 hours), wings (6 to 8 hours); pork chops or cutlets (3 to 4 hours), spare ribs (6 to 8 hours)

Smoked Pepper Marinade for Seafood

This marinade imports a subtle smoked flavor without grilling, but you will need a water smoker or covered kettle grill to complete this recipe. Use this marinade with grilled or broiled fish. Lightly heated, the leftover marinade makes a wonderful sauce.

2 yellow bell peppers
1/4 cup fresh lime juice
1 tablespoon grated lime zest
1 jalapeño pepper, seeded, with veins removed,
   and diced
1/4 cup white wine vinegar
1/2 cup olive oil
1/4 cup chopped chives
1/4 cup chopped fresh cilantro leaves
Kosher salt and cracked black peppercorns, to
   taste

Smoke the peppers for no longer than 2 hours in a water smoker with presoaked smoking chips like mesquite or hickory. If you are using a covered kettle grill instead, smoke the peppers as above over low indirect heat with a water pan. Note that high heat will result in blistered skins that will impart a burnt taste.

Cool and seed the peppers, then puree in a food processor with the lime juice and zest, jalapeño, and vinegar. Drizzle in the oil in a steady stream and pulse in the chives, cilantro, salt, and pepper until blended.

Yield: 2 cups

Recommended cuts: Shrimp (2 to 3 hours), fish fillets (1 to 2 hours)

Adobo Red Chili Marinade

Traditionally, adobo is a spicy red sauce that's used as both a marinade and a sauce for pork and poultry in Mexico. I've used this marinade as a substitute for barbecue sauce with the Marinated Pork Spare Ribs on page 198 with spectacular results.

6 dried ancho chilies
3 dried guajillo (New Mexican) chilies
2 tablespoons peanut oil or lard
1/2 cup diced white onion
4 to 5 garlic cloves, pressed
1/2 cup fresh orange juice
1/2 cup fresh lime or lemon juice
1/4 cup olive oil
1 teaspoon dried oregano (preferably Mexican)
1/4 teaspoon ground cumin
1/2 teaspoon cinnamon
1/2 teaspoon freshly ground black pepper
3 tablespoons dark brown sugar

To prepare the dried chilies, toast on a moderately hot dry griddle, cast iron frying pan, or comal by pressing them against the hot metal with the back of a spoon until they become plump and begin to soften. Do not let them burn or become crisp. The process will take a few minutes. Devein and seed the chilies. Place them in a deep saucepan and cover with a small plate or bowl. Add 2 cups of boiling water to cover and soak the chilies for about 30 minutes. Drain and discard all but a cup of the soaking liquid.

In a food processor, puree the chilies and the soaking liquid. Heat the oil or lard in a heavy-bottom frying pan, add the onions and garlic, and saute until they are translucent. Add the chili puree and fry the chile puree for about 5 minutes over medium heat. Place the chili mix in a food processor and add orange and lemon juice. With the motor running, drizzle in the oil. Stir in the oregano, cumin, cinnamon, and brown sugar. Place the mix in a nonreactive saucepan and simmer the marinade on low heat for about 1 hour, stirring occasionally. Remove from the heat and cool before marinating poultry or meat.

To use the marinade as a sauce, bring the marinade to a low boil and simmer over low heat until ready to use. Spoon about 1/3 cup of warm sauce on each portion.

Yield: 2 1/2 cups

Recommended cuts: Chicken breasts (2 to 4 hours), wings (6 to 8 hours); beef tenderloins or filets (4 to 6 hours); pork chops or cutlets (3 to 4 hours), spare ribs (6 to 8 hours)

Orange-Chipotle Marinade

This marinade has one of my favorite culinary combinations—the sweet-sour taste of citrus against the heat of smoky chipotle peppers. You can substitute seeded jalapeños or serrano peppers, but it won't have the same smoky flavor. Use this marinade on beef, kid, or pork tenderloins.

3/4 cup fresh orange juice (about 2 to 3 oranges)
1 tablespoon grated orange zest
1/4 cup fresh lime juice (2 to 3 limes)
1 canned chipotle pepper
1/3 cup Orange Chipotle Oil (see page 34) or
  safflower oil
3 garlic cloves, minced or pressed
2 tablespoons chopped fresh cilantro leaves
Kosher salt, to taste

Combine the orange juice, orange zest, lime juice, and chipotle pepper in a blender or food processor and process enough to blend. Transfer the puree to a nonreactive mixing bowl and whisk in the oil a little at a time. Add the garlic, cilantro, and salt.

Yield: 1 1/2 cups

Recommended cuts: Beef tenderloins (2 to 3 hours); kid (young goat) tenderloin (3 to 4 hours); pork chops and tenderloin (4 to 6 hours)

Yucatecan Citrus Marinade

The seasoning style of the Yucatan Peninsula mixes tangy citrus with piquant spices. This marinade will work with chicken breasts, fish such as tuna, swordfish, and grouper, or shrimp. It also can act as a base for seviche made with shrimp, bay scallops, or any firm-fleshed fish.

1/2 cup fresh orange juice
1 tablespoon grated orange zest
1/4 cup fresh lime juice
1 teaspoon grated lime zest
1/4 cup fresh lemon juice
1 teaspoon grated lemon juice
1/4 cup avocado oil or safflower oil
2 tablespoons Chipotle Seasoning (see page 38)
1 teaspoon dried oregano (preferably Mexican)
3 to 4 garlic cloves, minced or pressed
1 tablespoon finely diced jalapeño pepper
3 to 4 tablespoons chopped fresh cilantro leaves
Kosher salt and cracked black peppercorns,
  to taste

Combine the orange juice and zest, lime juice and zest, and the lemon juice and zest in a nonreactive mixing bowl. Whisk in the oil a little at a time. Add the chipotle seasoning, oregano, garlic, jalapeño, cilantro, salt, and pepper.

Yield: 1 1/2 cups

Recommended cuts: Shrimp (2 to 3 hours), bay scallops for seviche (overnight), fish filets (2 to 3); chicken breasts (2 to 4 hours)

Yucatecan Achiote Marinade

Chef Lou Sackett uses this Yucatecan Achiote Marinade at Zocalo, a contemporary Mexican restaurant in West Philadelphia. It's great on chicken, pork, duck, and any strong-flavored fish. It is especially wonderful on kid and roast suckling pig. For the classic Yucatecan dish, Pibil (pi-BEEL), marinate any of the above meats overnight, sear over hot charcoal, wrap in banana leaves, and steam bake.

4 ounces (about 1/2 cup) achiote paste
4 to 5 garlic cloves, minced or pressed
1/2 cup apple cider vinegar
2 teaspoons freshly ground pepper
2 ounces gold tequila
3 bay leaves (crushed)
1/2 teaspoon anise seeds, toasted and crushed
1 teaspoon cumin seeds, toasted and ground
2 teaspoons dark brown sugar
4 one-inch cinnamon sticks, ground
2 teaspoons kosher salt

In a food processor, puree the achiote paste, garlic, and vinegar until smooth. Stir in pepper, tequila, bay leaves, anise, cumin, brown sugar, cinnamon, and salt. Let the marinade stand for several hours or overnight for the flavors to develop.

Yield: 3 cups

Recommended cuts: Shrimp (2 to 3 hours), fish fillets (2 to 3 hours); chicken breasts (2 to 4 hours); lamb kabobs (4 to 6 hours); pork chops (3 to 4 hours)

Chipotle Marinade

The smoky flavor of chipotle peppers adapts well to barbecued ribs. The slow-cooked onions caramelize nicely and give the ribs a hint of sweetness. The marinade has the consistency of a loose paste—a little goes a long way.

2/3 cup chopped white onion
4 to 6 garlic cloves, minced or pressed
2 canned chipotle peppers
1/2 cup white wine vinegar
1/2 cup fresh orange juice
1 tablespoon grated orange zest
1/3 cup olive oil
1 teaspoon Mexican oregano
1 teaspoon ground cumin seeds
2 tablespoons coarsely cracked black peppercorns
Kosher salt, to taste

Puree the onion, garlic, and chipotles in a food processor or blender. Then mix in the vinegar, juice, orange zest, oil, and seasonings.

Yield: 2 cups

Recommended cuts: Chicken wings (6 to 8 hours); spare ribs (6 to 8 hours)

Pineapple-Chili Marinade

The sweet flavor of fresh pineapple tempers the New Mexican chili powder, while the cilantro adds an herbal aroma. I've used this marinade on grilled chicken and grouper in the microwave with splendid results. The marinade is on the mild side, but by adding additional jalapeños you can have it walk on the wild side.

1/2 cup unsweetened pineapple juice
1/4 cup fresh lime juice
2 tablespoons light soy sauce
2 tablespoons New Mexican chili powder
1/3 cup dry white wine
1/3 cup avocado oil
2 tablespoons diced jalapeño
1/4 cup chopped fresh cilantro leaves
1/4 cup chopped red onion
1/2 cup diced fresh pineapple
Kosher salt, to taste

Combine the pineapple juice, lime juice, soy sauce, chili powder, and white wine in a nonreactive mixing bowl. Whisk in the oil a little at a time. Add the jalapeño, cilantro, onion, pineapple, and salt. The marinade will keep in an airtight jar for 1 week in the refrigerator.

Yield: 2 1/2 cups

Recommended cuts: Shrimp (2 to 3 hours), fish fillets (2 to 3 hours); chicken breasts (2 to 4 hours); pork chops or cutlets (3 to 4 hours), spare ribs (6 to 8 hours)

Sofrito Marinade

Sofrito is the spicy tomato base of many Puerto Rican recipes. Its sweet spices benefit from a nice slow simmer. With the addition of lime juice, you can make a good marinade for baked pork chops in winter, as well as for a Caribbean mixed grill in the summer. You can substitute canola oil for the salt pork and slab bacon or pancetta for the smoked ham.

2 to 3 tablespoons of diced salt pork
1/4 pound diced smoked ham
1/2 cup chopped onions
1 tablespoon diced fresh jalapeño
2 garlic cloves, minced or pressed
1 tablespoon Annatto Oil (see page 35)
1/2 teaspoon cinnamon
1/4 teaspoon ginger
1/4 teaspoon ground cloves
1/4 teaspoon cumin
1/2 teaspoon ground coriander seeds
12-ounce can tomatoes
1/2 cup fresh lime juice (about 3 to 4 fresh limes)
1/4 cup chopped fresh cilantro leaves

In a large nonreactive saucepan, render the salt pork, then remove the salt pork and discard. Add the smoked ham, onion, jalapeño, garlic, and annatto oil and saute over high heat until the onions start to brown and ham becomes crisp, 5 to 6 minutes. Add the cinnamon, ginger, cloves, cumin, and coriander. Cook for about 3 minutes more, stirring and scraping the pan well. Reduce the heat, add the tomatoes, and simmer, partially covered, for about 1 hour. Remove from heat and cool. At this point you have the basic recipe for sofrito. To use as a marinade, add the fresh lime juice and cilantro. This marinade freezes well.

Yield: 2 1/2 cups

Recommended cuts: Chicken breasts (4 to 6 hours); pork tenderloin or chops (6 to 8 hours), baby back ribs (6 to 8 hours)

Passion Fruit Marinade

Passion fruit need not be relegated to the dessert side of a menu. This cumin-scented light marinade is perfect for chicken breasts or firm-textured fish, like grouper or monkfish. Since no oil is added, you can reduce the marinade for a sauce or use the marinade in parchment recipes or as a baste for grilled shrimp or chicken cutlets.

With passion fruit, wrinkled means ripe. Look for heavy wrinkled fruit about the size of jumbo or extra-large eggs.

6 passion fruit
1/2 cup orange juice
2 tablespoons dark rum or passion fruit liqueur
1 teaspoon Jamaican hot sauce (or tabasco)
2 tablespoons molasses
2 to 3 garlic cloves, minced
1/2 teaspoon ground coriander seeds
1/4 teaspoon ground cumin
1/4 cup fresh lime juice
2 tablespoons chopped fresh cilantro leaves

Cut the passion fruit with a serrated knife over a nonreactive mixing bowl. Scoop out the seeds and pulp and combine with the orange juice. Place the seeds and juice in a small nonreactive saucepan and simmer for about 3 to 5 minutes, or microwave in a glass or pottery bowl on high for 3 minutes. Strain the juice, discard the seeds, and cool to room temperature. Combine the passion fruit juice with the remaining ingredients.

Yield: 1 1/2 cups

Recommended cuts: Shrimp (2 to 3 hours); chicken breasts (2 to 4 hours); spare ribs (6 to 8 hours)

Yellow Hell®(Mango Marinade)

One of my biggest weaknesses is the sweet fire of Caribbean cuisine. This recipe flirts with the palate with the initial sweetness of the mango and coconut; then the ginger, coriander, and cumin kick in like a steel band. But it's the Scotch bonnet (habañero) chili pepper that gives the mix its tropical heat. My friends call this mango marinade "Yellow Hell," but they always call for seconds.

The marinade can be used as a dipping sauce for grilled shrimp.

2 ripe (yellow-skin) mangoes, peeled and chopped (about 1 1/2 cups)
1 whole Scotch bonnet (habeñero) chili pepper
1 tablespoon dark rum
1 teaspoon Jamaican hot sauce (Pick-a-peppa, Belinda's, or tabasco)
2 garlic cloves, minced or pressed
1 tablespoon grated fresh ginger root
1/4 cup dry unsweetened coconut flakes
1/2 teaspoon ground coriander seeds
1/4 teaspoon ground cumin
1/2 cup canned coconut milk
1/4 cup fresh lime juice
2 tablespoons chopped fresh cilantro leaves

Puree the mango, chili pepper, rum, and the hot sauce in a blender or food processor. Combine the mango puree with the garlic, ginger, coconut, coriander, and cumin in a heavy nonreactive pot and bring to a boil. Reduce the heat and simmer for about 20 minutes. Remove from the heat and cool. Stir in the coconut milk, lime juice, and cilantro.

This marinade freezes well.

Yield: 2 1/2 cups

Recommended cuts: Shrimp (2 to 3 hours); chicken breasts (4 to 6 hours); pork chops (6 to 8 hours)

The Dreaded Red Menace®

For Philadelphia's Book and the Cook event, I wanted to streak some red sauce paint through pools of Yellow Hell marinade for a dish called Mango Shrimp from Hell (see page 129). Well, the red sauce never made it to the shrimp—it tasted so good that we marinated chicken breasts with it instead. People are initially fooled by the sweet raspberry flavor, but this marinade packs a fair amount of heat. We started referring to the marinade in the restaurant as the "Dreaded Red Menace." It's wonderful as a dipping sauce too.

3 dried habañero chilies
1 tablespoon grated orange zest
1 cup raspberry vinegar
1 1/2 cups of fresh or frozen unsweetened raspberries
1/3 cup fresh orange juice

Combine the chiles, orange zest, and vinegar in a heavy nonreactive pot and bring to a boil. Reduce the vinegar to 1/3 cup, strain, and discard the solids. Return the vinegar to the saucepan. Puree the raspberries in a food processor fitted with a plastic dough blade. (A steel blade will crush the seeds, which will lend a bitter taste to the food.) Then strain. Add the raspberry puree to the vinegar and simmer over low heat for 20 minutes. Cool to room temperature and add the orange juice. The marinade will keep in the refrigerator in an airtight jar for 1 to 2 weeks.

Yield: 1 1/2 cups

Recommended cuts: Shrimp (2 to 3 hours); chicken breasts (4 to 6 hours)

Variation

Smoky Red Menace. You can substitute 3 to 4 dried chipotle for the habeñero chilies for a smokier taste.

Lemon Marinade

My friend Barbara Boswell makes a Lemon Marinade that picks up an additional citrus appeal by way of orange juice. The marinade pulls the lemon from three different levels of flavor. The first level of taste comes from the marmalade, which enables the marinade to work as a glaze, the second is from the zest, which gives a fresh lemon flavor, and the third is from the juice, which gives the marinade a nice tang and tempers the sweetness of the marmalade.

1/2 cup lemon marmalade
2 tablespoons water
2 to 3 tablespoons fresh orange juice
1/2 teaspoon grated lemon zest
1/4 cup fresh lemon juice
1/2 cup canola oil
1 1/2 tablespoons diced fresh ginger root
3 garlic cloves, minced or pressed
1/2 teaspoon dried basil
1/2 teaspoon fresh ground pepper
1 tablespoon fresh sage

In a small nonreactive saucepan, heat the marmalade, water, and orange juice until the marmalade dissolves. Cool to room temperature and combine with the fresh lemon juice. Whisk in the canola oil a little bit at a time. Add the ginger, garlic, basil, pepper, and sage.

Yield: 2 cups

Recommended cuts: Chicken breasts (2 to 4 hours), wings (6 to 8 hours), Cornish hens (4 to 6 hours), quail (4 to 6 hours)

Lime Marinade

This is my favorite marinade to use when I am smoking chicken breasts. The sweet citrus flavor cuts and balances the hickory or mesquite smoked flavor. This marinade works particularly well with grilled chicken or quail. The jalapeño-lime version that follows makes scrumptious Southwestern grilled chicken or swordfish.

1/2 cup lime marmalade
1/3 cup water
1/2 cup rice wine vinegar
1/4 cup fresh lime juice
1 tablespoon grated lemon zest
1/2 cup safflower oil
1 garlic clove, minced
1-inch fresh ginger root, minced
6 scallions, white part only, chopped
1 teaspoons crushed black peppercorns
3 to 4 sprigs Mexican mint marigold or fresh
   tarragon

Heat together the marmalade and water in a small saucepan until the marmalade dissolves; then remove from the heat and cool. Combine the cooled marmalade mixture, vinegar, lime juice, and zest in a nonreactive mixing bowl. Whisk in the oil a little at a time. Add the garlic, ginger, scallions, peppercorns, and mint marigold.

Yield: 2 cups

Recommended cuts: Swordfish or tuna (2 to 3 hours); chicken breasts (2 to 4 hours), quail (4 to 6 hours)

Variation

Jalapeño-Lime Marinade. Substitute jalapeño or red chili pepper jelly for the lime marmalade. Add 1 1/2 teaspoons diced jalapeño and proceed with the recipe as above.

Hot Chili Lime Marinade

This chili-infused marinade will fool you. It starts off sweet, sour, and savory. Then the jalapeño arrives, and a wonderful wild ride of flavors begins. Although chicken wings are the perfect match for this marinade, the mix also puts a shine on oven-roasted spare ribs.

1/2 cup jalapeño jelly
2 tablespoons freshly grated lime zest
1/2 cup freshly squeezed lime juice (about 3 to 4
   limes)
1/4 cup olive oil
2 to 3 garlic cloves, minced or pressed
1/3 to 1/2 cup finely chopped white onion
1/2 teaspoon ground cumin
Kosher salt and cracked black peppercorns,
   to taste

Dissolve the jelly in a microwave at 50 percent power for 3 minutes, or bring it to a low simmer in a heavy-bottom enamel sauce pan. Let the jelly cool to room temperature. It should be thick like ketchup, but not solid.

Combine the jelly with the lime zest and juice in a blender. With the motor running, drizzle in the oil a little bit at a time. Stir in the garlic, onion, cumin, salt and pepper.

Yield: 1 1/2 cups

Recommended cuts: Chicken wings (6 to 8 hours); spare ribs (6 to 8 hours)

Lemon Ginger Marinade

This marinade glazes chicken breasts and pork chops with a wonderful tinge of gold. The zesty combination of lemon and ginger contrasts the sweetness of the honey, and the chopped mint adds a gust of coolness to the overall flavor.

1/2 cup lemon juice (2 to 3 lemons)
2 tablespoons grated lemon zest
1/3 cup oriental or wildflower honey
1/4 cup safflower oil
1 tablespoon chopped fresh mint
2 tablespoons freshly grated ginger root
2 garlic cloves, minced or pressed

Combine the lemon juice, zest, and honey in a nonreactive mixing bowl. Whisk in the oil a little at a time. Add the mint, ginger, and garlic. This marinade will keep for about 1 week in an airtight jar in the refrigerator.

Yield: 2 cups

Recommended cuts: Chicken breasts (2 to 4 hours), wings (6 hours to overnight); pork chops or tenderloins (4 to 6 hours), spare ribs (6 hours to overnight)

Espresso Lemon Marinade

This is my Italian version of the Southern breakfast specialty, red-eye gravy. Not only do I marinate chicken breasts and pork chops in this robust marinade, I deglaze the skillet and create a wonderful sauce with it. The espresso flavor really comes through, tempered by the sweet tang of the balsamic vinegar and musky molasses. Lemon peel and espresso go naturally in a demitasse cup. They also balance one another nicely in this recipe.

1 tablespoon instant, freeze-dried espresso
1 cup freshly brewed espresso
1/4 cup balsamic vinegar
1/2 cup unsulphured molasses
1/4 teaspoon red pepper flakes
1 tablespoon low-sodium soy sauce
Julienned peel of 1 lemon
1/4 cup freshly squeezed lemon juice
1/4 teaspoon ground cardamom

Dissolve the instant espresso into the brewed espresso and cool to room temperature. Combine the espresso, balsamic vinegar, molasses, red pepper, soy sauce, lemon peel, lemon juice, and cardamom in a nonreactive mixing bowl.

Yield: 2 cups

Recommended cuts: Chicken breasts (2 to 4 hours), wings (6 hours to overnight); pork chops or tenderloins (4 to 6 hours), spare ribs (6 hours or overnight)

Orange Ginger Marinade

I like the type of marinade that you can make before you go to the market. Whatever you return with, be it chicken, ribs, or tuna steaks, this make-ahead marinade will always come through with flying colors. By combining the Mediterranean flavors of orange, olive oil, and balsamic vinegar with the Oriental tang of ginger, the marinade's flavor is constantly unraveling, bite after bite.

2/3 cup fresh orange juice (about 2 oranges)
1 tablespoon balsamic vinegar
2 tablespoons low-sodium soy sauce
1/4 cup light olive oil
1 1/2 tablespoons grated orange zest
2 tablespoons minced fresh ginger root
1 teaspoon dry mustard
Freshly ground black pepper, to taste

Combine the orange juice, balsamic vinegar, and soy sauce in a nonreactive mixing bowl. Whisk in the olive oil a little at a time. Add the orange zest, ginger, dry mustard, and pepper. This marinade will keep in an airtight jar in the refrigerator for at least a week.

Yield: 1 1/2 cups

Recommended cuts: Tuna or salmon steaks (2 to 3 hours); chicken breasts (2 to 4 hours), wings (6 hours or overnight); pork chops or tenderloins (4 to 6 hours), spare ribs (6 hours or overnight)

Variation

Orange Ginger Glaze. To use this marinade as a glaze for chicken wings or pork ribs, over low heat gently heat the orange juice with either 1/4 cup of orange marmalade or ginger jelly. Cool and complete the recipe as above.

Orange Tarragon Marinade

The bittersweet flavor of Seville oranges in the marmalade pairs nicely with the tarragon in this recipe. Use the marinade on roast chicken or Cornish hens and then glaze carrots with the pan juices and remaining marinade.

1 cup fresh orange juice
1/2 cup Seville orange marmalade
1/3 cup tarragon vinegar
1/2 cup canola oil
2 tablespoons chopped shallots
1 tablespoon chopped fresh tarragon
1 teaspoon coarsely cracked white peppercorns
1 teaspoon coarsely cracked black peppercorns
Kosher salt, to taste

In a heavy-bottom enamel saucepan, bring the orange juice to a low simmer and stir in the marmalade until dissolved. Remove the saucepan from the heat and cool to room temperature.

In a blender or food processor, blend the vinegar into the marmalade mixture. With the motor running, drizzle in the oil a little at a time. Stir in the shallots, tarragon, and peppercorns. Add salt, to taste.

Yield: 2 1/2 cups

Recommended cuts: Whole chicken (6 to 8 hours), Cornish hens (6 to 8 hours, quail (4 to 6 hours)

Bitter Orange Marinade

This Cuban-style marinade is perfect on pork. Seville oranges can sometimes be found in Spanish grocery stores during the winter. The allure of this marinade comes from the sourness of the bitter orange, which really isn't orange tasting at all.

1/2 cup bitter orange juice
1/2 cup canola oil or Orange Chipotle Oil (see page 34)
1 teaspoon ground cumin
2 teaspoons dried Mexican oregano
3 to 4 garlic cloves, minced or pressed
1/4 cup finely diced white onion

To make the marinade, pour the orange juice into a nonreactive mixing bowl. Whisk in the oil a little at a time. Add the cumin, oregano, garlic, and onion.

Williams-Sonoma sells Seville oranges for marmalades. But if you're in a hurry, here's a workable substitute from Diana Kennedy's cookbook, *The Cuisines of Mexico*. Combine 1 teaspoon grated grapefruit zest, 3 tablespoons fresh orange juice, 3 tablespoons fresh grapefruit juice, and 2 tablespoons fresh lemon juice in a nonreactive mixing bowl to make 1/2 cup.

Yield: 1 1/2 cups

Recommended cuts: Pork chops (6 to 8 hours), whole pork tenderloin (8 hours or overnight)

Orange Saffron Marinade

The electric yellow color of this marinade matches its highly charged flavor. The sweet wines counteract the strong flavor of the saffron, while the orange gives the dish a citrus bite that makes the marinade perfect for fish or shrimp. Don't overdo the saffron or the dish will turn medicinal. This marinade makes the transition to a sauce effortlessly. Saute fish or shrimp and deglaze the pan with the remaining marinade.

1/8 teaspoon saffron threads, crushed
2 tablespoons boiling water
1/2 cup fresh orange juice
1 to 2 tablespoons grated orange zest
1 teaspoon coarse-grain mustard
2/3 cup Sauternes or Essina Orange Muscat wine
1/3 cup grapeseed oil
2 to 3 tablespoons chopped shallots
1 teaspoon cracked black peppercorns
Kosher salt, to taste
3 to 4 tablespoons chopped fresh parsley

Combine the saffron with the boiling water and cool to room temperature. Combine the saffron liquid, orange juice, zest, mustard, and wine in a nonreactive mixing bowl. Whisk in the oil a little at a time. Add the shallots, peppercorns, salt, and parsley.

Yield: 1 3/4 to 2 cups

Recommended cuts: Shrimp or scallops (2 to 4 hours), salmon steaks or fillets (2 to 3 hours)

Apricot Marinade

Not only does this apricot marinade make a perfect glaze for chicken wings and spare ribs, it's one of my favorite marinades for Cornish hens.

1/2 cup diced dried apricots or 1 cup fresh apricots, peeled and diced
1 cup dry white wine or fresh orange juice
1/2 cup apricot preserves
2 tablespoons Dijon-style mustard
1/2 cup white wine vinegar
2/3 cup canola oil
1 tablespoon low-sodium soy sauce
1 teaspoon coarsely cracked black peppercorns

In a heavy-bottom enamel saucepan, simmer the apricots in the wine for about 30 minutes, or microwave on high for 8 minutes. Remove the saucepan from the heat, stir in the preserves until dissolved, then let cool to room temperature.

In a blender or food processor, puree the apricot mix, mustard, and vinegar. With the motor running, drizzle in the oil a little at a time through the feed tube. Stir in the soy sauce and peppercorns.

Yield: 2 cups

Recommended cuts: Chicken breasts (4 to 6 hours), kebabs (3 to 4 hours); pork ribs (8 hours to overnight), chops (3 to 4 hours)

Plum-Cassis Marinade

Whether you use this on grilled pork chops or a smoked pork tenderloin, the flavor is sublime. You can use this also as a basting sauce for barbecued ribs and oven-roasted turkey breast.

The yield for this marinade is just right for a whole turkey when marinated in a large roasting bag. Since this recipe freezes well, use half the recipe on ribs and pork chops and save the rest in your freezer.

6 fresh plums, pitted and coarsely chopped
1/4 cup crème de cassis liqueur
1/3 cup cider vinegar
1/4 cup dry Madeira wine
2 cloves garlic, minced or pressed
1 teaspoon dry mustard
1 tablespoon dark brown sugar
1/4 teaspoon freshly grated nutmeg

Combine the plums and the cassis in a heavy enamel pot. Bring to a boil, reduce the heat, and simmer for about 20 minutes. Remove from the heat and let cool to room temperature. Combine the plum mixture with the vinegar, Madeira, garlic, mustard, brown sugar, and nutmeg in a blender or food processor and puree. This marinade will keep in an airtight jar in the refrigerator for 1 week, or in your freezer for a longer stretch of time.

Yield: 3 cups

Recommended cuts: Whole chicken and Cornish hens (4 to 6 hours), turkey (8 hours to overnight), duck breasts (4 to 6 hours); pork chops, tenderloin, or spare ribs (6 to 8 hours)

Cranberry Marinade

I love the tart flavor of cranberries so much that I've often substituted them for fresh currants with wonderful results. I often pair this recipe with turkey breasts, but the marinade can fly to greater heights with roast pork tenderloin, roast chicken, and, especially, chicken wings. Since cranberries freeze so well, stock up on extra bags for the summer grilling months.

12 ounce bag of cranberries, fresh or frozen
1 cup fresh orange juice
1 tablespoon grated orange zest
1/3 cup black currant or raspberry vinegar
1/3 cup canola oil
2 tablespoons unsulphured molasses
1 tablespoon Chambord or crème de cassis
2 tablespoons chopped shallots
Kosher salt and cracked black peppercorns,
to taste

Combine the cranberries and orange juice in a heavy enamel saucepan. Bring to a low boil, and then simmer for about 10 minutes until the berries burst. Remove from the heat and puree in a food processor. Strain the cranberry puree through a fine sieve, and let cool in the refrigerator before combining it with the other ingredients.

Combine the cranberry puree, grated orange zest, and vinegar in a nonreactive mixing bowl. Whisk in the oil a little at a time. Add the molasses, Chambord, shallots, salt and pepper. The marinade will keep in an airtight jar for 1 week in the refrigerator.

Yield: 3 cups

Recommended cuts: Whole chicken (6 to 8 hours), wings (6 to 8 hours), turkey breasts (8 to 10 hours); pork tenderloin (8 hours or overnight)

Variation
Red Currant Marinade. Substitute 1 1/2 cups fresh red currants for the cranberries and proceed with the preceding recipe.

Blueberry Marinade

I was pleasantly surprised to learn how well blueberries work in a savory context. The blueberry flavor is heightened by port wine, which gives the marinade its hints of sweetness. I've used this marinade on roast guinea hen, as well as on Cornish hens, with excellent results.

1 cup tawny port
12-ounce bag frozen unsweetened blueberries
(defrosted)
1/3 cup blueberry vinegar (or other fruit vinegar)
1 teaspoon grated orange zest
1/4 cup fresh orange juice
1 tablespoon chopped shallots
1/2 teaspoon Herbes de Provence (see page 37)
1/4 teaspoon ground coriander seeds
1/2 teaspoon coarsely ground black pepper

In a nonreactive saucepan, combine the port and blueberries, and simmer for 20 minutes. Pour into a blender or food processor and puree. Strain the puree and let it cool to room temperature. Combine it with the remaining ingredients. Makes enough for 2 guinea or Cornish hens.

Yield: 1 1/2 cups

Recommended cuts: Chicken breasts (3 to 4 hours), Cornish hens (4 to 6 hours), guinea hens (4 to 6 hours), quail (3 to 4 hours)

Raspberry Marinade

This recipe is perfect to use when you are smoking duck breasts. You're not limited to raspberries; blackberries, strawberries, or even cooked cranberries will work too.

1/3 cup raspberry vinegar (or balsamic if you're using strawberries)
1 1/2 cups fresh or frozen raspberries
1/4 cup fresh lemon juice
1 to 2 tablespoons chopped shallots
1 tablespoon maple syrup
1 garlic clove, minced
1 teaspoon crushed black peppercorns
1/2 teaspoon kosher salt
3 to 4 fresh herb sprigs, such as tarragon or rosemary
1/3 cup canola or grapeseed oil

Puree the raspberries in a food processor fitted with a plastic dough blade. (A steel blade will crush the seeds which will lend a bitter taste to the food.) Then strain. Combine all the ingredients in a blender or food processor.

Yield: 2 cups

Recommended cuts: Chicken breasts (4 to 6 hours), turkey, duck, or goose breasts (8 to 10 hours), quail (3 to 4 hours)

Beaujolais-Raspberry Marinade

This is one of my favorite marinades for game such as venison, wild duck, quail, and grouse, but chicken breast takes to it just as well. The berry-like flavor of the Beaujolais complements the raspberries, and the aromatics give the marinade a savory contrast which stands up to meat or game birds.

12 ounce bag frozen unsweetened raspberries
1 cup Beaujolais (or other light fruity red wine)
1/4 cup fresh orange juice
2 tablespoons soy sauce
1/4 cup light olive oil or canola oil
2 to 3 garlic cloves, minced or pressed
1/4 cup chopped scallions
1 bay leaf, crumbled
2 to 3 cloves, crumbled
1 teaspoon cracked peppercorns
1/2 teaspoon ground coriander seeds
1/2 teaspoon nutmeg

Puree the raspberries in a food processor fitted with a plastic dough blade. (A steel blade will crush the seeds which will lend a bitter taste to the food.) Combine the raspberry puree, wine, orange juice, and soy sauce in a nonreactive mixing bowl. Whisk in the oil a little at a time. Add the garlic, scallions, bay leaf, cloves, peppercorns, coriander, and nutmeg.

Yield: 3 3/4 cups

Recommended cuts: Chicken breasts (3 to 4 hours), game birds such as wild duck, quail, and grouse (4 to 6 hours); loin of venison (8 hours or overnight)

Sage-Port Wine Marinade

The slight sweetness of port is underscored by savory sage. Ginger perks up the flavor even more to make this marinade a perfect traveling companion for beef tenderloins on their way to the grill. Gently warmed, this marinade makes a delicious, light sauce.

1 1/2 cups ruby port
1/3 cup balsamic or good-quality red wine
  vinegar
2 tablespoons fresh lemon juice
1/2 cup olive oil
2 to 3 tablespoons chopped shallots
2 garlic cloves, minced or pressed
1 tablespoon diced fresh ginger root
3 to 4 tablespoons chopped fresh sage or 1 to 2
  dried sage leaves, crumbled
Kosher salt and cracked black peppercorns,
  to taste

Combine the port, vinegar, and lemon juice in a nonreactive mixing bowl. Whisk in the oil a little at a time. Add the shallots, garlic, ginger, sage, salt, and pepper.

Yield: 2 1/2 cups

Recommended cuts: Beef (6 to 8 hours)

Madeira Marinade

The almonds complement the nut-like quality of sherry vinegar in this marinade, but it's the Madeira that gives the marinade its signature. The marinade is a delight for a cold winter dinner of roasted eye round of beef, as well as for a summer grilling of beef filets.

1/2 cup sherry vinegar
1 cup Madeira wine
1/4 cup almond or hazelnut oil
1/4 cup chopped shallots
2 to 3 garlic cloves, minced or pressed
3 whole cloves, crushed
3 whole bay leaves, crumbled
1 tablespoon freshly cracked black peppercorns
1 tablespoon Herbes de Provence, crushed (see
  page 37)
1 tablespoon allspice berries, crushed
2 tablespoons roasted almond slivers
Kosher salt, to taste

Combine the vinegar and Madeira in a nonreactive mixing bowl. Whisk in the oil a little at a time. Add the shallots, garlic, cloves, bay leaves, peppercorns, Herbes de Provence, allspice, juniper berries, almonds, and salt.

Yield: 2 cups

Recommended cuts: Beef (6 to 8 hours)

Asian Sauternes Marinade

My favorite marinades combine flavors from both Eastern and Western cuisines. The Asian flavors of lemongrass and ginger are a delight with the French flavors of Sauternes and calvados. Because of its high sugar content, Sauternes is a high-acid wine (to balance the sugar) that can cut your marinating time in half. It will take about an hour for shrimp, 2 to 3 hours for poultry, a great marinade for those in a hurry.

3/4 cup Sauternes
3 tablespoons calvados
3 tablespoons lemon juice
1/3 cup canola oil
1 tablespoon soy sauce
1/4 teaspoon ground nutmeg
2 to 3 tablespoons diced fresh ginger root
1/4 cup chopped lemongrass (6-inch stalks)
3 to 4 tablespoons chopped parsley
Kosher salt and cracked black peppercorns,
   to taste

Combine the Sauternes, calvados, and lemon juice in a nonreactive mixing bowl. Whisk in the oil a little at a time. Add the soy, nutmeg, ginger, lemongrass, parsley, salt and pepper.

Yield: 1 1/2 cups

Recommended cuts: Shrimp and scallops (2 to 3 hours); chicken breasts (4 to 6 hours)

Amber Beer Marinade
for Braised Ribs

What makes this marinade a winner is the presence of lime zest, which cuts the bitterness of the beer. People rave about its flavor. Since braising cuts down the cooking time of the ribs, you can brown them over a hot grill and serve in a matter of minutes. After braising, reduce the marinade for a zesty sauce.

12-ounce bottle of amber or dark beer or stout
1/2 cup fresh lime juice (3 to 4 medium limes)
1 to 2 tablespoons grated lime zest
1/4 cup dark brown sugar
1/4 teaspoon cayenne pepper
2 tablespoons worcestershire

Combine the beer, lime juice and zest, sugar, cayenne pepper, and worcestershire in a nonreactive bowl or blender. The recipe will make enough to marinate 2 pounds of ribs.

Yield: 2 cups

Recommended cuts: Baby back, spare, and beef ribs (8 hours or overnight)

Spicy Beer Marinade

Chef Kevin von Klaus of the White Dog Cafe in West Philadelphia combines the flavor of garden-fresh tomatoes with a spice and a surprise ingredient, beer. This tomato-based marinade gets its heat from the tabasco. This marinade is especially good for the grill.

1 cup lager beer
1 cup beef broth
1 teaspoon fresh thyme leaves
3 tomatoes, peeled, seeds removed, and diced
2 teaspoons worcestershire
1 teaspoon tabasco
2 bay leaves, crumbled
3/4 teaspoon freshly cracked black peppercorns
1/4 cup chopped fresh parsley

Combine all of the ingredients in a nonreactive bowl.

Yield: 3 cups

Recommended cuts: Filet mignon (3 to 4 hours), sirloin steak (6 to 8 hours); pork loin or chops (6 to 8 hours)

Cassis Marinade

I use this sweet marinade on duck or goose breast, but I don't stop there. The marinade plays nicely with a hickory-smoked turkey breast and works as a light baste for grilled pork chops. The dried currants give the marinade a bit of texture when you reduce it for a sauce.

1/2 cup dried currants
1/2 cup dry red wine
3/4 cup crème de cassis
3 tablespoons chopped shallots
1 teaspoon cracked black peppercorns
1 bay leaf
1 teaspoon Herbes de Provence (see page 37)
1/4 cup fresh lemon juice

Soften the currants by combining them with the red wine in a nonreactive saucepan and bring to a low boil. Simmer for 10 minutes. Or microwave for 4 to 5 minutes on high. Bring to room temperature. Combine the currants and wine, cassis, shallots, peppercorns, bay leaf, Herbes de Provence, and lemon juice in nonreactive bowl. The marinade will keep in the refrigerator in an airtight jar for up to 3 days.

Yield: 2 1/4 cups

Recommended cuts: Chicken breasts (2 to 4 hours), turkey, duck, or goose breasts (8 to 10 hours); pork chops 6 to 8 hours)

Cointreau-Orange Marinade

This marinade is the essence of orange, from the bright orange color to the intense orange flavor. It is a good marinade for chicken wings or breasts, as well as for glazing pork chops or basting spareribs.

1/2 cup Cointreau (or other orange liqueur)
1/2 cup fresh orange juice
2 tablespoons grated orange zest
2 tablespoons Dijon-style mustard
2 tablespoons Madeira wine
1/4 cup light olive oil
2 cloves garlic, minced or pressed
1 teaspoon cracked black peppercorns
1/2 teaspoon kosher salt
1/4 cup chopped fresh herbs (sage, rosemary, thyme, parsley, etc.)

Combine the Cointreau, orange juice, mustard, and Madeira in a nonreactive mixing bowl. Whisk in the oil a little at a time. Add the garlic, pepper, salt, and chopped herbs. The marinade will keep for about 1 week in a tightly covered jar in the refrigerator.

Yield: 2 cups

Recommended cuts: Chicken breasts (2 to 4 hours), turkey, duck, or goose breasts (8 to 10 hours)

Hazelnut-Galliano Marinade

Sweet vanilla-flavored Galliano balances the nutty flavor of the hazelnuts and the tart lemon zest in this seafood marinade. The marinade works particularly well with firm-textured fish, such as tuna, swordfish, or mackerel.

3 tablespoons Galliano
1/4 cup fresh lemon juice
1 tablespoon grated lemon zest
1/4 cup hazelnut oil
1/4 cup chopped fresh parsley
2 to 3 tablespoons chopped shallots
1/4 cup toasted hazelnuts, skin removed

Combine the Galliano and lemon juice in a nonreactive mixing bowl. Whisk in the oil a little at a time. Add the parsley, shallots, and hazelnuts.

Yield: 1 1/4 cups

Recommended cuts: Fish steaks (2 to 4 hours)

Vodka-Dill Marinade

Vodka provides a savory complement to dill, which is highlighted by the freshness of lemon zest. This is a perfect marinade for salmon or tuna steaks broiled indoors.

1/4 cup vodka
1/3 cup fresh lemon juice
1 tablespoon grated lemon zest
1/4 cup canola oil
1/4 cup pure or virgin olive oil
1/4 cup chopped fresh dill
1/4 cup chopped scallions, white part only
1/2 teaspoon sugar
Kosher salt and freshly ground black pepper,
  to taste

Combine the vodka, lemon juice, and lemon zest in a nonreactive mixing bowl. Whisk in the oils a little at a time. Add the dill, scallions, and sugar. Season to taste with salt and pepper.

Yield: 1 1/2 to 2 cups

Recommended cuts: Salmon or tuna steaks (2 to 4 hours)

Juniper-Lemon Marinade

Try this marinade with sauteed haddock, flounder, or halibut. The marinade has a nice tartness with touches of a savory gin and lemon flavor mixed with herbs.

1 tablespoon juniper berries, crushed
1/4 cup fresh lemon juice
1 tablespoon grated lemon zest
3 tablespoons gin
1/3 cup safflower oil
2 shallots, minced
1 bay leaf, crushed
1/2 teaspoon chopped fresh thyme
2 to 3 tablespoons chopped flat-leaf parsley

Combine the juniper berries, lemon juice, lemon zest, and gin in a nonreactive mixing bowl. Whisk in the oil a little at a time. Add the shallots, bay leaf, thyme, and parsley.

Yield: 1 cup

Recommended cuts: Fish steaks (2 to 4 hours)

Scotch Whiskey Marinade

This light marinade glazes chicken breasts with a golden sheen, fragrant with scotch and fresh oranges. You can also use the marinade to baste chicken breasts while they are on the grill, or you can reduce the marinade for a light sauce.

1/3 cup scotch whiskey
1 tablespoon coarse-grain dark mustard
1/2 cup fresh orange juice
1 tablespoon grated orange zest
1/4 teaspoon freshly grated nutmeg
1 tablespoon worcestershire
1/4 cup chopped scallions (white part only)
2 tablespoons dark brown sugar
Kosher salt and fresh cracked black peppercorns, to taste

Combine the scotch, mustard, orange juice and zest, nutmeg, worcestershire, scallions, brown sugar, and salt and pepper in a nonreactive bowl. This marinade will keep for a week in an airtight glass jar in the refrigerator.

Yield: 1 1/2 cups

Recommended cuts: Salmon fillets (2 to 3 hours); chicken breasts 4 to 6 hours)

Maple Bourbon Marinade

This marinade gives pork chops a caramel-colored glaze. The sweet flavors of maple syrup and bourbon are gently tempered by orange so that the marinade doesn't taste overly sweet but deep and savory.

1 cup pure maple syrup
1/2 cup bourbon or sour mash whiskey
1/2 cup cider vinegar
1/2 cup fresh orange juice
1 tablespoon grated orange zest
1 tablespoon dark brown sugar
2 tablespoons Dijon-style mustard
1/4 cup low-sodium soy sauce

Combine all of the ingredients in a nonreactive mixing bowl.
Note: Since the acid is slightly higher in this marinade to offset the sweetness, marinating times can be shorter.

Yield: 2 cups

Recommended cuts: Chicken wings (6 to 8 hours); pork chops or cutlets (4 to 6 hours), spare ribs (6 to 8 hours)

Rum-Rosemary Marinade

The sweet combination of rum and rosemary pairs nicely with both shrimp and scallops. It works great with chicken breast as well.

1/3 cup dark rum (preferably Myer's)
1/4 cup dry vermouth
3 tablespoons tarragon vinegar
1/4 cup fresh lemon juice
1/2 cup Olio Rosmarino (see page 32) or grapeseed oil or virgin olive oil
1 tablespoon Herbes de Provence (see page 37)
1 to 2 tablespoons chopped fresh rosemary

Combine the rum, vermouth, vinegar, and lemon juice in a nonreactive mixing bowl. Whisk in the oil a little at a time. Stir in the Herbes de Provence and rosemary.

Yield: 1 1/2 cups

Recommended cuts: Scallops or shrimp (2 to 3 hours); chicken breasts (2 to 3 hours)

Hot Chili Rum Marinade

On the first pass, you taste the tropical flavors of sweet rum and zesty lime. Then the Scotch bonnet kicks in with a blast of heat. You can substitute jalapeño or serrano chili in the recipe for a cooler and milder breeze. The marinade provides a nice glaze for basting chicken wings or spare ribs.

1 Scotch bonnet (habañero) chili pepper (or 1 tablespoon diced jalapeño or serrano), seeds, stem, and veins removed
1/2 cup dark rum
1/4 cup fresh lime juice
1 tablespoon grated lime zest
3/4 cup Asian or domestic cold-pressed peanut oil
1/4 cup chopped fresh cilantro leaves
3 garlic cloves, minced or pressed
Kosher salt and pepper, to taste

Puree the chili pepper, rum, and lime juice in a blender or food processor. With the motor running, add the peanut oil a little at a time. Add the cilantro and garlic. The marinade will keep for in an airtight jar for about 1 week in the refrigerator.

Yield: 1 3/4 cups

Recommended cuts: Chicken wings or spare ribs (6 to 8 hours)

Spicy Yogurt Marinade

This Indian-style marinade gives lamb kebabs a tart and spicy taste. Savory yogurt marinades do not require oil—they keep lamb moist and fragrant whether the meat is grilled or broiled. See the variation below for an equally flavorful Mediterranean marinade.

1/4 cup finely chopped fresh mint
1-inch cube fresh ginger root, minced
1/2 cup chopped onion
2 garlic cloves, minced or pressed
1/2 teaspoon Garam Marsala (see page 38) or
  curry powder
1/2 teaspoon ground coriander seeds
1/2 teaspoon ground cardamom
Pinch cayenne pepper
1/2 teaspoon kosher salt
1 1/2 cups plain yogurt

Combine the ingredients in a nonreactive bowl.

Yield: 2 cups

Recommended cuts: Chicken kebabs (3 to 4 hours); lamb kebabs (4 to 6 hours)

Variation

Yogurt-Mint Marinade. Omit the garam masala and coriander. Add 3 tablespoons lemon juice, 1 tablespoon grated lemon zest, and 1 teaspoon dried Greek oregano.

Yogurt Dill Marinade

This marinade seems to cry out for salmon. Mustard, dill, and hints of horseradish in a wrapper of yogurt will cover salmon steaks or whole salmon trout with a blanket of flavor. I had a request from a friend to use this marinade as a sauce for smoked brook trout at brunch, and I obliged.

1/4 cup chopped fresh dill
1 cup plain yogurt
2 tablespoons grated horseradish
1 tablespoon coarse-grain mustard
2 tablespoons sherry vinegar
3 tablespoons olive oil

Combine the dill, yogurt, horseradish, mustard, and vinegar in a nonreactive mixing bowl. Whisk in the oil a little at a time.

Yield: 1 1/2 cups

Recommended cuts: Salmon steaks or fillets, salmon trout or fresh brook trout (2 to 4 hours)

5. Dry Marinades, Rubs, and Pastes

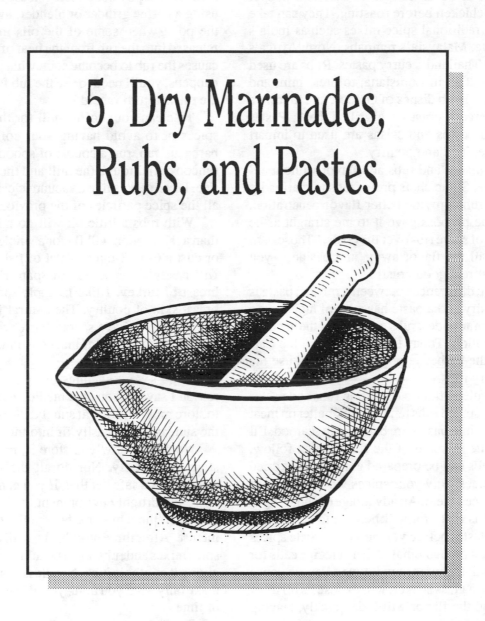

Dry marinades, pastes, and rubs are age-old mixes that infuse food with flavor. The ingredients can be as simple as salt and pepper rubbed on a chicken before roasting. They can take the form of traditional spice mixes such as India's garam masala, Malaysia's rempahs, North Africa's berbere, and Thailand's curry pastes. Rubs are used to blacken redfish in Louisiana, to press mint and lemon into the lamb dishes of Greece, and to form a mixed peppercorn crust on a grilled steak. Pastes such as herb pestos and salsas are used to impart flavor into seafood and poultry.

Dry marinades and rubs add flavor without excess moisture. Some chefs prefer rubs to marinades because the rubs provide better flavor penetration. One barbecue pit boss gave it to me straight as he tossed a side of spare ribs over the coals, "Those darn baths wash all the flavor away, and besides—you don't get that real good crust!"

The basic differences between a rub and paste is that a rub is dry and a paste has a bit of moisture to bind it. Like marinades, rubs grew out of the need for food preservation. Today the jerk joints of the Caribbean and the barbecue pits of Texas still use the traditional dry rubs.

A loose rule of thumb regarding rubs and pastes is that highly spiced rubs tend to work better on meat and poultry, while pastes are better with seafood. I'll break this rule in some of the recipes that follow, however. Rubs can be prepared entirely from dried herbs and spices. Buy your spices whole and grind them as you need them. An advantage of shopping at a spice shop is that you will be able to smell (and maybe even taste) before you purchase. Stale spices will taste bitter or medicinal. When a recipe calls for pepper, avoid the preground type. Pepper, once ground and in a glass shaker, will expose its oil to air and light, and the flavor will fade quickly, leaving you with gray sawdust.

Preparing rubs is easy—the only equipment you need is a blender or a coffee grinder, although the time-honored tradition of mortar and pestle is still preferred by some cooks. A rub need not be pulverized to a fine powder for it to release flavor. If you are using a coffee grinder or blender, avoid grinding to the point when some of the oils in the spices are released into the rub from the heat of the motor. This causes the rub to become somewhat pasty. Once that happens, you'll need to use the rub fairly quickly, as the oil will turn rancid.

To clean your coffee mill for the next batch of spices or to avoid having your coffee taste like a barbecue rub, run a couple of spoonfuls of dry rice (uncooked) through the mill and then throw out the rice. Dry rice acts like a vacuum cleaner and collects all the spice particles of the previous mix.

With rubs a little bit will go a long way. Less than a tablespoon will flavor a whole chicken breast or dust a 6- to 8-ounce fillet of fish. A quarter cup will easily cover a side of spare ribs, or a whole breast of turkey. I like to apply the rub under the breast skin of poultry. The natural juices mix with the rub to provide a savory baste when it hits a hot grill or broiler. And it makes wonderful crackling, too.

A rub's worst enemies are light and heat. For that reason I save old opaque medicine bottles in which to store rubs. The lids fit snugly; the bottles block out the sun, and they easily fit into the refrigerator.

No matter how you store it, no spice mix will store indefinitely. Nor do all the ingredients age evenly. It's a safe bet that, if you can store a dry rub in a cool airtight environment, it'll maintain flavor for two to three months, but the flavor will not be as intense. After three months, I usually shake leftover spice mixes and rubs into a breading for fried chicken giving it an ethnic kick. Needless to say, it's smart to make only what you think you'll use in a short period of time.

Pastes have moisture. The moisture can come from fresh herbs or aromatics such as onions, shallots, or garlic. Pastes can be bound together with wine, citrus juices, or oils. But since most pastes are generally mixed from fresh ingredients, their shelf life is short. Pastes tend to be less piquant than rubs—they work well with seafood without overpowering it.

Here's a trick that I learned from Chef Jon Jividen of Ridgewell's Catering in Washington, D.C., for getting deeper flavor penetration with pastes. After rubbing fish or meat with a paste, tightly wrap it with lightly oiled cling wrap before you cook it. The liquid and seasonings will be absorbed into the food's surface.

Mixed Peppercorn Rub for Beef

I have a pretty simple attitude when it comes to grilling steaks, namely that less is more. In this case, the ingredients of the rub complement the steak, instead of competing with it. When grilling or broiling using high heat, the peppercorns caramelize and sear into the crust, thus helping to lock the flavor of a good fillet inside a thin, savory, crisp shell.

2 tablespoons black peppercorns
2 tablespoons white peppercorns
1 tablespoon pink peppercorns
1 tablespoon mustard seeds
1 teaspoon garlic powder
1 teaspoon kosher salt

Combine all the ingredients in a spice grinder or blender and grind to a coarse meal.

Yield: 1/2 cup

Recommended cuts: Beef, such as filet mignon, top loin, sirloin (3 to 4 hours)

Rosemary Seasoning Rub

I began using this rub on grilled chicken and liked the combination of rosemary and cracked peppercorns so much I started to use it on lamb dishes and then proceeded to use it on grilled swordfish. This is a great all-purpose rub. Coat your fish or meat with a tablespoon of olive oil, then apply this rub, let stand for 2 to 3 hours, and you're ready to go.

4 tablespoons chopped fresh rosemary
2 teaspoons kosher salt
1 tablespoon fresh cracked black peppercorns
1/2 tablespoon fresh cracked white peppercorns
1/4 teaspoon cayenne
1 teaspoon dry mustard powder
1 teaspoon dried oregano
1 teaspoon garlic powder

Combine all the ingredients in a spice mill or blender and grind to a coarse powder. Stored in an airtight jar, this will keep in the freezer for 3 to 4 months.

Yield: 1/2 cup

Recommended cuts: Swordfish (2 to 4 hours); chicken breasts (4 to 6 hours); lamb (3 to 6 hours)

Chipotle Rub

The Madeira and orange add a sweet-sour flavor to the spicy kick of the chipotle rub. Just a tablespoon of this dry marinade goes a long way. I've used this on eye rounds for indirect cooking in a covered grill as well as on a roast for a Sunday night dinner in winter.

1/4 cup Madeira wine
2 tablespoons low-sodium soy sauce
1 tablespoon worcestershire
1/4 cup Chipotle Seasoning (see page 38)
1 1/2 tablespoons grated orange zest
4 to 5 garlic cloves, minced or pressed

Combine the Madeira, soy sauce, worcestershire, Chipotle Seasoning, orange zest, and garlic in a blender or food processor. Process until smooth. This rub will keep in an airtight jar for 2 to 3 weeks in the refrigerator.

Yield: 1 cup

Recommended cuts: Beef (up to 8 hours)

Achiote Chipotle Rub

This incendiary Achiote Chipotle Rub uses tangy dried chipotles to give a smoky, outdoor taste to chicken, ribs, and hamburger. The heat of the chili is tempered with cinnamon and orange-cumin dust, while the aromatic achiote seeds give the rub its Latin soul.

2 tablespoons achiote seeds
2 sticks cinnamon (2 to 3 inches each)
2 dried chipotle pepper
2 tablespoons epozote
2 tablespoons Orange Cumin Dust (see page 39)
  or 2 to 3 teaspoons dried orange zest and 1
  teaspoon ground cumin
2 tablespoons black peppercorns

Combine all the ingredients in a spice grinder or blender and process until ground. Store in an airtight container in the freezer for about 3 months.

Yield: 1/2 cup

Recommended cuts: Chicken breasts (4 to 6 hours), wings (6 to 8 hours); hamburger (4 to 6 hours), beef kabobs (4 to 6 hours); spare ribs (8 hours to overnight)

Yucatecan Rub

One of the essential flavor elements of the Yucatan Peninsula is citrus. This rub combines the flavors of orange, coriander, and cumin with a wisp of heat from the cayenne. I like to mix this rub with yogurt for a Southwestern tandoori chicken.

1 tablespoon achiote seeds
1 1/2 teaspoons whole coriander seeds
1 tablespoon Orange Cumin Dust (see page 39) or
  1 1/2 teaspoons dried orange zest and 1 1/2
  teaspoons ground cumin
1 tablespoon whole black peppercorns
1 tablespoon paprika
1 teaspoon cayenne

Combine all the ingredients in a spice mill or blender and grind to a coarse powder. Store in an airtight jar in the freezer for up to 6 months.

Yield: 1/3 cup

Recommended cuts: Chicken breasts (4 to 6 hours); pork chops (3 to 4 hours); beef steak (6 to 8 hours)

Cinnamon-Chili Rub for Poultry

I've used this rub under the skin of turkey breasts and then smoked them under mesquite and fruit woods for 3 to 4 hours. The flavor is wonderful. The heat is balanced by the cinnamon and orange. This rub works just as well on grilled chicken breasts.

2 tablespoons ancho chili powder (ground ancho
  chili pepper)
2 tablespoons New Mexican chili powder
2 cinnamon sticks or 1 tablespoon ground
  cinnamon
2 teaspoons ground cumin
2 teaspoons dried oregano
2 teaspoons kosher salt
2 to 3 dried chipotle peppers
2 tablespoons ground dried orange peel, (peel of
  1 juice orange, white pith removed, dried in the
  oven overnight, then ground in a spice mill)

Combine all the ingredients in a spice mill or blender and grind to a coarse powder. Store in an airtight jar in the freezer for up to 6 months.

To serve with turkey breasts, peel back the skin and rub the spice mix onto the turkey breast. Replace the skin, cover with plastic cling wrap, and refrigerate for at least 4 to 6 hours before cooking.

Yield: 1/2 cup

Recommended cuts: Chicken breasts (4 to 6 hours), wings (6 to 8 hours), turkey breast (8 hours to overnight)

Cumin Spice Rub

Lately, cooks have become more aware of spicy food from Southeast Asia and the Southwest. The North African spices are just as complex, maybe even more so. The emphasis there is on sweet spices that once were traded throughout the Orient, with a bit of heat added. A little bit of this rub goes a long way. A tablespoon per chicken breast is all you need, or about 1/4 cup for a pound of shrimp.

1/4 cup ground cumin
2 tablespoons paprika
2 tablespoons ground cardamom
1 tablespoon ground cinnamon (or a 2-inch stick)
1 tablespoon dark brown sugar
1 tablespoon freshly cracked black pepper
1 tablespoon cayenne pepper
2 tablespoons dried oregano

Combine all the ingredients in a spice mill or blender and grind to a coarse powder. Store in an airtight jar. It will keep in the freezer for up to 6 months.

Yield: 3/4 cup

Recommended cuts: Shrimp (2 to 4 hours); chicken breasts (4 to 6 hours), kabobs (3 to 4 hours); beef or lamb kabobs (4 to 6 hours)

Texas Dry Rub

The secret ingredient here is the dried wild mushroom, which lends it a savory muskiness. The dried chipotles add hints of smoke, along with the heat. Use as a dry rub for beef brisket or beef or pork ribs.

3 tablespoons coarsely cracked black peppercorns
2 tablespoons dried oregano
1 teaspoon cumin
1 teaspoon onion powder
2 to 3 dried chipotle chili peppers
1 tablespoon dried cilantro leaves
1 bay leaf
1 teaspoon ground dried orange peel
1 tablespoon chopped dried wild mushroom (cèpes)

Combine all the ingredients in a spice mill or blender and grind to a coarse powder. Store in an airtight jar in the freezer for up to 6 months.

Yield: 1/2 cup

Recommended cuts: Beef brisket (8 hours to overnight), flank steak (6 to 8 hours); pork ribs (8 hours to overnight)

Tumbleweed Spice Mix

I came across this recipe as part of a seasoning mix for Tumbleweed Onions in a recipe from Executive Chefs Bob Munich and Joe D'Aquila of Kinterra in Wayne, Pennsylvania. I had some left over and since I didn't want it to go to waste, I tried it as a rub on beef brisket. Now it goes with spare ribs and chicken wings as well.

2 tablespoons paprika
1 tablespoon cayenne
1 teaspoon dried thyme
1 teaspoon dried oregano
1 teaspoon freshly ground white pepper
1 teaspoon freshly ground black pepper
1 tablespoon kosher salt
1 tablespoon garlic powder
1 tablespoon onion powder

Combine all the ingredients in a small bowl. Store in an airtight jar. It will keep in the freezer for up to 6 months.

Yield: 1/2 cup

Recommended cuts: Chicken wings (6 to 8 hours); beef steaks (3 to 4 hours), brisket (8 hours or overnight); spare ribs (6 to 8 hours)

Southern Barbecue Rub

This rub will enable you to create ribs that a pit boss would be proud of. Rub it into a side of ribs and refrigerate overnight. Then slow smoke the ribs over indirect heat in a kettle grill, adding a couple of handfuls of presoaked hickory smoking chips. Serve with your favorite barbecue sauce and a side of coleslaw.

1/4 cup dark brown sugar
2 tablespoons kosher salt
1/4 cup black peppercorns
1/4 cup paprika
1 tablespoon powdered mustard
1 tablespoon onion powder
2 tablespoons garlic powder
1 to 2 teaspoons cayenne pepper, or to taste

Combine all the ingredients in a spice mill or blender and grind to a coarse powder. Store in an airtight jar in the freezer for up to 6 months.

Yield: 1 cup

Recommended cuts: Beef brisket (8 hours to overnight), flank steak (6 to 8 hours); pork ribs (8 hours to overnight)

Sour Mash Pink Peppercorn Rub

The sour mash in this rub is none other than Jack Daniels, but I've taken the spice portion of the recipe and combined it with scotch, cognac, or armagnac, and they worked well, too. This is an elegant rub to dress salmon fillets bound for the grill or the broiler.

3 tablespoons pink peppercorns
2 tablespoons black peppercorns
2 tablespoons white peppercorns
1 teaspoon whole yellow mustard seeds
1 teaspoon whole coriander seeds
2 tablespoons finely diced shallots
1 tablespoon chopped fresh dill, or 1 teaspoon
 dried dill, crumbled
3 tablespoons Jack Daniels
1 tablespoon honey

Combine the peppercorns, mustard seeds, and coriander seeds in a spice mill or blender and grind to a coarse powder (about 3 to 4 pulses). Place in a nonreactive bowl and add the shallots and dill.

To use as a rub, combine the Jack Daniels and honey. Brush onto 2/3 to 1 pound of fish fillets, flesh side up. Press the spice mix into the surface of the fish and marinate in the refrigerator for 1 to 2 hours. Grill or broil the fillets. This recipe will make enough rub for 2 to 4 servings.

Yield: 1/2 cup

Recommended cuts: Salmon fillets (2 to 4 hours); beef fillets (6 to 8 hours)

Jerk Rub

Jerk! That single word is to Caribbean cuisine as the word "blackened" is to Cajun cuisine. This fiery hot recipe is from my friend Dunstan Harris's cookbook, *Island Cooking*. What it delivers in fire power, it matches in flavor. Jerk marinade is also good on fish, chicken, and pork chops.

2 tablespoons Jamaican pimento (allspice),
 crushed
1/4 teaspoon freshly grated nutmeg
1 teaspoon ground cinnamon
12 scallions, white part chopped
6 Scotch bonnet peppers or 12 jalapeño peppers,
 halved with seeds
1/3 cup red wine vinegar
2 tablespoons canola oil
1 tablespoon kosher salt
1 teaspoon freshly ground black pepper
2 tablespoons soy sauce
Jamaican hot pepper sauce or tabasco (optional)

Combine all the ingredients in a blender or food processor, adding hot pepper to taste. Process to liquify, about 1 to 2 minutes. Pour into a jar and refrigerate overnight to let the flavors develop. The sauce will keep for 3 to 4 weeks, covered, in an airtight jar in the refrigerator.

Yield: 1 cup

Recommended cuts: Shrimp (2 to 4 hours); chicken breasts (4 to 6 hours); beef kabobs (4 to 6 hours); pork chops (3 to 4 hours), spare ribs (8 hours to overnight); lamb kabobs (4 to 6 hours)

Cajun Rub

This rub uses peppers in three different ways. The three different peppers, black, white, and cayenne, hit you in three different areas in your mouth. Each pepper caramelizes differently when seared over high heat. This enables them to encrust chicken, pork chops, and firm-flesh fish with a savory shell of flavor. But flame without flavor is not very interesting. It's the accompanying spices that give this rub its staying power. I use the rub under the skin of grilled chicken breasts, on flank steak, lamb kabobs, and spare ribs.

2 tablespoons black peppercorns
2 tablespoons white peppercorns
1 to 2 tablespoons cayenne (start with 1 table-
   spoon; if you like it hotter, add the second)
3 tablespoons paprika
1 tablespoon brown sugar
1 tablespoon kosher salt, or to taste
2 teaspoons garlic powder
2 teaspoons onion powder
2 teaspoons dried oregano
1 teaspoon dried sage
1 teaspoon dried thyme

Combine all the ingredients in a blender or spice grinder and grind to a coarse powder. Makes enough for 2 pounds of chicken, flank steak, or a side of spare ribs.

Yield: 2/3 cups

Recommended cuts: Chicken breasts (4 to 6 hours); beef flank steak (6 to 8 hours); spare ribs (8 hours to overnight)

Sambal Mint Paste

Indonesian sambals are incendiary blends that can be added sparingly to perk up the flavor of blander dishes and sauces. This particular version is a little gentler on the tongue due to the mint and cilantro. The paste is great for grilled shrimp.

1/2 cup (1 bunch) tightly packed mint leaves
1/2 cup (1 bunch) tightly packed cilantro leaves
1/4 cup unsalted cashew pieces
1/2 cup Tamarind Juice (see page 25)
4 to 5 Thai bird peppers or 3 to 4 dried red chili
   peppers, seeds removed

Combine all the ingredients in a food processor and blend to a paste. The paste will keep for a week refrigerated.

Yield: 1 cup

Recommended cuts: Shrimp (2 to 4 hours); chicken breasts (4 to 6 hours); spare ribs (8 hours to overnight)

Wasabi Rub

This recipe is the perfect match for grilled flank steak. The heat in this marinade is from the Japanese horseradish powder called wasabi. The spices are Chinese, with mustard seeds added.

1 tablespoon white peppercorns
1 tablespoon black peppercorns
1 tablespoon yellow mustard seeds
1 tablespoon five spice powder
1 teaspoon star anise, crushed
1 teaspoon wasabi powder
3 to 4 teaspoons warm water
1/4 cup sake
1/4 cup low-sodium soy sauce
1/4 cup mirin

Combine the white peppercorns, black peppercorns, mustard seeds, five spice powder, and star anise in a spice mill or blender. Grind to a coarse powder.

In a small bowl, stir the warm water into the wasabi powder until it's smooth, adding additional water (1/2 teaspoon at a time) if necessary. Let the wasabi stand uncovered for 15 minutes until the flavor develops. Combine the spice mix, wasabi, sake, soy, and mirin. The mix will keep for 1 week.

You can use this paste to marinate flank steak overnight in the refrigerator; grill and serve with the Japanese dipping sauce.

Yield: 1 cup

Recommended cuts: Beef steaks (6 to 8 hours), brisket and flank steak (8 hours to overnight)

Hoisin Sesame Paste

This combination of sweet and savory spices works well with chicken, pork tenderloins, and shrimp. It gives them a tasty glaze. The chilies are a nice foil for the sweetness from the hoisin and the ketjap manis. The sesame seeds provide an added nutty crunch.

1/3 cup toasted sesame seeds
1 tablespoon oriental sesame oil
4 tablespoons hoisin sauce
3 tablespoons sweet soya sauce (ketjap manis) or molasses
2 tablespoons soy sauce
2 to 3 dry red chilies, seeded and crushed
2 tablespoons grated orange sauce
1 teaspoon ground coriander seeds
1/2 teaspoon cumin
1 tablespoon shrimp paste
2 to 3 garlic cloves, minced or pressed

Combine all the ingredients in a nonreactive mixing bowl. The paste will last for about a week in the refrigerator.

Yield: 1 cup

Recommended cuts: Shrimp (2 to 3 hours); chicken (4 to 6 hours); pork tenderloins (8 hours to overnight)

Herb Pesto Rub

This rub (created by Chef Jon Jividen) is truly sublime when placed under the skin of chicken breasts or on a leg of lamb. You can covert this to a rub for beef by substituting 1/4 cup Madeira for a 1/4 cup of the olive oil.

1/4 cup fresh thyme
1/4 cup fresh rosemary
1/2 cup fresh oregano
1 cup fresh parsley
1 tablespoon kosher salt
1 teaspoon freshly ground black pepper
1/2 cup olive oil

Strip the thyme and rosemary leaves from the stems and remove the leafy parts from the oregano, sage, and parsley (you should have approximately 3 cups of loose herbs after cleaning). Place the herbs, salt, and pepper in a food processor. With the motor running, slowly add the olive oil and process until the pesto is blended. The mix will keep for 1 week refrigerated.

Yield: 2 cups

Recommended cuts: Firm fish fillets (3 to 4 hours); chicken breasts (4 to 6 hours); lamb chops (3 to 4 hours), leg of lamb (overnight)

Charmoula

Charmoula or (chermoulla) can best be described as Moroccan pesto. There are many variations. The sweet spices of cinnamon, ginger, and cumin, along with the heat from cayenne and paprika, are what differentiates this from Italian pesto. Olive oil or fresh lemon juice can be added should you want a lighter consistency.

1/2 cup chopped fresh parsley
1/2 cup chopped fresh cilantro (or mint) leaves
1 tablespoon ground cinnamon
1 tablespoon ground ginger
1 tablespoon paprika
1 teaspoon freshly ground black pepper
1/2 teaspoon ground cumin
1/2 teaspoon ground thyme
1/2 teaspoon cayenne pepper

Combine all the ingredients in a food processor and puree to a smooth paste. The paste will last about 1 week refrigerated.

Yield: 1 1/2 cups

Recommended cuts: Shrimp (2 to 3 hours), fish (2 to 3 hours); chicken breasts (2 to 3 hours), quail (2 to 3 hours)

Roasted Garlic and Jalapeño Paste

Sometimes it's the simple ingredients that pack the most flavor. Chef Bruce Cooper of Jake's in the Manyunk section of Philadelphia roasts garlic and jalapeño together, then adds extra-virgin olive oil for a taste that is far more complex than it seems. It performs culinary marvels on grilled tuna and swordfish.

1 pound jalapeño peppers, stemmed, seeded, and deveined
2 pounds peeled garlic cloves
1/2 cup water
1 cup extra-virgin olive oil

Preheat the oven to 350°F. Place the garlic and jalapeño in a roasting pan. Add the water and olive oil. Roast for 1 hour. Place the roasted garlic, jalapeño, and pan liquid in a food processor and puree.

Yield: 2 1/2 cups

Recommended cuts: All seafood (2 to 4 hours)

Tamarind Chipotle Paste

What's nice about this low-acid paste is that the longer it sits on chicken or lamb, the better the flavor. Chef Lou Sackett of Zocalo in West Philadelphia has isolated two basic building blocks in Mexican cuisine: sour tamarind and smoky chipotle chili, softened by just the right amount of honey. The recipe calls for fresh tamarind (not the seedless concentrate) which can be found in Asian and Spanish grocery stores.

12 ounces soft tamarind pulp
3 cups boiling water
4 dried chipotle chili peppers
1 cup boiling water
1/2 white onion, chopped
1 tablespoon chopped garlic
2 tablespoons honey
2 teaspoons kosher salt

Place the tamarind in a small nonreactive bowl and pour 3 cups boiling water over the pulp. Let stand for 20 minutes, stirring occasionally. Add more boiling water if the mixture is too stiff. Push the tamarind mixture through a sieve, extracting and discarding seeds, but retaining the pulp.

Place the chipotles in a small bowl and pour 1 cup boiling water over the chilies. Let stand for 20 minutes or until the chilies are softened.

Place the tamarind pulp, the chilies, their soaking water, and all the remaining ingredients in a blender or food processor and blend to a smooth paste. Makes enough for at least 2 pounds of chicken, lamb, or tuna.

Yield: 4 cups

Recommended cuts: Firm fish steaks or fillets (2 to 4 hours), tuna steaks (4 to 6 hours); chicken breasts (4 to 6 hours); lamb (3 to 6 hours)

New Mexican Red Pepper Paste

This paste, created by Chef Jon Jividen, is ideal for beef brisket, chicken breasts, and spare ribs. You can also add a couple of tablespoons of the paste to any of the basic marinades or to your favorite barbecue sauce to liven up the flavor.

4 dried ancho chili peppers, stems, veins, and seeds removed
2 dried New Mexican chili peppers (guajillo), stems, veins, and seeds removed
2 canned chipotle chili peppers
1/2 cup chopped onion
4 garlic cloves
2 teaspoons ground cumin
2 tablespoon dried oregano (preferably Mexican)
1 teaspoon kosher salt

Soak the ancho and New Mexican chili in hot water to cover for about 1 hour. Remove the chilies from the water and reserve 2 cups of soaking water. Combine the chilies, reserved soaking water (as needed), chipotle, onion, garlic, cumin, oregano, and salt in a food processor and puree until all the ingredients are blended into a smooth thick paste. Use the soaking liquid as needed to moisten the mixture in a paste form. Store in an airtight jar in the refrigerator for 3 or 4 weeks.

Yield: 2 to 3 cups

Recommended cuts: Chicken breasts (4 to 6 hours), wings (6 to 8 hours); beef brisket (8 hours to overnight); spare ribs (8 hours to overnight)

Cilantro Ginger Pesto

Place this herb paste under the skin of a whole chicken breast bound for the grill or the broiler, or coat shrimp with the pesto by tossing it in a zip-lock bag for an entree or appetizer. You can even toss a couple of tablespoons with pasta for an oriental pasta salad.

1/4 cup chopped garlic
1/2 cup chopped fresh ginger root
1 1/2 cups chopped fresh cilantro
1 teaspoon ground nutmeg
1 teaspoon five spice powder
1 tablespoon dark brown sugar
3 tablespoons light soy sauce
2 tablespoons sherry vinegar
1/4 cup light peanut oil

Combine the garlic, ginger root, cilantro, nutmeg, five spice powder, sugar, soy sauce, and vinegar in a blender or food processor and puree to a smooth paste. Add the oil a little bit at a time. The pesto will last for 1 week refrigerated.

Yield: 1 1/2 cups

Recommended cuts: Shrimp (2 to 4 hours); chicken kabobs (3 to 4 hours)

Lemon-Cumin Paste

This paste is perfect for flavoring grilled shrimp with a zest of spice and mild heat. The lemon acts as a refreshing coolant against the spicy cumin and cayenne in this savory North African paste.

1 tablespoon lightly crushed cumin seeds
1 tablespoon lemon zest
2 to 3 tablespoons freshly squeezed lemon juice
1/2 teaspoon white peppercorns
2 to 3 tablespoons dried parsley
1/4 cup olive oil
1/4 cup finely chopped onion
1 teaspoon sugar
1/2 teaspoon kosher salt
1/2 teaspoon cayenne pepper

Heat the cumin seeds in a nonstick frying pan until roasted but do not burn. Combine the cumin seeds with the rest of the ingredients and blend in a blender or food processor. The paste will last for a week refrigerated.

Yield: 2/3 cup

Recommended cuts: Shrimp and scallops (2 to 4 hours); beef and lamb kabobs (4 to 6 hours)

Indian Spice Paste

You'd be surprised how much flavor this paste has when pressed into chicken or tossed with shrimp. Marinate either for a couple of hours before grilling. The cilantro cools for the spicy curry and cayenne, and the cashews give the right amount of savory density.

1/2 cup tightly packed cilantro leaves
1/3 cup fresh lemon juice
2 tablespoons curry powder
1 tablespoon Garam Masala (see page 38) or curry
1/2 teaspoon cayenne pepper
4 garlic cloves, minced or pressed
1/4 cup roasted cashew pieces
1/4 cup cold-pressed peanut oil

Combine all the ingredients in a food processor or blender and puree to a smooth paste. Will last for up to 1 week refrigerated.

Yield: 1 1/2 cups

Recommended cuts: Shrimp and scallops (2 to 4 hours); chicken breasts (4 to 6 hours); lamb kabobs (4 to 6 hours)

6. Vegetables

We're in the middle of a vegetable renaissance. In trying to find alternatives for rich cream sauces and animal fats, cooks are turning more and more to vegetables, which are becoming main-course options. Marinades enable you to pickle, season, stir-fry, or grill vegetables, turning them into a mouth-watering blend of colors, textures, and flavors. Vegetables laced with olive oil and Mediterranean herbs can be found in the antipastos of Italy, in the tapas of Spain, and on the meze tables of the Middle East. Asia is no stranger to cold marinated vegetables. Kimchee, a spicy pickled cabbage from Korea (a forerunner of sauerkraut), and Pak Dong, pickled vegetables from Thailand, work as condiments.

Vegetables contain a carbohydrate that gives them a structure called cellulose, instead of muscle tissue like fish or meat, which means the rules of "tenderizing" or denaturizing do not apply. Most vegetables need a combination of heat and moisture to soften them. Marinades can be used before or after the cooking process. Vegetables are softened by blanching, steaming, or grilling.

The following section walks you through a whole storehouse of traditional and not so traditional ways of flavoring vegetables with marinades. The first section deals with veggies as openers or appetizers. I've also included a couple of marinated cheeses, both of which I like to serve wrapped in marinated sweet peppers or over salad greens. These starters are the ultimate in nibble food. Full portions of these recipes never make it to my buffet, in part because I insist on testing (consuming) every second tidbit to maintain my strict quality control.

Marinated Goat Cheese

A mild chevre marinated in an oil of Herbes de Provence makes great picnic food for open-air concerts or warm weather buffets. The marinade in this recipe also does double duty as a flavored oil, and it can be used to marinate chicken breasts or tuna fillets.

Provence Marinade

1/2 cup grapeseed oil
1 1/2 cup virgin or pure olive oil
1/4 cup fresh lemon juice (1 to 2 lemons)
2 garlic cloves, minced or pressed
1 tablespoon chopped fresh parsley
2 tablespoons Herbes de Provence (see page 37)
1 tablespoon coarsely cracked black pepper
Kosher salt, to taste

To make the marinade, mix in a nonreactive bowl the grapeseed oil, olive oil, lemon juice, garlic, parsley, Herbes de Provence, black peppercorns, and salt. The marinade will keep for up to 1 week in an airtight jar in the refrigerator.

Yield: 2 1/2 cups

Cheese

10-ounce log mild goat cheese

Place the goat cheese in the freezer for about 30 minutes to firm up before slicing. Slice it into 1/2-inch rounds and place in a flat pyrex dish or a clean wide-mouth glass jar. Pour the marinade over the cheese and refrigerate overnight. The cheese will keep for up to 1 week in the refrigerator. Serve with crusty French bread.

Yield: 6 to 8 appetizer servings

Mozzarella with Sun-Dried Tomato Marinade

Marinated mozzarella is rapidly becoming a staple in our home. It finds its way between slices of fresh tomatoes, it is tossed in pasta, mixed with salad greens, and often slapped on a chunk of crusty Italian bread as a quick snack. The marinade is certainly an all-purpose one. It can be used also with roasted sweet peppers, marinated mushrooms, olives, or even drizzled over pizza.

Sun-Dried Tomato Marinade
1/2 cup white wine
3 tablespoons lemon juice
1/2 cup extra-virgin olive oil
5 to 6 sun-dried tomatoes, packed in oil
1 teaspoon dried oregano
2 tablespoons chopped fresh basil
2 tablespoons chopped fresh flat-leaf parsley
1 teaspoon (or to taste) crushed red pepper or red pepper flakes
2 cloves garlic, diced

Combine the wine and lemon juice in a nonreactive bowl. Mix in the olive oil a little at a time. Add the sun-dried tomatoes, basil, parsley, pepper, and garlic.

Yield: 1 1/2 cups

Cheese

1 pound fresh mozzarella

Slice the mozzarella into 1/2-inch rounds. Place the cheese in a flat pyrex dish or a clean wide-mouth glass jar (large peanut butter or mayonnaise jars are ideal). Pour the marinade over the cheese and refrigerate overnight. The cheese will keep for up to 1 week in the refrigerator.

Serve with crusty Italian bread or fresh tomatoes.

Yield: 6 to 8 appetizer servings

Marinated Crimini Mushrooms

My wild mushroom source in Philadelphia's Italian Market, Michael Anastasio, pointed me towards these mushrooms one afternoon. Crimini mushrooms look like small brown button mushrooms. We both remembered our fathers bringing home brown paper bags of what they called "creamers" and sauteing them with veal and Madeira. Their flavor is sublime when marinated in sweet balsamic vinegar. If you can't find criminis, white button mushrooms will also work in this Italian marinade.

2 pounds fresh crimmini mushrooms, tough base stem removed and caps brushed
2 tablespoons fresh lemon juice
Kosher salt, to taste
1 cup balsamic vinegar
1/2 cup olive oil
4 to 5 garlic cloves, minced or pressed
1/4 cup chopped parsley
1 tablespoon diced pimento
1 tablespoon capers, drained

In a nonreactive saucepan, combine the mushrooms, lemon juice, and salt in water to cover. Simmer for 15 minutes or until they are tender. Drain and put into a bowl. In a nonreactive saucepan, combine 2/3 cup of the balsamic vinegar, the olive oil, and garlic and simmer for 20 minutes.

Pour the warm marinade over the drained mushrooms. Cool to room temperature and add the remaining 1/3 cup balsamic vinegar, the parsley, pimento, and capers. The mushrooms will keep for 1 week in the refrigerator (if you can resist snacking).

Yield: 6 to 8 servings

Italian Marinated Mixed Vegetables

Verdura Mista Marinata, Italian marinated vegetables, are traditionally marinated in olive oil and vinegar. In Philadelphia's Italian Market, vats of marinated vegetables, olives, mushrooms, and sweet peppers scent the air. These marinated vegetables are an essential part of antipasto platters and make great summer picnic food. The marinade also can be used on tuna and swordfish steaks.

Italian Marinade

6 to 8 anchovy fillets
2 tablespoons balsamic vinegar
1/3 cup fresh lemon juice
1/3 cup extra-virgin olive oil
1/4 cup chopped red onion
1/4 cup chopped fresh flat-leaf parsley
1 tablespoon nonpareil capers
Cracked black peppercorns, to taste

Puree the anchovies with the balsamic vinegar and lemon juice in a blender. With the motor running, add the oil a little at a time. Pour the marinade into a nonreactive bowl and stir in the onion, parsley, capers, and pepper.

Yield: 1 1/2 cups

Vegetables

1 teaspoon salt
2 tablespoons fresh lemon juice or vinegar (to maintain color)
1 cup carrots sliced 1/4 inch thick
1 cauliflower head, broken into florets and sliced in half
1 small fennel bulb, chopped (1/2 cup)

Add the salt and lemon juice (or vinegar) to 2 quarts of water in a saucepan, bring to a rolling boil. Add the carrots and the cauliflower and blanch for 3 to 5 minutes. Drain, then plunge them into a bowl of ice water to stop the cooking action. The vegetables should be firm and crisp. Drain the carrots and cauliflower, and place them with the fennel in a nonreactive container or a 1-gallon zip-lock plastic bag. Pour the marinade over the vegetables and refrigerate for at least 4 hours. The vegetables will keep for a week.

Yield: 4 to 6 servings (about 1 quart)

Asparagus with
Sherry-Hazelnut Marinade

A marinade of toasted hazelnuts, nutty Spanish sherry, and fresh lemon is the finest way that I can think of to welcome spring asparagus. Try this recipe as an appetizer or serve it to accompany freshly grilled salmon. Use pencil-thin asparagus if possible.

Sherry-Hazelnut Marinade

1/4 cup dry sherry
3 tablespoons sherry vinegar
3 to 4 tablespoons fresh lemon juice
1 tablespoon grated lemon zest
1/4 cup hazelnut oil
1/3 cup sunflower oil
1 tablespoon chopped shallots
1/4 cup peeled and roasted hazelnuts, coarsely
    chopped
Cracked black peppercorns and kosher salt,
    to taste

To make the marinade, combine the sherry, vinegar, lemon juice, and lemon zest in a nonreactive mixing bowl. Whisk in the oil a little at a time. Add the shallots, hazelnuts, pepper and salt.

Yield: 1 1/2 cups

Asparagus

1/2 pound asparagus

Trim the asparagus, breaking off any rough ends, and scrape the rough outer stalk with a vegetable peeler. Blanch in boiling water to cover until the asparagus is cooked but still crisp, 2 to 3 minutes. Immediately plunge the asparagus into a bowl of ice water to stop the cooking, then drain. Place the asparagus into a long, shallow glass baking dish, add the marinade, and refrigerate for at least 4 hours. The asparagus will keep for a little over a week.

Yield: 4 servings

To peel hazelnuts, combine 2 tablespoons baking soda with 2 quarts water in a saucepan and bring to a rolling boil. Blanch the hazelnuts for 5 minutes and drain in a colander. Run cold water over the nuts and peel. Toast the hazelnuts to a light brown in a dry frying pan over medium heat.

Zucchini and Yellow Squash with Lemon-Rosemary Marinade

Combining the flavors of lemon and rosemary with julienned slivers of green zucchini and yellow squash on a bed of red radicchio will give you a stunning dish that lives up to its good looks. Small to medium zucchini (about 4 to 6 inches long) work well. However, if you have access to tiny zucchini and yellow squash, you'll find that they're more tender (and look prettiest when sliced in half lengthwise).

Lemon-Rosemary Marinade

1/4 cup dry white wine
1/4 cup fresh lemon juice
2 tablespoons grated lemon zest
1 teaspoon Dijon-style mustard
1/4 cup safflower oil
1 tablespoon coarsely chopped fresh rosemary
1/2 teaspoon fresh thyme (or pinch of dried thyme)
Kosher salt and pepper, to taste

Combine the wine, lemon juice, lemon zest, and mustard in a nonreactive mixing bowl. Whisk in the oil a little at a time. Add the rosemary, thyme, and salt and pepper.

Yield: 1 cup

Squash

1 teaspoon salt
2 tablespoons vinegar or fresh lemon juice (to maintain color)
2 medium-size zucchini, julienned, or 1/2 pound tiny zucchini, sliced in half lengthwise
2 medium-size yellow squash, julienned, or 1/2 pound tiny yellow squash, sliced in half lengthwise
1 head radicchio, for garnish

Add the salt and vinegar to 2 quarts water in a nonreactive saucepan and bring to a rolling boil. Add the vegetables and blanch for 1 to 2 minutes, then drain. Plunge the vegetables into a bowl of ice water to stop the cooking action. Do not overcook—the vegetables should be firm and crisp. Drain the vegetables and place them in a nonreactive container or a 1-gallon zip-lock plastic bag. Pour the marinade over the vegetables and refrigerate for at least 4 hours. The zucchini will keep for 1 week in the refrigerator.

To serve, line the bottom of a salad plate with radicchio leaves, add the zucchini and yellow squash, and serve.

Yield: 4 to 6 appetizer servings

Chickpeas in a Lemon Basil Balsamic Marinade

The nutty flavor of chickpeas makes them a popular staple all over the Mediterranean region and India. I've served this salad in cups of bright red radicchio leaves, garnished with whole basil leaves. And it has been equally popular tossed in a green salad with small pieces of soppressata sausage, or diced prosciutto, or feta cheese. The marinade also can be used to marinate swordfish or salmon for either the grill or broiler.

Lemon Basil Balsamic Marinade

1/4 cup balsamic vinegar
2 tablespoons fresh lemon juice
1/2 cup extra-virgin olive oil
1 teaspoon grated lemon zest
1 tablespoon cracked black peppercorns
2 to 3 garlic cloves, minced or pressed
1/4 cup chopped fresh basil

To make the marinade, combine the balsamic vinegar and lemon juice in a nonreactive bowl. Whisk in the olive oil a little at a time. Add the lemon zest, peppercorns, garlic, and basil.

Yield: 1 cup

Chickpeas

1 cup dry chickpeas

Cover the chickpeas with 3 to 4 inches of cold water and leave them overnight. Discard the water, put the chickpeas in a 4-quart saucepan, and cover with 2 quarts water. Cook over low heat for 3 to 4 hours, until tender. Remove the chickpeas from the heat and let them cool to room temperature. Drain and discard the cooking liquid.

Toss the chickpeas with the marinade. This dish keeps getting better the longer it sits. It will keep refrigerated for up to 2 weeks. Serve the salad as part of an antipasto platter.

Yield: 8 to 10 servings

Marinated Olives

Mention olives, and I automatically think of Mediterranean food. In the following recipes I've tried to keep the flavor of each marinade regionally correct by suggesting regional olives and their corresponding olive oils. Substitutions are perfectly acceptable; however, there's one rule that should be followed when purchasing olives. Keep the pits in! I've never eaten an olive that tasted good with the pit out.

Marinating olives takes the brining process of olives one step further and infuses the olives with even more flavor. Marinated olives last indefinitely, and they'll provide you with a constant source of garnish.

With marinated olives, the longer they sit, the better they taste. Use them to accompany tapas, meze-style appetizers, antipasto, or for just plain snacking.

Italian Marinated Black Olives

2/3 cup extra-virgin olive oil
2 to 3 garlic cloves, pressed
3 to 4 anchovy fillets, mashed
1 tablespoon capers
1 teaspoon dried oregano
1 pound black olives (preferably the brown black Liguria type)

Combine the oil, garlic, anchovies, capers, and oregano in a ceramic baking dish or glass jar. Add the olives and toss to coat. Refrigerate for 2 to 3 days before serving. These will last several weeks in the refrigerator. Bring to room temperature before serving.

Yield: 2 cups

Rosemary Marinated Olives

1/2 teaspoon Herbes de Provence (see page 37)
2 tablespoons chopped fresh rosemary
1/2 cup French olive oil or Rosemary-Infused Oil (see page 32)
1 tablespoon balsamic vinegar
1/2 teaspoon cracked peppercorns
1 teaspoon grated lemon zest
1 pound Niçoise olives

Combine the herbs, oil, vinegar, peppercorns, and zest in a ceramic baking dish or glass jar. Add the olives and toss to coat. Refrigerate for 2 to 3 days before serving. These will last several weeks in the refrigerator. Bring to room temperature before serving.

Yield: 2 cups

Moroccan Olives

1 teaspoon whole cumin seeds
1 tablespoon cracked coriander seeds
1 tablespoon red pepper flakes
1/2 cup olive oil (preferably Greek or Tunisian)
3 to 4 tablespoons fresh lemon juice
1 tablespoon grated lemon zest
1/2 teaspoon cracked peppercorns
1 pound round black or Moroccan olives

Combine the cumin, coriander, red pepper flakes, oil, lemon juice and zest, and peppercorns in a ceramic baking dish or glass jar. Add the olives and toss to coat. Refrigerate for 2 to 3 days before serving. These will last several weeks in the refrigerator. Bring to room temperature before serving.

Yield: 2 cups

Greek Marinated Olives

2/3 cup Greek olive oil
1/4 cup fresh lemon juice
1 tablespoon grated lemon zest
1 to 2 garlic cloves, pressed or minced
2 teaspoons dried oregano
1 teaspoon anise seeds
Cracked black peppercorns
1 pound Kalamata olives

Combine the oil, lemon juice and zest, garlic, oregano, anise, and peppercorns in a ceramic baking dish or glass jar. Add the olives and toss to coat. Refrigerate for 2 to 3 days before serving. These will last several weeks in the refrigerator. Bring to room temperature before serving.

Yield: 2 cups

Marinated Green Spanish Olives

2/3 cup Spanish olive oil
2 bay leaves
3 to 4 garlic cloves, pressed
1 teaspoon brandy
1/3 cup sherry vinegar
1 teaspoon cumin seeds
1 teaspoon dried oregano
2 to 3 tablespoons diced pimento
3 anchovy fillets, mashed
1 pound green unpitted Sicilian-style Spanish
  olives

Combine the oil, bay leaves, garlic, brandy, vinegar, cumin, oregano, pimento, and anchovies in a ceramic baking dish or glass jar. Add the olives and toss to coat. Refrigerate for 2 to 3 days before serving. These will last several weeks in the refrigerator. Bring to room temperature before serving.

Yield: 2 cups

Tomatoes with Basil Balsamic Vinegar Marinade

This is my favorite way to prepare garden-fresh tomatoes. The marinade not only amplifies the sweet flavor of tomatoes, but also keeps the palate charged. Don't use anything but ripe summer tomatoes in this simple recipe.

Basil Balsamic Vinegar Marinade

1/2 cup extra-virgin olive oil
1/4 cup balsamic vinegar
1/4 cup chopped fresh basil
Salt and coarsely cracked peppercorns, to taste

In a nonreactive mixing bowl, whisk the oil into the vinegar a little at a time. Add the basil, salt and pepper.

Yield: 1 cup

Tomatoes

1 1/2 pounds fresh tomatoes (2 to 3 large or 3 to 4
  medium)
Aged dry provolone cheese, for garnish

Lay the tomatoes in a long, shallow glass baking dish or in a wide-mouth glass jar and cover with the marinade. Refrigerate for at least 4 hours. The tomatoes will keep for 3 days. To serve, scrape the cheese with a vegetable peeler to form curls; place on top of the tomatoes.

Yield: 4 servings

Jicama with Lime-Cilantro Marinade

This simple dish is positively habit forming. The marinade has the flavors of lime and cilantro, with a gentle chili kick. The jicama should be firm, not mushy. When it is julienned into the size of french fries, it's always the first vegetarian appetizer to be totally consumed at a buffet. Julienned into matchstick size, jicama makes a nice relish for grilled seafood. I have also served a version of this recipe with dollops of avocado sorbet at Philadelphia's Book and the Cook event.

Lime-Cilantro Marinade
1/4 cup fresh lime juice
1 tablespoon lime zest
3 tablespoons fresh lemon juice
1/4 cup fresh orange juice
1/2 teaspoon red pepper flakes
1/4 cup chopped fresh cilantro leaves
3 tablespoons avocado oil

Combine the lime juice, lime zest, lemon juice, orange juice, red pepper, cilantro, and avocado oil in a nonreactive container.

Yield: 1 cup

Jicama
1 pound jicama

Peel the jicama and julienne into a french fries size if using as an appetizer, matchstick size if you are preparing a salad or relish.

Toss the jicama with the marinade in a nonreactive mixing bowl or a 1-gallon zip-lock plastic bag. Refrigerate for least 4 to 6 hours before serving. The marinated jicama will last for 2 to 3 days in the refrigerator; after that the flavor will stay but the dish will lose its crunch.

Yield: 4 servings

Pickled Haricots Verts

This recipe uses a marinade as part of the pickling process. This is the ultimate in refreshing, savory snack foods. I also use this as an accompaniment to grilled seafood. There is a very pleasant bite to the pencil-thin fresh string beans, which comes from the mustard oil. The aromatic mustard oil carries hints of horseradish and mustard. The two levels of tang in this recipe come from the champagne vinegar and the lemon juice which is added at the last minute.

Haricots Verts
1/2 to 2/3 pound haricots verts (or garden fresh string beans), ends trimmed

Champagne-Vinegar Marinade
1 tablespoon mustard oil
1 teaspoon capers
1/3 cup champagne vinegar
1/3 cup water
Julienned zest of 2 lemons, white pith removed
1 tablespoon black peppercorns
1 teaspoon Herbes de Provence (see page 37)
1 teaspoon sugar
1/3 cup fresh lemon juice

Rinse and drain the haricots verts; then blanch in boiling water to cover for about 3 minutes. Refresh the beans in a bowl of ice water. They should be crisp. Pack the beans upright in a sterile pint jar, spoon the mustard oil (available in Indian food stores) and capers over the beans.

In a small nonreactive saucepan, bring to a boil the vinegar, water, lemon zest, peppercorns, Herbes de Provence, and sugar. Reduce the heat and simmer for 10 minutes. Pour the vinegar mixture over the beans, top with the lemon juice, and seal the jar immediately. Keep refrigerated. Let the beans marinate for at least 1 week before using. These keep for 2 months if unopened and refrigerated.

Yield: 6 to 8 servings

Thai Pickled Vegetables

This is my favorite Thai condiment. This Thai version of the Italian giardiniera makes an excellent cooling contrast to the hot flavors of traditional Thai marinades.

Thai-Infused Vinegar Marinade

4 to 5 garlic cloves, minced or pressed
6 dried red chili peppers, seeded and crumbled
3 to 4 tablespoons finely diced shallots
1 tablespoon grated fresh ginger root
2 to 3 tablespoons Asian or domestic cold-pressed peanut oil
3 1/2 cups rice wine vinegar
1 tablespoon sugar
1/4 cup chopped lemongrass

To make the marinade, combine the garlic, chili peppers, shallots, and ginger in a blender or food processor and blend to a smooth paste. Heat the oil in a wok and stir-fry the paste for several minutes. Cool the paste to room temperature. Bring the vinegar to a boil, add the sugar and lemongrass, reduce the heat, and simmer for 20 minutes. Add the paste.

Yield: 4 cups

Vegetables

1 cup baby corn
1 cup broccoli florets, rough stems removed
1 cup carrots, sliced into 1/4-inch diagonal rounds
1/2 cup sliced bok choy, white part only
1 cup cucumbers, seeded, cut into 3-inch by 1/4-inch strips
1/2 cup fresh cilantro leaves
2 to 3 tablespoons toasted sesame seeds

Bring 4 quarts water to a rolling boil in a large pot. Place the vegetables in a colander or large strainer, set them in the boiling water, and blanch for 2 to 3 minutes. Refresh them in a bowl of cold water to stop the cooking process, then drain. Place the vegetables into a nonreactive mixing bowl and pour the marinade over them. Cool to room temperature. Stir in the cilantro and sesame seeds. This will keep for 1 week in the refrigerator.

Yield: 8 to 12 servings

Marinated Indonesian Carrot Sticks

Served cold, this makes a great summertime snack food. Or stir-fry the marinated carrots and serve hot for an Indonesian rijsttafel (buffet). The marinade is excellent for grilling shrimp. The sambal ulek (a seasoning mix) and shrimp paste are both available where Asian foods are sold.

Indonesian Tamarind Marinade

1/2 cup Tamarind Juice (see page 25)
1 tablespoon soy sauce
1/4 cup rice wine vinegar
1 tablespoon sambal ulek
1 tablespoon shrimp paste
3 tablespoons chopped fresh cilantro leaves
3 to 4 tablespoons chopped fresh mint
1 tablespoon brown sugar

To make the marinade, combine all the ingredients in a nonreactive mixing bowl.

Yield: 1 cup

Carrots

1 pound carrots, julienned into 2-inch-long pieces
2 to 3 tablespoons peanut oil (if stir-frying)

Blanch the carrots in a pot of salted boiling water for 1 to 2 minutes. Refresh the carrots in a bowl of cold water to stop the cooking process. Combine them with the marinade and refrigerate overnight. Serve at room temperature. The carrots will keep for at least a week refrigerated.

To stir-fry, marinate the carrot sticks for at least 6 hours. Heat the peanut oil over high heat. Drain the carrots and stir-fry in 2 to 3 tablespoons of marinade for 3 to 4 minutes or until firm (not crisp). The remaining marinade can be warmed separately and served as a sauce.

Yield: 8 to 10 appetizer or 6 side-dish servings

Marinated Cucumber Salad

This salad combines crunch with cool—coconut with lime and chilies. The salad picks up flavors from Southeast Asia, but the ingredients are as much at home in the Caribbean. This makes a wonderful accompaniment to grilled shrimp.

Coconut Chili Marinade

3 tablespoons rice wine vinegar
2 tablespoons shredded unsweetened coconut
1 tablespoon shredded fresh ginger root
3 tablespoons fresh lime juice
1 tablespoon grated lime zest
4 to 5 fresh Thai bird peppers (or 1 habañero), seeded and diced
2 teaspoons sugar
1/8 teaspoon ground cumin

Salad

1 cup julienned jicama (matchstick size)
1 medium cucumber, peeled, seeded, and julienned into matchsticks
2 to 3 tablespoons chopped fresh basil

Warm the vinegar and add the coconut and ginger to soften them. Combine the coconut-ginger mix with the lime juice, lime zest, chilies, sugar, and cumin. Toss with the jicama, cucumber, and basil. Place the salad in a nonreactive container and marinate in the refrigerator for 2 hours before serving.

Yield: 6 servings

Marinated Black Bean Salad

I asked my good friend Nina Blum to work on a black bean recipe. Half expecting a Southwest black bean relish, I was absolutely delighted with this oriental tour de force. The marinated black beans taste as good as they look. This salad accompanied Tamarind-Marinated Pompano Steamed in Banana Leaves at a dinner we still haven't stopped talking about. By the way, the method for cooking black beans is foolproof for holding their shape.

Oriental Marinade

4 tablespoons peanut oil
1 teaspoon finely diced fresh ginger root
1 teaspoon minced garlic
1/2 teaspoon hot chili oil
1 teaspoon oriental sesame oil
1/4 cup rice wine vinegar
1 1/2 tablespoons light soy sauce
1 tablespoon sherry

Heat 1 tablespoon of peanut oil in a saute pan. Add the ginger and garlic and saute for 1 to 2 minutes. Remove from heat and cool. Combine with the rest of the ingredients.

Yield: 1/2 cup

Salad

1 cup uncooked black beans
1/2 cup diced red bell pepper
1/3 cup chopped scallions (white part only)
1/2 cup canned water chestnuts or jicama, diced
1 medium cucumber (preferably seedless), peeled, for garnish
Radicchio leaves, for garnish
1 red bell pepper, sliced into 1/4-inch-wide rings, for garnish

Preheat oven to 550°F. Place the black beans in a deep casserole (2 quarts) and cover with 1 quart of boiling water. Place the beans in the oven for 20 minutes. Then reduce the heat to 200°F and continue to cook for 1 hour. Remove the beans from the oven, drain in a colander, and cool to room temperature. You should have about 3 cups.

Combine the cooled black beans with the red pepper, scallions, and water chestnuts. Toss with the marinade and refrigerate for 3 to 4 hours.

To serve, use a vegetable peeler to shave the cucumber into long, flat strips working around its core. Line 6 salad plates with radicchio. Form a nest with the shaved cucumber strips and top with about 2/3 cup of black beans. Garnish with red pepper rings.

Yield: 6 servings

Braised Chanterelles

When I was told by my mushroom merchant, Mike Anastasio in South Philadelphia's Italian Market, that the only chanterelles he had in that day were the large tough ones, I took them anyway telling Mike that I would think of something. The apricot flavor of chanterelles comes through with a nudge from the Sauternes and diced dry apricot. By the way, this is an excellent marinade for chicken breasts.

Sauternes-Apricot Marinade

1/2 cup Sauternes
1 tablespoon diced dried apricot
1 tablespoon cognac
1/2 cup full-bodied poultry stock
1 teaspoon cracked black peppercorns

Combine the Sauternes, cognac, apricot, poultry stock, and peppercorns in a nonreactive mixing bowl.

Yield: 1 1/4 cups

Chanterelles

1 1/2 pounds fresh chanterelles
2 to 3 tablespoons unsweetened butter or canola oil
1/4 cup julienned leeks
Kosher salt and freshly cracked black pepper, to taste

Clean and slice the chanterelles in half sideways. Place the chanterelles in a nonreactive container or a 1-gallon zip-lock plastic bag, pour the marinade over the chanterelles, and refrigerate for at least 6 hours, or preferably overnight.

Heat the butter or oil in a Dutch oven or large saucepan with a lid and saute the leeks until translucent. Drain the mushrooms from the marinade, reserving the marinade; add to the leeks and saute for 2 to 3 minutes over medium-high heat. Add the remaining marinade, reduce the heat to low, cover, and cook for 1 to 1 1/2 hours.

Serve with sauteed goose or duck breast.

Yield: 4 to 6 servings

Variation

Quick Braised Chanterelles. Saute the leeks in a large skillet, drain the chanterelles, and add them to the sauteed leeks. Add the reserved marinade and saute over medium heat until the liquid evaporates.

Grilled Shitake Mushrooms

Fresh shitake mushrooms are the next best thing to hamburgers on a grill. They grill crisp and meaty, sealing inside the gills the oriental flavors of the marinade. With sprouts and pita bread, they make a great vegetarian standby at a barbecue. Go for the largest mushroom caps you can find. But if you can't find shitakes, cèpes or oyster mushrooms will be as tasty.

Lemon Oriental Marinade

1/3 cup fresh lemon juice (2 to 3 lemons)
1 teaspoon grated lemon zest
2 tablespoons light soy sauce
2 tablespoons sherry
1 tablespoon brown sugar
1/2 teaspoon hot chili oil
1 tablespoon oriental sesame oil
1/4 cup Asian or domestic cold-pressed peanut oil
1 teaspoon diced fresh ginger root

To make the marinade, combine the lemon juice, lemon zest, soy sauce, sherry, and brown sugar in a nonreactive mixing bowl. Whisk in the oils a little at a time. Add the ginger.

Yield: 1 cup

Mushrooms

1/2 to 3/4 pound shitake mushrooms

If the mushrooms are dirty, rub their surfaces gently with a cloth or paper towel. Place them in a nonreactive container or a 1-gallon zip-lock plastic bag, pour the marinade over the mushrooms, and refrigerate for 6 to 8 hours, preferably overnight.

Remove the mushrooms from the marinade and bring the marinade to a low boil in a nonreactive saucepan, or microwave the marinade for 3 minutes on high. Use for basting.

To grill, lightly brush the grill with vegetable oil and grill the mushrooms stem side down first, then the cap for a total of 3 to 5 minutes, while basting with the warm marinade. Don't overcook!

To cook indoors, pan fry the mushrooms, cooking both sides in a skillet over medium high heat for no longer than 3 minutes total. Don't overcook!

Yield: 4 appetizer or 2 side-dish servings

Grilled Vegetable Kabobs

There are a couple of tricks to marinating vegetables for the grill. By lightly scoring firm vegetables with a paring knife, you enable the marinade to bite into the veggies before they hit the coals. The second tip is to separate the hard and soft vegetables. Soft vegetables, such as cherry tomatoes, should have their own skewers, as they cook faster than harder veggies such as zucchini.

Grilled vegetable kabobs have brilliant colors with taste to match. I've included a choice of marinades for your kabobs should you want to match them with another marinated dish.

Feel free to use either recipe as a marinade for grilled vegetables of any type.

Basic Marinade for Grilled Vegetables

2/3 cup olive oil
1/4 cup fresh lemon juice
1 tablespoon chopped fresh basil
1 tablespoon chopped fresh parsley
1 tablespoon chopped fresh thyme
1 tablespoon grated lemon zest
1 teaspoon kosher salt, or to taste

Combine all the marinade ingredients in a nonreactive mixing bowl.

Yield: 1 cup

Basic Asian Marinade for Grilled Vegetables

1/2 cup Asian or domestic cold-pressed peanut oil
3 tablespoons oriental sesame oil
1/4 cup fresh lime juice
2 to 3 tablespoons light soy sauce
1 tablespoon chopped fresh basil
1 tablespoon chopped fresh mint
2 to 3 tablespoons chopped fresh cilantro leaves
1 tablespoon grated lime zest
1 teaspoon chili oil

Combine all the marinade ingredients in a nonreactive mixing bowl.

Yield: 1 cup

Vegetable Kabobs

1 red bell pepper, cut into 1-inch squares
1 red or yellow pepper, cut into 1-inch squares
1 zucchini, scored and cut into 1/2-inch slices
1 yellow squash, scored and cut into 1/2-inch slices
12 red pearl onions, peeled
12 white pearl onions, peeled
12 peeled garlic cloves

Skewer and alternate the vegetables for color on 6 presoaked skewers. Marinate the kabobs for about 1 hour.

To cook, lightly brush the grill with oil and cook the kebabs for 3 to 5 minutes or until the vegetables are tender, while basting with the remaining marinade.

Serve with lemon aioli or a light caper mayonnaise.

Yield: 6 servings

Roasted Tri-Color Sweet Peppers with Chipotle-Lime Marinade

Charcoal-grilled or roasted over a stove, these marinated sweet peppers are the closest thing to a Southwestern antipasto. The secret ingredient in the recipe is the chipotle pepper, which is a smoked jalapeño canned in adobo sauce. The marinade is a combination of fire and smoke, tempered by fresh lime juice and cilantro. Equally good (but less incendiary) is the robust Italian variation that follows below.

Chipotle-Lime Marinade

1/3 cup fresh lime juice
1/4 cup white wine
1 canned chipotle pepper
3 garlic cloves, minced or pressed
1 teaspoon Orange-Cumin Dust (see page 39) or
1/2 teaspoon ground cumin and 1/2 teaspoon
ground dried orange peel
1/4 cup chopped fresh cilantro leaves

To make the marinade, combine the lime juice, wine, and chipotle pepper in a blender and puree. In a nonreactive mixing bowl, combine the chipotle mixture with the garlic, cumin, and cilantro.

Yield: 1 cup

Peppers

2 sweet red peppers
2 sweet yellow peppers
2 sweet green peppers

Roast the peppers over the stove or charcoal grill until the skin is charred or blackened. Be careful not to burn. Immediately place the peppers in a 1-gallon zip-lock bag and put the peppers in the freezer for 10 minutes to loosen the skin and stop the cooking process. Peel the peppers (do not rinse underwater as the pepper will lose flavor). Remove the stem and seeds and cut the peppers into 1-inch or 2-inch strips.

Place the peppers in clean jar, add the marinade, and refrigerate for at least 6 hours.

Yield: 8 to 10 servings

Variation

Marinated Sweet Pepper Antipasto. Stir together 1/4 cup lemon juice and 1/3 cup balsamic vinegar. Whisk in 1/2 cup light extra-virgin olive oil a little at a time. Add 1 tablespoon capers and 1/4 cup chopped flat-leaf parsley. Then follow the same procedure for roasting the sweet peppers, and proceed with the recipe as above.

Grilled Tofu with Mango Chutney Marinade

This has always been a staple for my vegetarian friends, but now the meat eaters have caught on to it, too. The secret ingredient in the recipe is the concentrated tomato paste (available in a tube) that gives the marinade an additional surge of flavor.

Mango Chutney Marinade

1/2 cup Major Grey's mango chutney
1 tablespoon tomato paste concentrate
1/3 cup fresh lemon juice
1/3 cup olive oil
1 serrano chili, seeded, deveined, and diced
2 garlic cloves, minced or pressed
1/2 teaspoon coarsely cracked black pepper

To make the marinade, combine the chutney, tomato paste, and lemon juice in a food processor or blender and puree. With the motor running, drizzle in the oil a little at a time. Mix in the serrano, garlic and pepper.

Yield: 1 cup

Tofu

14-ounce to 18-ounce block firm tofu

Cut the tofu into 1-inch squares and put them into a nonreactive container or a 1-gallon zip-lock plastic bag. Pour the marinade over the tofu and refrigerate for at least 24 hours, preferably 2 to 3 days. Remove the tofu from the marinade and reserve the marinade for basting. Thread the tofu onto a pair of presoaked bamboo skewers for each serving.

To grill, lightly brush the grill with vegetable oil and grill the tofu for about 12 to 15 minutes, turning often and basting with the warm marinade.

Yield: 6 to 8 appetizer servings

Stir-Fried Carrots in a Cinnamon Marinade

This is a glazing marinade for a carrot stir-fry. For a pretty presentation, lightly channel the carrots by running the tip of a sharp paring knife lengthwise down the sides. The carrot will slice into florets.

Cinnamon Marinade

1 1/2 cups dry white wine
1 cup fresh orange juice
2 tablespoons grated orange zest
1 teaspoon cinnamon
6 tablespoons olive oil
1/4 cup chopped shallots
12 garlic cloves, minced or pressed
1/2 teaspoon dried thyme
1 teaspoon dried oregano
1/2 teaspoon ground coriander seeds
1 bay leaf

To make the marinade, combine the wine, orange juice and zest, and cinnamon in a nonreactive mixing bowl. Whisk in the oil a little at a time. Add the shallots, garlic, thyme, coriander and bay leaf.

Yield: 2 1/2 cups

Carrots

1 pound carrots, peeled and sliced into 1/4-inch pieces
1/4 cup golden raisins

Place the carrots in a nonreactive container or a 1-gallon zip-lock plastic bag. Pour the marinade over the carrots and refrigerate for 4 to 6 hours. Remove the carrots from the marinade and set aside.

In a wok or deep-sided saute pan, cook over high heat to reduce the marinade to one-third. Add the carrots to the pan and stir-fry for 2 to 3 minutes. Stir in the raisins and cook until heated, 3 to 4 minutes. The carrots should be firm but not crisp.

Yield: 4 servings

Stir-Fried Snow Peas with Balsamic Ginger Marinade

This East-meets-West marinade combines the Mediterranean flavors of balsamic vinegar, olive oil, and Dijon-style mustard with the Orient's soy sauce and ginger. The combination works so well that I occasionally stir-fry shrimp in this marinade.

Balsamic Ginger Marinade

1 tablespoon dark soy sauce
3 tablespoons balsamic vinegar
1 teaspoon Dijon-style mustard
1/3 cup grapeseed or canola oil
3 tablespoons olive oil
3 garlic cloves, minced or pressed
2 tablespoons grated fresh ginger root
1 scallion, white part only, chopped
1/2 teaspoon kosher salt
1 teaspoon coarsely cracked black pepper

To make the marinade, combine the soy sauce, vinegar, and mustard in a nonreactive mixing bowl. Whisk in the oils a little at a time. Add the garlic, ginger, scallion, salt, and pepper.

Yield: 1 1/4 cups

Snow Peas

1 pound snow peas, ends trimmed
1 tablespoon toasted sesame seeds or 2 tablespoons toasted pine nuts

Place the snow peas in a nonreactive container or a 1-gallon zip-lock plastic bag, pour the marinade over, and refrigerate for at least 6 hours. Remove the snow peas from the marinade and set aside.

In a wok or deep-sided saute pan, cook the marinade over high heat to reduce its volume to one-third. Add the snow peas and stir-fry for 3 to 4 minutes. Stir in the sesame seeds or pine nuts and cook for 3 to 4 minutes more. Serve immediately.

Yield: 4 servings

Coconut Curried Cauliflower

Cauliflower is one of my favorite vegetables because it absorbs marinades like a sponge. Locked in the florets will be wonderful bursts of curry, coconut, and zesty lime waiting only to be released by the steam of your wok. The Coconut Curry Marinade also can be used on grilled chicken or shrimp kabobs.

Coconut Curry Marinade

12-ounce can Asian or Thai unsweetened coconut milk
1/2 cup toasted dried coconut
2 teaspoons curry powder
1/3 cup lime juice
1 tablespoon lime zest
2 garlic cloves, minced or pressed
1/4 teaspoon cayenne pepper
1 teaspoon dark brown sugar

To make the marinade, combine the coconut milk, coconut, and curry in a nonreactive saucepan and simmer over low heat for 20 minutes. Remove from heat and cool to room temperature. Add the lime juice, zest, garlic, cayenne, and brown sugar.

Yield: 2 1/2 cups

Cauliflower

1 head cauliflower
2 tablespoons Asian or cold-pressed domestic peanut oil

Rinse and trim the cauliflower and break into florets. Slice them in half lengthwise and place in a nonreactive container or a 1-gallon zip-lock plastic bag. Pour the marinade over the cauliflower and refrigerate for 4 to 6 hours.

Bring the marinated cauliflower to room temperature. Heat the peanut oil in the wok. Add cauliflower and the marinade and toss for 3 to 4 minutes over high heat. Serve as a side dish with seafood.

Yield: 4 servings

7. Fish and Shellfish

*I*t all started with seafood. The Romans first preserved fish in a salt-water brine, in a process they called "marinara," meaning "of the sea." Fish take to marinades the way they take to water. Luckily, we have better ways of flavoring fish with marinades than the Romans did, and better reasons to do so.

It is a common assumption among inexperienced cooks that marinades repair food. There is no repairing spoiled food. A marinade simply heightens food in good condition. A good marinade is like a setting for a jewel. If the seafood is fresh, the recipe will sparkle. All the seasoning in the pantry is not going to make old fish taste fresh. Old fish will still have that fishy odor along with the marinade's flavors. Usually, you can tell which whole fish are fresh just by, as my fish monger puts it, "Lookin' 'em in the eye." The eyes of whole fresh fish should be bright, clear, and bulging out. Old fish have glassy, cloudy eyes which are sunken inward, much like harried commuters during rush hour. But what about fillets and steaks that are sitting under glass at your fishmonger's? How do you know what's fresh and what's better off used as bait?

Unless you live on the coast, most "fresh" salt-water fish has an 8- to 12-day trek from the net to your dinner plate. Aquaculture speeds the processing and distribution system up a bit, but not that much. Fresh is what you catch yourself. Fresh, when it applies to store-bought fish, simply means unfrozen. The seafood industry calculates a refrigerated shelf life of 10 to 12 days for most fish.

Some fish are fresher than others. Here's how to check. Look. As mentioned before, the eyes will tell a great deal with whole fish. What happens if one eye is cloudy and the other eye is clear? One possibility is that the cloudy eye could have been caused by its lying on the ice.

With fillets and steaks, the skin should be shiny, with an almost metal-like gleam. The skin should look smooth, not puckered in areas. Look at the flesh. It should be clean of spots. The flesh should be translucent, no matter what the color, be it white, purple (tuna), or deep orange (salmon), and have a sheen. Once the shine goes from fish, so goes the freshness.

Smell. Fresh fish will have a clean smell, without a fishy odor, a little like seaweed. Avoid off odors like sulfur or ammonia. Avoid medicinal odors from shrimp or shellfish. Fishy odors indicate old fish. A marinade won't hide that.

Touch. The flesh should feel firm and bounce back. With old fish, your finger may make a lasting impression. The flesh shouldn't separate into large flakes. When touching the skin, the surface shouldn't slide away from the flesh. It should be tight.

If everything checks out at this point, the question is how much seafood to buy. Depending on the number of courses and accompaniments, and the company you keep, here are some basic guidelines. Fillets should weigh in around 6 to 8 ounces per serving, with about 1 cup marinade per 1 1/2 pound to 2 pounds of fish. With oilier fish, such as salmon or tuna, you can lean toward lighter portions, 4 to 6 ounces per serving. If using whole fish, allow 12 to 16 ounces per serving with 1 1/2 cups marinade per pound. Shrimp should weigh in at or about 1/2 to 3/4 pound per serving, but, truthfully, the more shrimp you put out, the more everyone will eat. Figure a cup of marinade per pound of shrimp.

After you've landed the right catch, how do you keep it fresh, especially if you're not going to start marinating it until the next day?

First, unwrap it. Seafood wrapped in paper or plastic has no air circulating around it. Because wrapping acts as insulation, the fish is not evenly chilled. Pack a deep baking dish with crushed ice cubes, lay the fish on top of the ice (skin side down if there is skin) and cover with plastic wrap, leaving about 1/2 inch headroom. Place the fish on the bottom part of your refrigerator (where it's the coldest). Your fish will stay fresh a little longer that way.

Unless you're close to the Gulf of Mexico, most shrimp that you find will be frozen. Should you be lucky enough to find fresh shrimp with heads on, please don't marinate them. Cook them as is, it's a rare treat. Go for the large (16 to 20 count per pound) unpeeled shrimp and allow 4 to 5 per serving. The smaller sizes aren't as tasty and you'll likely get bored peeling them. Some shrimp aficionados will tell you that by peeling shrimp you also peel flavor away. Perhaps, but a marinade or a rub won't penetrate the shell. And when you ultimately peel the shell away from cooked shrimp, so goes your marinade. However, I use rubs to spice up crawfish and crab boils and get raves over my "secret" ingredients.

When preparing fish for marinades, rinse the fish lightly under cold water. Remove the bones with a set of tweezers or needle-nose pliers if your cut of fish is a fillet. Also, if you are marinating salmon fillets, remove the dark gray fat area if necessary. With tuna, marlin, or swordfish steaks, the skin carries the oil and fat, which can be removed before marinating. Go for thick cuts, as these fish may dry out quickly over high heat grilling or broiling.

If you are going to make a seviche, for safety's sake, freeze the fish overnight in a 0°F freezer, defrost, and then marinate. This will kill any parasites that may be present.

Fish takes about 10 minutes per inch to cook. But on the grill, cooking times vary with the cut and texture of the fish, how long it's been marinating, and the heat of the fire. If you are sauteing indoors, the heat of the skillet affects timing. The center of the cooked fish shouldn't look translucent or raw, but have a steamy opacity. It should not be a dry, brittle white (which may indicate that your fish is overcooked). You want to hold some of that wonderful moisture in the center for flavor.

There are several ways to judge when a fish is done.

Look. Fish flesh turns from translucent to opaque. In the case of deep-colored fish, such as tuna or salmon, it actually changes hue from dark to light.

Smell. That's the easy part when you are grilling or sauteing. The air changes with fragrance. When that fragrance of cooking hits the air, start touching to test for doneness.

Touch. Fish becomes firmer when cooked, then it flakes. Touch the fish with a fork. If it separates with a little pressure along its natural grain, it's done. If it starts to separate in sections, it's overdone.

The minimum for cooking temperature should be around 140°F to kill off parasites.

The recipes that follow are in two parts. The first part is the marinade and the second part is a particular cooking technique. Feel free to exchange marinades in the recipes. The only recipe that should not be altered is Grapefruit Scallop Seviche, which needs a high acid marinade. If you would like to use a marinade from Chapter 4 or a paste from Chapter 5, refer to the charts in Appendix II, Marinades at a Glance, for marinating times and recommended cuts.

Marinated Calamari Tapas

Seafood marinades play an important role in tapas of Spain. This recipe combines tender calamari (squid) in sherry, citrus, and olive oil. To achieve perfectly tender calamari, there is no middle ground in cooking time. Squid sauteed longer than 2 to 3 minutes or less than 20 minutes will have the consistency of rubber bands. After 20 minutes, the squid begins to soften again, but it will have lost some of its initial flavor. The trick is to blanch the squid, then let it marinate. No further cooking is required.

The marinade recipe also will work as a seviche marinade for bay scallops and as a marinade for smoked mussels or cooked shrimp.

Sherry-Seviche Marinade

3 tablespoons dry sherry
1 tablespoon Spanish brandy or cognac
1/2 cup dry white wine
1/4 cup fresh lemon juice
2 tablespoons fresh lime juice
2 tablespoons light extra-virgin olive oil, preferably Spanish
1/4 cup chopped red onion
2 to 3 garlic cloves, minced or pressed
2 tablespoons chopped flat-leaf parsley
1 teaspoon dried oregano
1 teaspoon paprika

To make the marinade, combine the sherry, brandy, wine, lemon juice, and lime juice in a nonreactive bowl. Whisk in the olive oil a little bit at a time. Add the onion, garlic, parsley, oregano, and paprika.

Yield: 1 1/2 cups

Squid

2 pounds fresh squid, cleaned and cut into 1-inch rings
3 quarts water
2 tablespoons salt

In a large saucepan, bring about 3 quarts water and the salt to a rolling boil. Blanch the squid for 60 seconds and immediately plunge the squid into a bowl of ice water to stop the cooking process. Drain the squid and place in a nonreactive bowl or zipper-lock plastic bag and marinate in the refrigerator overnight.

Serve the squid on a small bed of greens.

Yield: 4 to 6 appetizer servings

To clean squid, separate the tentacles from the body by holding the sack in one hand and the tentacles in the other hand, and pulling. Squeeze out the bony beak from the sack and remove the bone from the body tube. Peel off the dark skin and discard. Rinse the squid with water.

Marinated Mussels

In this tapas-style marinade, mussels pick up the flavor of the Iberian peninsula—brandy, almonds, and oranges, amplified by the sweetness of the sherry vinegar. The recipe calls for 1 cup of cooked mussels, which is the yield from a 2 1/2-pound bag of mussels in the shell. I prefer using smoked mussels in this marinade. The mussels are already cooked and their smoky flavor works well with the orange in the recipe. Small shrimp (51 to 60 count) also work well in this recipe.

Brandy Marinade

1 tablespoon olive oil
1 tablespoon sherry vinegar
1/4 cup fresh orange juice
2 tablespoons chopped pimento
1/4 cup finely chopped flat-leaf parsley
2 tablespoons brandy
1 tablespoon green peppercorns, drained
2 tablespoons slivered almonds, toasted

Stir together the marinade ingredients.

Yield: 3/4 cup

Mussels

1 cup steamed or smoked mussels

Place the mussels in a small ceramic or glass baking dish. Add the marinade and toss. Refrigerate overnight.

Serve on a bed of greens or radicchio, with crusty bread.

Yield: 4 to 6 appetizer servings

Grapefruit Scallop Seviche

The mixture of limes and grapefruit in seviche is better than limes or lemons alone.

1 pound bay scallops
4 scallions, chopped, (white part only)
1/2 cup fresh grapefruit juice
1 tablespoon grated grapefruit zest
1/3 cup fresh lime juice
2 tablespoons grated lime zest
6 to 8 tablespoons extra-virgin olive oil
1/4 cup finely chopped red onion
1/4 cup finely chopped red bell pepper
1 tablespoon finely chopped fresh cilantro leaves
1/4 cup finely chopped fresh parsley
1 teaspoon dried oregano
Kosher salt and freshly ground black pepper, to taste
Crushed red pepper, to taste

Combine all the ingredients in a nonreactive mixing bowl. Place the seviche in a nonreactive container or a 1-gallon zip-lock plastic bag and refrigerate overnight.

Before serving, drain well and discard the marinade. Serve on salad greens.

Yield: 6 to 8 appetizer servings

Pesce Bianco alla Siciliana
(Whitefish or Smelts in the Sicilian Style)

I first had this traditional antipasto in the home of Italian cooking instructor Dorothy Marcucci on New Year's Day, and I spent the rest of the day raving about it. Like Caribbean escovitched fish, the whitefish is cooked first and then marinated, which harkens back to the day when marinades were used as a preservative. Unlike the marinades with escovitched fish, this marinade uses raisins—their sweetness undercuts the sourness of the lemon and vinegar.

If whitefish is not available, use small (51 to 60 count) shrimp.

Sicilian Marinade

3 to 4 tablespoons olive oil
1 small bulb fennel, sliced in thin strips
1 red pepper, seeded and cut into narrow strips
1 green pepper, seeded and cut into narrow strips
2 garlic cloves, minced or pressed
3 scallion tops, finely chopped
5 tablespoons chopped fresh flat-leaf parsley
2 tablespoons golden raisins
2 tablespoons balsamic vinegar
1 cup dry Italian white wine, Corvo
3 tablespoons lemon juice (1 medium lemon)
2 teaspoons grated lemon zest

Heat the oil over medium heat in a large skillet. Add the fennel and saute it until it is translucent. Add the peppers and cook for 3 to 4 minutes more. Add the garlic, scallions, parsley, raisins, and balsamic vinegar and simmer for 5 minutes more. Keep the marinade warm. Add the wine, lemon juice, and zest just before adding it to the fish.

Yield: 2 cups

Whitefish

1 pound smelts or whitefish, cleaned
1/2 cup unbleached flour
2 to 3 tablespoons olive oil

Dust the fish with flour. Heat the olive oil over medium heat and brown the fish in the hot oil. With a slotted spoon, remove the fish to a glass or ceramic baking dish.

Pour the hot marinade with the vegetables over the fish and cool to room temperature. Add the wine, lemon juice and zest; cover and refrigerate for 2 to 3 days. Serve at room temperature over greens or radicchio.

Yield: 8 to 10 appetizer servings

Mango Shrimp from Hell with Southwestern Tabbouleh

The title of this recipe sounds as though it should be appearing at a drive-in movie instead of on a salad plate, but the flavor of this mango-marinated shrimp is pure heaven. The Southwestern tabbouleh is a variation of the Middle Eastern favorite with ginger, cilantro, and serrano chili adding the accents.

Shrimp

1 pound large shrimp (16 to 20 count to the pound), peeled and deveined
Yellow Hell (see page 71)
8 bamboo skewers soaked in water for at least 30 minutes
2 tablespoons Asian or cold-pressed domestic peanut oil (for cooking indoors)

Place the shrimp in a nonreactive container or a 1-gallon zip-lock plastic bag, pour the marinade over the shrimp, and refrigerate for 2 to 4 hours.

Southwestern Tabbouleh

8 ounces medium-fine bulgur (cracked wheat)
3/4 cup canned tamarind nectar (see note)
1/4 cup fresh lime juice
1/4 cup light olive oil
2 tablespoons grated lime zest
1 medium tomato, peeled, seeded, and diced
2 serrano chili peppers, diced with stem, seeds, and vein removed
1 tablespoon grated fresh ginger root
1/2 teaspoon ancho chili powder
1/2 teaspoon New Mexican chili powder
4 to 6 tablespoons chopped fresh cilantro leaves
4 to 6 tablespoons chopped fresh mint

An hour before you are ready to serve, soak the bulgur in the tamarind nectar and lime juice for about 15 minutes, or until the liquid is absorbed. Add the olive oil, lime zest, tomato, serrano, ginger, chili powders, cilantro, and mint. Refrigerate 1 to 2 hours before serving.

Remove the shrimp from the marinade. Reserve at least 1 cup of the marinade for a dipping sauce and use the remainder for basting. Divide the shrimp into 4 portions and run a presoaked skewer through each shrimp so that it is skewered in two places. Bring the marinade to a low boil in a nonreactive pan, or microwave the marinade for 3 minutes on high. Use for basting and as a dipping sauce.

To grill, lightly brush the grill with vegetable oil and grill the shrimp for about 3 to 4 minutes, turning often, basting with the warm marinade.

To cook indoors, arrange the shrimp skewers on a foil-lined baking sheet and broil about 6 inches from the flame for about 6 to 8 minutes, turning the skewers every few minutes, basting with the warm marinade. The shrimp is done when the flesh becomes opaque.

To serve, pack the tabbouleh into cups or ramekins, cover with a spatula, and invert onto the center of a salad plate. Slide the spatula free and remove the ramekin. Spoon 1 tablespoon of sauce onto the 4 corners of the salad plate and top each pool with 1 shrimp each, tail up.

Yield: 4 first-course salad servings

Note: For the canned tamarind nectar you can substitute 3/4 cup Tamarind Juice (see page 25) plus 2 tablespoons sugar.

Indonesian Shrimp

The Indonesian marinade is a combination of sweet coconut, fragrant lemongrass, and tangy chili, playing off the nutty flavor of the oriental sesame oil. The only problem you may encounter is the eventual shrimp shortage as guests clamor for more. This recipe can be doubled, and often is, the next time you serve it.

Indonesian Marinade

1/4 cup fresh lime juice (about 2 limes)
1 tablespoon grated lime zest
2 tablespoons nam pla (fish sauce)
1/2 cup oriental sesame oil
1/4 cup grated unsweetened coconut
2 tablespoons grated fresh ginger root
1 stalk lemongrass, chopped (about 1/4 cup)
2 dried red peppers, crumbled (about 1 table-spoon)
1 serrano chili, seeds removed and diced
3 garlic cloves, minced or pressed
3 scallions, white part only, chopped

Combine the marinade ingredients in a nonreactive mixing bowl.

Yield: 1 3/4 cups

Shrimp

1 1/2 to 2 pounds large shrimp (16 to 20 count to the pound), shelled and deveined
2 tablespoons Asian or cold-pressed domestic peanut oil (for cooking indoors)
1 1/2 tablespoons oriental sesame oil

Rinse the shrimp under cold water. Place the shrimp in a nonreactive container or a 1-gallon zip-lock plastic bag, pour the marinade over the shrimp, and refrigerate for 2 to 4 hours.

Remove the shrimp from the marinade and run a presoaked skewer through each shrimp so it is skewered in 2 places. Bring the marinade to a low boil in a nonreactive saucepan, or microwave the marinade for 3 minutes on high. Use for basting.

To grill, lightly brush the grill with vegetable oil and grill the shrimp for 3 to 4 minutes, turning often and basting with the warm marinade.

To cook indoors, arrange the shrimp skewers on a foil-lined baking sheet and broil about 6 inches from the flame for about 6 to 8 minutes, turning the skewers every few minutes after basting with marinade.

The shrimp is done when the flesh becomes opaque.

Yield: 4 to 8 appetizer servings

Scallops with
Tequila-Almond Marinade

The flavors of the lime and tequila are enhanced by the toasted almonds. When cooking indoors, I use the marinade to deglaze the pan, resulting in a wonderful light sauce. Made outdoors on the grill, this recipe gets raves not only with scallops but also with shrimp and chicken breasts.

When cooking scallops on the grill, thread scallops with 2 skewers instead of one. This keeps the scallops from sliding around on the skewers when you turn them.

Tequila-Almond Marinade

1/2 cup tequila
3/4 cup dry white wine
1/4 cup lime juice
1 tablespoon grated lime zest
1/3 cup canola oil
1/4 cup chopped fresh cilantro leaves
1/4 cup almond slivers, toasted until brown and
   coarsely crushed

To make the marinade, pour the tequila into a nonreactive saucepan, ignite with a match, and flame the tequila to reduce it by a third. Remove from the heat and cool. Combine the tequila, wine, lime juice, and lime zest in a nonreactive mixing bowl and whisk in the oil a little at a time. Add the cilantro and almonds.

Yield: 1 1/2 cups

Scallops

1 1/2 pounds large sea scallops
1 tablespoon butter (for cooking indoors)

Place the scallops in a nonreactive container or a 1-gallon zip-lock plastic bag. Pour the marinade over the scallops and refrigerate for 4 to 6 hours.

Remove the scallops from the marinade and bring the marinade to a low boil in a nonreactive saucepan or microwave the marinade for 3 minutes on high.

To grill, thread the scallops onto the skewers. Lightly brush the grill with vegetable oil and grill the scallops until light brown, about 2 to 3 minutes per side, turning often and basting with the warm marinade.

To cook indoors, heat the butter in a heavy skillet, add the scallops, and cook over high heat for about 30 seconds per side, shaking the skillet. Add the remaining marinade, bring to a boil, and simmer for about 2 to 3 minutes. Remove the scallops from the skillet with a slotted spoon, and place in a warm oven (300°F). Continue cooking the marinade until it is reduced to a glaze. Return the scallops to the skillet and gently saute the scallops until firm. Serve at once.

Yield: 4 main-course servings

Soft-Shell Crabs with Thai Coconut Marinade

Soft-shell crabs taste best when they're cooked within a few hours of being cleaned. These crabs are infused with coconut and spicy lemongrass, with accents of curry and chili oil. This Indonesian-style marinade also can be used with shrimp and scallops. Asian canned coconut milk, nam pla, and Thai chili oil are available wherever Asian groceries are sold.

Thai Coconut Marinade

1 1/2 cups Asian canned coconut milk (12-ounce can)
3 tablespoons fresh lime juice
1 teaspoon grated lime zest
3 tablespoons chopped fresh basil
1 stalk lemongrass, chopped (about 1/4 cup)
2 garlic cloves, minced
1 teaspoon ground coriander
2 tablespoons nam pla (fish sauce)
1/2 teaspoon Thai chili oil
2 teaspoons brown sugar

To make the marinade, combine the marinade ingredients in a nonreactive mixing bowl.

Yield: 2 cups

Soft-Shell Crabs

4 jumbo soft shell crabs, or 8 "hotel" size
2 tablespoons Asian or domestic cold-pressed peanut oil (for cooking indoors)
1 1/2 tablespoons oriental sesame oil (for cooking indoors)

To clean soft-shell crabs, place the crabs on a clean cutting surface and cut off the face section (about 1/4 inch). Lift up the sides of the back and scrape away the feather-like gills with a knife. Turn the crabs on their backs and remove the apron flap. Wash the crabs and pat dry.

Place the soft-shell crabs in a nonreactive container or a 1-gallon zip-lock plastic bag. Pour the marinade over the crabs and refrigerate for 2 to 4 hours.

Remove the crabs from the marinade and bring the marinade to a low boil in a nonreactive saucepan. Or microwave the marinade for 3 minutes on high.

To grill, lightly brush the grill with vegetable oil and grill the crabs for 5 to 8 minutes, turning often and basting with the warm marinade.

To cook indoors, heat the peanut and sesame oils in a large skillet, add the crabs, and saute over medium high heat for 4 to 5 minutes on each side until brown, adding more oil if needed. Place the crabs in a 300°F oven and deglaze the pan with the remaining marinade. Over low heat, reduce the marinade to about half the original volume.

To serve, cover the surface of each plate with the reduced marinade. Add the crab and serve immediately.

Yield: 4 main-course servings

Marinated Crab with Jicama and Avocado

This first-course salad could easily double as a light main course. Jicama gives the dish its texture. The flavor of the dish bounces around the lime juice, smooth avocado, and breezy cilantro.

Cilantro-Avocado Marinade

1/2 cup fresh lime juice
2 teaspoons grated lime zest
1/3 cup avocado oil
2 tablespoons extra-virgin olive oil
1/4 cup chopped fresh cilantro leaves
1 tablespoon diced serrano chili pepper, seeds, stem, and veins removed
2 garlic cloves, minced or pressed

Combine the lime juice and zest in a nonreactive mixing bowl. Whisk in the oils a little at a time. Add the cilantro, serrano, and garlic.

Yield: 1 cup

Crabmeat

1 pound jumbo lump crab meat, picked over
1 small Hass avocado (the larger ones do not have the same flavor), peeled and diced into 1/2-inch pieces
1 cup finely diced jicama
Radicchio leaves and cilantro sprigs, for garnish

Combine the crabmeat, avocado, and jicama in a glass bowl. Pour the marinade over the crab salad, cover, and refrigerate for 6 to 8 hours.

To serve, line 6 salad plates with the radicchio. Pack the marinated crab salad into coffee cups or ramekins (to use as a mold) and invert onto the individual plates. Garnish with cilantro sprigs.

Yield: 6 first-course servings

Escovitched Marlin

Dunstan Harris mentions in *Island Cooking* that escovitched fish comes from the tapas-like dish pescado en Escabeche. The method of pickling fish is very old and predates refrigeration. We've served this particular recipe at Philadelphia's Book and the Cook dinner and received raves. The recipe works as a snack, finger food, or full meal and travels well for outdoor picnics.

3 pounds marlin steaks (or swordfish, red snapper, tuna), cut into 1/2-inch pieces
2 limes, sliced
1 tablespoon kosher salt
1 tablespoon freshly ground black pepper
1/4 cup all-purpose flour
1 cup canola oil
1 bay leaf, crumbled
1/2 cup malt vinegar
1 teaspoon allspice berries, crushed
2 large red or white onions, sliced into thin rings
1 Scotch bonnet chili pepper (habañero), sliced

Wash the fish thoroughly in cold water, rinse, and pat dry with paper towels. Rub the fish with the lime slices, then season with the salt and pepper and allow to stand for 30 minutes.

Dust the pieces with a thin coating of flour. Heat the oil in a large skillet and fry the fish on both sides until crisp and brown. Let it cool to room temperature in a glass or ceramic baking dish.

Combine the bay leaf, vinegar, allspice, onions, and Scotch bonnet pepper in a saucepan and cook until the onions are tender. Cool, then pour the mixture over the fish and cover. Refrigerate for at least 2 hours, preferably overnight. Serve cold or at room temperature. Spoon the marinade and spices over the fish as you serve.

To make this a complete meal, serve with a vegetable salad and French bread.

Yield: 6 servings

Juniper Gin-Cured Gravlax

When setting up a buffet table, I like to have a few anchor dishes, such as homemade prosciutto, a smoked turkey breast, and a side of salmon, each surrounded by a collection of condiments for folks to build their own platters. Gravlax is always one of those anchor dishes. You can make it days ahead of time, and it always comes across as truly sophisticated fare.

The following are three different versions. The basic method is the same, but the cure/rub is where the fun begins. Traditionally, Gravlax calls for aquavit or perhaps vodka. I've replaced that with gin in the first version. The juniper berries pair wonderfully well with the lemon zest. The third variation has a Southwestern kick to it; you can omit the serrano if you wish.

2 one-pound center cut salmon fillets, including skin
2 tablespoons gin
1/3 cup sugar
1/3 cup kosher salt
2 tablespoons crushed white peppercorns
6 to 8 coarsely crushed juniper berries
1 teaspoon freshly grated lemon zest
1/2 cup packed dill sprigs, chopped

Rinse the salmon briefly under cold water and pat dry with a paper towel. With a pair of tweezers, remove any small bones that run up the center. Lay the salmon fillets on top of one another, skin out (flesh in), on a cutting surface and trim evenly. Lay the salmon skin side down in large ceramic or glass baking dish.

Sprinkle each fillet with a tablespoon each of gin. Combine the remaining ingredients in a small bowl and evenly spread each fillet with the cure. Lay the salmon fillets on top of one another, skin out (flesh in). Wrap the salmon in foil, place it in a baking dish, and weight it down with a brick or heavy cans. You need to make sure that the weight is evenly distributed. Refrigerate for 2 to 3 days, turning approximately every 12 hours.

To serve, unwrap the salmon and slice it very thin on the bias.

Yield: 10 to 12 servings

Variations

Lemon Mint Cured Brook Trout. Omit the juniper berries. Replace the gin with lemon juice and the dill with fresh mint. Substitute 2 brook trout, boned and filleted for the salmon (about 2 pounds). Proceed with recipe as above.

Lime-Cilantro Gravlax. Replace the lemon juice and lemon zest with equal amounts of lime juice and lime zest. Replace the juniper berries with 1/2 teaspoon crushed coriander seeds, a pinch of cumin, and 1 teaspoon seeded and diced serrano chilies. Replace the dill with fresh cilantro leaves. Add 1 ground ancho chili pepper (seeds and stem removed), and 1/2 cup chopped unpeeled ginger. Proceed with recipe as above. Garnish with streaks of Smoked Pepper Sauce (see page 204).

Smoked Salmon with Tangerine-Pink Peppercorn Marinade

This easy recipe has the prettiest presentation in the book, rosettes of translucent orange salmon on bouquets of dill branches. And the wonderful flavor of the dish lives up to its looks. The tangerine tempers the smoke flavor and cuts the saltiness of the salmon.

Tangerine-Pink Peppercorn Marinade

1 cup fresh tangerine juice
1 teaspoon grated tangerine zest
1/4 cup fresh lemon juice
1 teaspoon coarsely crushed coriander seeds
2 teaspoons coarsely crushed pink peppercorns
1 tablespoon (from 1 bunch) fresh dill, chopped

Combine all the marinade ingredients in a nonreactive mixing bowl.

Yield: 1 1/3 cups

Salmon

1/2 pound good-quality smoked salmon (Alaskan or Scottish), thinly sliced into 1-inch to 2-inch strips
1 bunch chives
1 1/2 to 2 cups alfalfa sprouts
1 bunch fresh dill (less dill used in marinade recipe)

Place the salmon in a flat glass baking dish, add the marinade, and refrigerate for no longer than 2 hours.

To serve, arrange 3 long chives at the ten o'clock position on each salad plate. Finely dice the remaining chives and sprinkle along the outer edge of the plates. Form a nest with the sprouts in the middle of each plate. Break the remaining dill into branches and place them in the center of the sprouts to form a bouquet. Gently roll the salmon strips into rosettes and place 3 to 4 of them in the center of the dill branches. Spoon the remaining marinade over the salmon and serve.

Yield: 4 appetizer servings

Barbecued Salmon

One would think that strong-flavored barbecue sauces would overpower salmon fillets. Not so. I was amazed by the flavor combination. This sweet tomato-based sauce makes a perfect marinade for salmon.

Rum Barbecue Sauce

2 tablespoons peanut oil
1 medium onion, chopped
1 garlic clove, chopped
1 1/2 cups tomato ketchup
1/3 cup worcestershire
1/4 cup cider vinegar
1/2 cup dark rum
2 tablespoons ancho or New Mexican chili
  powder
2 tablespoons paprika
1/4 to 1/2 teaspoon cayenne
1/2 teaspoon ground cumin
1/2 teaspoon ground coriander seeds

Heat the oil in a saucepan over medium heat, add the onions and garlic, and saute until tender. Add the remaining ingredients and simmer over low heat, stirring occasionally. Remove from heat and cool to room temperature. The barbecue sauce will last refrigerated for 3 to 4 months.

Yield: 3 cups

Salmon

4 salmon fillets, about 2/3 pound each

Brush the fillets with a thin coating of barbecue sauce. Marinate the fish in the refrigerator for 2 hours.

To grill, lightly brush the grill with vegetable oil and barbecue the salmon, skin side down in a covered grill for about 15 minutes per inch of thickness.

Close the vents during the last 4 to 5 minutes for a smoke flavor.

To cook indoors, preheat the broiler to its highest setting. Arrange the salmon on a foil-lined baking sheet and broil for 4 to 5 minutes per side or until the fillets are opaque in the center and are slightly firm.

Serve the salmon with a tart red cabbage slaw.

Yield: 6 servings

Cider-Marinated Grilled Salmon Fillets

The flavor match of the apple cider marinade with the salmon is marvelous. You can grill the salmon outdoors or broil it indoors, using the marinade as part of the sauce.

Cider-Calvados Marinade

1 cup fresh apple cider
2 tablespoons calvados
1/4 cup dry white wine
1/4 cup fresh lemon juice
1/3 cup canola or grapeseed oil
2 tablespoons chopped tarragon
2 to 3 tablespoons chopped parsley

Combine the cider, calvados, wine, and lemon juice in a nonreactive mixing bowl. Whisk in the oil a little at a time. Add the tarragon and parsley.

Yield: 2 cups

Salmon

4 salmon fillets, (6 to 7 ounces each)

Place the salmon in a nonreactive container or a 1-gallon zip-lock plastic bag. Pour the marinade over the salmon and refrigerate for at least 4 hours.

Remove the salmon from the marinade and bring the marinade to a low boil in a nonreactive saucepan. Or microwave the marinade for 3 minutes on high.

To grill, lightly brush the grill with vegetable oil and grill the salmon for 4 to 5 minutes. Turn and grill for another 4 to 5 minutes, basting with the warm marinade. Test for doneness; the fillets should be opaque in the center and slightly firm.

To cook indoors, preheat the broiler to its highest setting. Arrange the salmon on a foil-lined baking sheet and broil for 4 to 5 minutes per side or until the fillets are opaque in the center and are slightly firm. In a nonreactive saucepan, reduce the marinade by half.

To serve, drizzle 3 to 4 tablespoons of the reduced marinade on each salmon portion and serve.

Yield: 4 main-course servings

Salmon Steamed in a Japanese Marinade

Japanese foods are marinated for only a short period of time with few ingredients so that one flavor doesn't overpower another. This exquisite dish can be assembled in no time at all and has the shortest marinating time in the book. Its presentation is a beautiful play of rosy pink salmon on a bed of clear bean thread noodles. The Japanese marinade also can work with chicken breasts or shrimp.

Japanese Marinade

2/3 cup sake
1/2 cup mirin
1/3 cup low-sodium soy sauce

To make the marinade, combine all the marinade ingredients in a nonreactive mixing bowl.

Yield: 1 1/2 cups

Salmon

2 four-ounce to six-ounce salmon fillets
1 (2-ounce) package bean thread noodles
2 tablespoons minced preserved ginger root or 2 tablespoons minced fresh ginger root and 1/2 teaspoon light brown sugar

Place the salmon fillets in a nonreactive container or a 1-gallon zip-lock plastic bag. Pour the marinade over the salmon and refrigerate for no longer than an hour.

While the salmon is marinating, soak the noodles in very warm water for about 30 minutes or until they are translucent. Plunge the noodles into a large pot of boiling water and boil them until they are clear (about 5 minutes). Remove the noodles and drain.

Remove the salmon from the marinade and bring the marinade to a high boil in a covered nonreactive saucepan with a vegetable steamer. Place the salmon fillets on the steamer, cover, and steam for 15 to 20 minutes. Remove the lid and, with a fork or the tip of a sharp knife, gently separate the flesh at its thickest point. If the interior of the fillet is opaque and just beginning to flake, the salmon is done.

Remove the salmon with a slotted spoon, place on warm plate, cover with a bowl, and place in warm oven (about 300°F). Add the ginger to the remaining marinade and reduce the marinade to about half.

To serve, place the noodles on the center of a plate, add the salmon fillets, and cover the fillets with the remaining marinade.

Yield: 2 servings

Orange Saffron Marinated Fish in Parchment

Here the moist seafood and succulent vegetables are wedded in the orange saffron marinade. The orange plays off the hints of licorice from lightly sauteed fennel. But it's the saffron that gently infuses the fish, vegetables, and steam with its perfume.

Any of the seafood marinades in this book will work well as a steaming medium for shrimp, scallops, or fish in parchment. For this recipe I recommend swordfish, red snapper, pompano, mackerel, or salmon. All their wonderful moisture and flavor is kept tightly wrapped until the minute you open the parcel.

Orange Saffron Marinade (see page 76)
2 fish fillets or steaks, about 1 inch thick (6 to 8 ounces each)
2 sheets parchment paper, measuring 12 inches by 16 inches each
1/4 cup canola oil
2 small leeks, white part only, julienned (3-inch strips)
2 carrots, julienned (3-inch strips) (about 1 cup)
1/2 cup diced fennel
1 juice orange, peeled, seeded, and cut into 1-inch pieces

Place the fish in a nonreactive container or a 1-gallon zipper-lock plastic bag. Pour the marinade over the fish and marinate for no longer than 2 hours in the refrigerator. Remove the fish from the marinade and reserve about 1 cup of the marinade.

Preheat the oven to 400°F. Fold the parchment paper in half and cut each sheet into a heart shape. Brush 1 tablespoon of the canola oil on the inside of each sheet.

In a heavy skillet, heat 2 tablespoons of canola oil over medium-high heat. Add the carrots, leeks, and fennel along with 2 to 3 tablespoons of the reserved marinade, and lightly saute until the marinade evaporates, 3 to 5 minutes in all.

Divide the orange sections into 2 portions and place each portion on the middle inside crease of the parchment. Divide the sauteed vegetables in half and place on top of the oranges. Top with the fish and spoon about 1/4 cup marinade over each portion.

To close the parchment, fold the paper over and crimp the edges well. Fold the paper over twice and twist the bottom part of the heart. Place the parcels on a baking sheet and bake for 20 minutes in a conventional oven, or microwave on high for 12 to 14 minutes.

To serve, remove the parcels from the oven (or microwave) and slide them onto a serving plate. At the table, cut an X in the parchment with a sharp pointed knife and peel back the leaves.

Yield: 2 main-course servings

Tamarind-Marinated Pompano Steamed in Banana Leaves

Steamed fish parcels know no borders. Both Mexican and Southeast Asian cuisines steam seafood in a natural wrapper of banana leaves to get an added burst of moist flavor. You can substitute parchment for the banana leaves, but the flavor is not the same. The other advantage to using banana leaves is the wonderful flavor that kicks in when the leaves are grilled. Banana leaves usually come frozen in 1-pound packages. You'll find them in Asian grocery stores.

The pompano is marinated in light Asian flavors primarily to highlight the fish and its savory companions. Green mango (yes, unripe mango) is used in the recipe to provide a fruity, yet tart counterpart to the julienned carrots.

6 rectangles of banana leaves, each measuring 12 inches by 18 inches
6 pompano fillets
Asian Tamarind Marinade (see page 49)
2 small unripe mangoes, peeled and julienned
1 1/2 cups blanched julienned carrots
2 whole limes, sliced 1/8 inch thick
1/2 to 2/3 cup toasted cashew pieces
1/2 cup chopped fresh mint or cilantro leaves

To prepare the banana leaves, defrost them in the refrigerator overnight. Heat each whole leaf section over a flame or dry skillet until it changes texture and becomes more pliable. Do not overheat or it will become brittle. Trim into 12-inch by 18-inch sections.

Place the fish in a nonreactive container or a 1-gallon zip-lock plastic bag. Pour the marinade over the pompano and refrigerate for 2 to 3 hours. Remove the pompano from the marinade, reserving about 1 1/2 cups of the marinade.

Lay out each banana leaf shiny side up. Divide the carrots and mangoes into 6 portions and place a portion in the center (middle third) of each banana leaf. Top with the fish and spoon about 1/4 cup marinade over each portion. Garnish with lime slices, cashews, and chopped herbs. Fold the flaps of the banana leaves over like an envelope and secure each side with a presoaked bamboo skewer. If the banana leaves begin to split, make a foil boat under them before you place them in the oven. You will still get the flavor of the leaves without losing the juices.

To cook indoors, preheat the oven to 450°F. Place the parcels on a baking sheet and bake for 20 to 25 minutes (or 10 to 12 minutes per inch of thickness).

To grill outdoors, grill over glowing coals. Allow 10 minutes per inch of thickness on each parcel, about 20 to 25 minutes total.

To serve, remove the parcels from the heat and slide them onto a serving plate. At the table, cut an X in the banana leaves with a sharp pointed knife and peel back the leaves.

Yield: 6 servings

Grilled Mahi-Mahi with Chardonnay Marinade

This marinade combines the buttery vanilla taste of chardonnay and lemon with a little heat. You can substitute other dry white wines (or even blush wines) in this marinade. But whatever you choose, keep an extra bottle around for serving at the table. This marinade is excellent with pompano, yellow fin tuna, and red snapper.

Chardonnay Marinade

1/4 cup fresh lemon juice (1 to 2 lemons)
1 tablespoon grated lemon zest
1 cup chardonnay
1 teaspoon vanilla extract
1/4 cup grapeseed oil
1/4 teaspoon kosher salt
1 teaspoon diced jalapeño pepper (deveined and seeded)
2 garlic cloves, pressed

To make the marinade, combine the lemon juice, lemon zest, vanilla, and chardonnay in a nonreactive mixing bowl. Whisk in the oil a little at a time. Add the salt, jalapeño, and garlic.

Yield: 1 1/2 cups

Mahi-Mahi

4 six-ounce mahi-mahi fillets

Place the mahi-mahi in a nonreactive container or a 1-gallon zip-lock plastic bag, pour the marinade over, and refrigerate for 1 to 2 hours.

Remove the mahi-mahi from the marinade. Bring the marinade to a low boil in a nonreactive saucepan or microwave the marinade on high for 3 minutes.

To grill, lightly brush the grill with vegetable oil. Grill and baste the mahi-mahi for about 5 minutes. Turn the fillets and grill for an additional 3 to 4 minutes or until the fish begins to flake when tested with a fork.

To cook indoors, preheat the oven to 350°F. Arrange the fish on a foil-lined baking sheet and bake for 7 to 8 minutes, or until the fish begins to flake when tested with a fork.

Yield: 4 main-course servings

Marinated Swordfish Kabobs

Marc Pauvert of Charcuterie Pour Vous in Philadelphia uses this simple, yet versatile marinade on swordfish. It goes with both fish and shellfish. This marinade is a good starting point if you want an effortless recipe to get you to the grill in no time, and the marinade can easily be made year-round.

Basic Seafood Marinade

1 tablespoon minced garlic
1 tablespoon minced fresh ginger root
1/3 cup fresh lemon juice (about 2 lemons)
2 cups canola or grapeseed oil
1 bay leaf, crumbled
Kosher salt and freshly cracked black pepper,
**   to taste**

Combine the garlic, ginger, and lemon juice in a nonreactive mixing bowl. Whisk in the oil a little at a time. Add the bay leaf and salt and pepper.

Yield: 2 1/2 cups

Swordfish Kabobs

2 pounds swordfish, cut into 1 1/2-inch pieces

Place the swordfish in a nonreactive container or a 1-gallon zip-lock plastic bag. Pour the marinade over the swordfish and refrigerate for 1 to 2 hours.

Remove the swordfish from the marinade and thread it onto presoaked bamboo skewers.

To grill, lightly brush the grill with vegetable oil. Lay the swordfish kabobs on the grill and cook for 6 to 8 minutes, turning often and basting with the warm marinade. Because of the high oil content of the marinade, baste sparingly to avoid grill flare-up.

To cook indoors, preheat the broiler to its highest setting. Arrange the swordfish kabobs on a foil-lined baking sheet and broil for 10 minutes, basting with the marinade and turning after the first 5 minutes.

Yield: 4 main-course servings

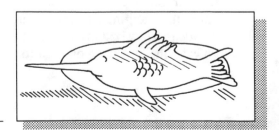

Lemon-Soy Swordfish Steaks with Pineapple Salsa

The tart flavor of Lemon-Soy Marinade is heightened by the Dijon-style mustard. By accompanying the steak with the Pineapple-Jalapeño Salsa, one gets a savory contrast with the sweet pineapple, earthy saffron, and spicy jalapeño. Chef Jon Jividen of Ridgewell's Catering in Washington created this recipe to use in two ways: as a main course with swordfish steaks and as an appetizer with skewered kabobs of swordfish around a bowl of salsa for dipping. You can also use the marinade on shark, mahi-mahi, and grouper.

Lemon-Soy Marinade

1/3 cup low-sodium soy sauce
1/4 cup fresh lemon juice
1 teaspoon grated lemon zest
2 teaspoons Dijon-style mustard
1/2 cup canola oil
1 garlic clove, minced or pressed

To make the marinade, combine the soy sauce, lemon juice, lemon zest, and mustard in a nonreactive mixing bowl. Whisk in the oil a little at a time. Add the garlic.

Yield: 1 1/2 cups

Swordfish

4 swordfish steaks, 6 ounces each
Pineapple-Jalapeño Salsa (see page 206)

Place the swordfish in a nonreactive container or a 1-gallon zip-lock plastic bag. Pour the marinade over the swordfish and refrigerate for no longer than 4 hours.

Remove the swordfish from the marinade. Prepare the marinade for basting by bringing it to a low boil, or microwave on high for 3 minutes.

To grill, lightly brush the grill with vegetable oil and grill the swordfish for 5 to 6 minutes, basting often with the warm marinade.

To cook indoors, preheat the broiler to its hottest setting. Arrange the swordfish on a foil-lined baking sheet and broil for 6 to 8 minutes on each side, basting often with the warm marinade.

Serve with the Pineapple-Jalapeño Salsa.

Yield: 8 appetizer or 4 main-course servings

Mediterranean Tuna Steaks
with Tomato Coulis

This recipe not only combines the flavors of Italy, but the colors as well: red tomato coulis, green basil butter on a field of white tuna. My friend Lisa Frank's tuna steaks deliver intense flavor to match their color.

Lemon Mediterranean Marinade

1/2 cup fresh lemon juice
2 tablespoons grated lemon zest
1 tablespoon extra-virgin olive oil
1 teaspoon freshly ground black pepper
1 teaspoon freshly ground white pepper

Combine the lemon juice, zest, and olive oil in a nonreactive bowl. Add the pepper.

Yield: 1/2 cup

Tuna Steaks

4 tuna steaks, 6 ounces each

Basil Butter

2 garlic cloves
Pinch salt
1/2 cup fresh basil leaves
4 tablespoons sweet (unsalted) butter, softened at
**   room temperature**
1/2 lemon, thinly sliced for garnishing

Place the tuna in a nonreactive container or a 1-gallon zip-lock plastic bag. Pour the marinade over the tuna and refrigerate for 4 hours.

Meanwhile, prepare the basil butter by processing the garlic into a paste with the salt in a food processor. With the motor running, add the basil leaves and process until finely chopped. Add the butter and process until well blended. Refrigerate until you're ready to serve.

Remove the tuna from the marinade and bring the marinade to a low boil in a nonreactive saucepan.

To grill, lightly brush the grill with vegetable oil. Grill the tuna steaks for 5 to 6 minutes. Turn and grill for 3 to 4 minutes more, or until the tuna flakes with a knife. Baste often with the warm marinade.

To cook indoors, preheat the oven broiler to its hottest setting. Arrange the tuna on a foil-lined baking sheet and broil for 8 to 10 minutes, or until the tuna flakes with a knife. Baste often with the warm marinade.

To serve, top each hot tuna steak with a dollop of basil butter and a thin slice of lemon. Garnish each plate with 2 to 3 tablespoons of warm tomato coulis.

Yield: 4 main-course servings

Tomato Coulis

3 ripe tomatoes, peeled, seeded, and diced
2 tablespoons balsamic vinegar
2 tablespoons tarragon vinegar
1 tablespoon dried parsley

In a heavy, nonreactive saucepan, combine the tomatoes, vinegars, and parsley. Reduce over medium heat until most of the liquid has evaporated and the coulis is quite thick. Keep warm until you're ready to serve.

Yield: 1 cup

Sauteed Tuna with Hazelnut-Peppercorn Crust

The seasoning here is a combination marinade and rub, slightly pasty in texture and perfect for lightly coating tuna or swordfish for an easy saute. This is a fast-acting marinade—the dish can be thrown together in an hour, but it tastes as if you've prepped all day. The hazelnut oil and sherry are perfect complements to the tarragon and chives in the paste, and the sauteed hazelnut coating stops dinner conversation as your guests devour each morsel.

Hazelnut-Peppercorn Rub
3 tablespoons dry sherry
1/3 cup hazelnut oil
1 tablespoon chopped fresh tarragon
2 tablespoons chopped chives
1 tablespoon minced garlic (about 2 cloves)

Whisk together the sherry and the oil in a nonreactive mixing bowl. Add the tarragon, chives, and garlic.

Yield: 1/2 cup

Tuna
2 tuna steaks, about 3/4 inch thick, 6 to 8 ounces each
1 tablespoon coarsely cracked black peppercorns
1 tablespoon coarsely cracked white peppercorns
1/2 cup hazelnuts, skinned, toasted and chopped coarsely (see page 107)
2 to 3 tablespoons clarified butter or canola oil

Place the tuna in a nonreactive container or 1-gallon zip-lock plastic bag. Pour the marinade over the tuna and refrigerate for 1 hour.

Combine the peppercorns and hazelnuts in a flat baking dish. Remove the fish from the marinade and coat evenly in the nut mixture.

Heat the butter or oil in a saute pan over medium heat, add the tuna, and saute on both sides until the crust is golden brown, 5 to 6 minutes per side.

Yield: 2 main-course servings

Orange Ginger Marinated Tuna

This recipe is a rollercoaster of taste sensations. Citrus and ginger pair off to cut the smokiness of the grilled tuna. The colorful corn salsa rounds out the dish with Southwestern flavors of corn, lime, cilantro, and a little bit of heat from the serrano.

4 tuna steaks, 6 ounces each
Orange-Ginger Marinade (see page 75)
Sweet Corn Salsa (see page 206)

Place the tuna steaks in a nonreactive container or a 1-gallon zip-lock plastic bag. Pour the marinade over the tuna and refrigerate for 4 hours.

Remove the tuna from the marinade and bring the marinade to a low boil in a nonreactive saucepan. Or microwave the marinade on high for 3 minutes.

To grill, lightly brush the grill with vegetable oil and grill the tuna for about 5 to 6 minutes, basting with the warm marinade, then turn and grill for 3 to 4 minutes more.

To cook indoors, preheat the broiler for about 8 to 9 minutes. Arrange the tuna on a foiled-lined baking sheet and broil about 4 inches from the heat source for 8 to 10 minutes, turning once.

Serve with 1/2 cup portions of the salsa.

Yield: 4 main-course servings

Tuna with Beaujolais Marinade

This particular recipe combines the flavors of the South of France with the flavors of our Southwest. The berry-flavored Beaujolais plays off the fresh lemon and woodsy flavor of the Herbes de Provence. The slight tang of the serrano chili gives the marinade added depth. Serve the tuna with your favorite pico de gallo or Peach Salsa.

Beaujolais Marinade

1 1/2 cups Beaujolais wine
1/4 cup fresh lemon juice (1 to 2 lemons)
1 tablespoon grated lemon zest
1/2 cup olive oil
1/4 cup chopped fresh parsley
1 tablespoon Herbes de Provence (see page 37)
1/2 teaspoon kosher salt
1/2 teaspoon coarsely cracked black peppercorns

To prepare the marinade, combine the wine, lemon juice, and lemon zest in a nonreactive mixing bowl. Whisk in the oil a little at a time. Add the parsley, Herbes de Provence, salt, and peppercorns.

Yield: 2 1/2 cups

Tuna

4 tuna steaks, about 6 ounces each
Peach Salsa (see page 207)

Place the tuna steaks in a nonreactive container or a 1-gallon zip-lock plastic bag, pour the marinade over the tuna and refrigerate for 4 hours.

Remove the tuna from the marinade and bring the marinade to a low boil in a nonreactive saucepan. Or microwave the marinade on high for 3 minutes.

To grill, lightly brush the grill with vegetable oil and grill the tuna for 3 to 4 minutes per side, basting often with the warm marinade.

To cook indoors, arrange the tuna on a foil-lined baking sheet and broil for 8 to 10 minutes, basting often with the warm marinade.

Serve with 1/3 to 1/2 cup of Peach Salsa on each plate.

Yield: 4 main-course servings

Red Snapper with Tomatillo Marinade

This Mexican marinade captures the flavor of salsa verde with tart tomatillos, cilantro, and lime, backed up with a little heat from the jalapeño. The marinade will be thick and actually becomes part of the sauce. You can use this marinade with swordfish, pompano, and even shrimp. Tomatillos are available in Hispanic grocery stores, as well as some supermarkets and greengrocers.

Tomatillo Marinade

1 pound fresh tomatillos, outer husks removed
1/2 cup light olive oil
1/4 cup avocado oil
3 tablespoons fresh lime juice
1 tablespoon grated lime zest
1/4 cup dry white wine
1 tablespoon diced fresh jalapeño
1 teaspoon sugar
1/4 cup chopped fresh cilantro leaves
3 to 4 garlic cloves, minced or pressed

To make the marinade, combine the tomatillos, the oils, lime juice, lime zest, and wine in a food processor, or puree in batches in a blender. Combine the tomatillo puree, jalapeño, sugar, cilantro, and garlic in a nonreactive mixing bowl.

Yield: 2 to 2 1/2 cups

Red Snapper

1 to 1 1/2 pounds red snapper fillets

Place the fish fillets in a nonreactive container, or a 1-gallon zip-lock plastic bag. Pour the marinade over the fish and refrigerate for 4 to 6 hours.

Preheat the oven to 400°F. Oil a long, shallow glass or enamel baking dish. Spoon a thin layer of marinade on the bottom of the baking dish. Add the fish and cover with the remaining marinade. Bake for 30 minutes or until the fish is opaque and flakes with a fork. Serve hot.

Yield: 4 main-course servings

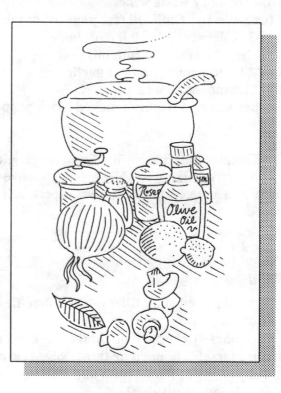

Braised Shad with White Wine Marinade

Writing cookbooks involves just as much time in front of a word processor as it does in front of a food processor. My wife Ellen bailed me out with this recipe for braised shad while I was busy writing the text for the book. The shad is marinated along with the vegetables and then braised in the marinade. The shad is succulent and the vegetables have just the right flavor and crunch.

White Wine Marinade for Seafood

1 1/4 cups dry white wine
1 teaspoon Hot Chili Oil (see page 35) or tabasco
2 to 3 tablespoons fresh lemon juice
3 tablespoons extra-virgin olive oil
1 to 2 tablespoons chopped garlic
1 1/2 teaspoons capers
Kosher salt and freshly cracked black pepper, to taste

Combine the wine, chili oil, and lemon juice in a nonreactive mixing bowl. Whisk in the olive oil a little at a time. Add the garlic, capers, salt and pepper.

Yield: 1 1/2 cups

Shad

2/3 to 3/4 pound shad fillet (or any firm-fleshed fish)
1 cup coarsely chopped or thinly sliced celery
1 cup coarsely chopped or thinly sliced carrots
3/4 cup chopped fennel bulb and stalks (save the fronds for garnishing)
3/4 cup chopped onion

Place the shad and the vegetables in a nonreactive container or a 1-gallon zip-lock plastic bag. Pour the marinade over the shad and refrigerate for 1 to 2 hours.

Preheat the oven to 350°F. Empty the contents of the container into a shallow glass baking dish, arranging the fish on top of the vegetables. Top the fish with fennel fronds, cover the dish with foil, place in the oven, and bake for 30 minutes. Serve over rice or couscous.

Yield: 2 servings

Pecan-Breaded Catfish with Mustard-Bourbon Marinade

This recipe has all of my favorite southern flavors: Creole mustard, bourbon, and the sweet taste of pond-raised catfish. Pecans have long enjoyed a savory relationship with catfish, and here they become part of the breading. Serve this dish with some sauteed zucchini and yellow squash.

Mustard-Bourbon Marinade

1 1/4 cups buttermilk
2 tablespoons Creole or coarse-grain brown mustard
1 to 2 tablespoons bourbon
2 tablespoons fresh lemon juice (about 1/2 lemon)
1 tablespoon grated lemon zest
1/4 cup chopped fresh herbs (parsley, thyme, rosemary)
1/4 teaspoon kosher salt
1/2 teaspoon coarsely ground black pepper

To make the marinade, combine all the marinade ingredients in a nonreactive mixing bowl.

Yield: 2 cups

Catfish

1/2 to 2/3 pound catfish fillets
1/2 cup crushed roasted pecans
2/3 cup Zatarain's Fish Fry (or finely ground yellow corn meal with 1 teaspoon grated lemon zest)
2 to 4 tablespoons peanut oil for pan-frying

Place the catfish fillets in a nonreactive container or a 1-gallon zip-lock plastic bag, pour the marinade over the catfish , and refrigerate for at least 4 hours.

Combine the ground pecans with the fish fry in a plastic or brown paper bag. Remove the catfish from the marinade and add it to the breading, gently shaking the bag to coat the fish evenly.

Heat 1/4 inch of peanut oil in skillet over medium-high heat to about 365°F (a cube of bread dropped into the hot oil will brown in 60 seconds.) Pan-fry the catfish for 8 to 10 minutes on each side, or until the crust turns golden brown. Drain on a paper towel before serving.

If you want to cut down on oil, coat the bottom of a cast iron or ovenproof frying pan with a little oil. Heat the oven to 500°F and bake the catfish for 8 to 10 minutes per side. The catfish will be as crisp as if it were fried.

Yield: 2 main-course servings

Grilled Halibut Steaks with a Sage Vermouth Marinade

Chef Dave Underwood from Virgil's Fish House in Bogalusa, Louisiana, has this recipe listed on his menu as Mason-Dixon Halibut. While the halibut's habitat may not be on the Mason-Dixon line, the marinade seems to be. It starts off as a savory soak of lemon and herbs, then the little bit of Louisiana hot sauce gives you a southern flavor exposure.

Dave says, "To find a good steak you may have to get a cross-section of the tail of a large fish, or choose a larger section from a smaller fish and divide it into its natural quarters."

Sage Vermouth Marinade

1 cup dry vermouth
1/3 cup fresh lemon juice
2 tablespoons Louisiana red pepper sauce
3/4 cup light olive oil
1/2 to 2/3 cup fresh chopped sage
3 tablespoons chopped chives
2 garlic cloves, chopped
2 teaspoons kosher or sea salt
1/4 teaspoon black pepper
1/4 teaspoon dried marjoram
1/4 teaspoon dried thyme

To make the marinade, combine the vermouth, lemon juice, and hot sauce in a nonreactive mixing bowl. Whisk in the oil a little at a time. Add the sage, chives, garlic, salt, pepper, marjoram, and thyme.

Yield: 2 1/2 cups

Halibut

4 halibut steaks, 8 ounces each

Place the halibut in a nonreactive container or a 1-gallon zip-lock plastic bag. Pour the marinade over the halibut and refrigerate for at least 8 hours, preferably overnight.

Remove the halibut from the marinade. Bring the marinade to a low boil in a nonreactive saucepan and simmer for about 10 minutes. Or microwave the marinade on high for 3 minutes.

To grill, lightly brush the grill with vegetable oil and grill the halibut for 8 to 10 minutes on each side, using the marinade as a baste. The fish flakes with a fork when done.

To cook indoors, preheat the broiler to its hottest setting. Arrange the halibut on a foil-lined baking sheet and broil for 6 to 8 minutes on each side, basting with the warm marinade. The fish flakes with a fork when done.

Yield: 4 main-course servings

8. Poultry, Game Birds, and Rabbit

Chicken breasts are the ultimate canvas for flavor painting with marinades. I often used chicken breasts as a litmus test while balancing the flavors of my marinades. They are versatile enough to handle most of the marinades in the front of this book. Once skinned and trimmed of fat, chicken breasts average about 200 calories per serving (before marinating). Most of of recipes that follow call for boneless chicken breasts, but since they tend to dry out fairly quickly, a good bet is to buy the breasts with the bone and skin intact if you are going to wait a day or two before you use them. Remove the skin before marinating to cut calories and for better flavor penetration. Soft as it may be, poultry skin is Nature's protective covering with a little bit of fat thrown in for insulation. For a slow oven roast I prefer to leave the bone in for more moisture and flavor.

Since most of the marinades in this section are low-acid baths, your poultry can be marinated for a little longer than the standard 4 hours. How long do you need to marinate chicken? Average timing can be 2 to 3 hours for light flavor, and 6 to 8 hours (but not longer than a day) for stronger flavor. The longer you leave chicken in a high acid marinade, the more shrinkage you'll have during cooking. For lengthy marinating times, go light on acids such as wine, lemon, or lime, or add them gradually during the marinating period. Too much acid will cook a chicken while it is marinating. The surfaces will turn white and opaque, and the chicken will cook unevenly.

To speed things up, you can always tenderize a boneless chicken breast before marinating by flattening it with a rolling pin or kitchen mallet between two pieces of waxed paper. The breast will cook more quickly and evenly, and your marinating times for chicken breasts will take half as long. One the nicest benefits of a marinade is the amount of flavor and moisture it can add to a frozen chicken. The chicken will, however, lose its moisture more quickly during the cooking process, so I suggest quick saute recipes over slow roasts. I love to marinate turkey breast. Since turkey is grown year-round (and frozen for the Thanksgiving rush), fresh, young, tender turkeys are more available in the summer months. They are great for large outdoor (and indoor) potluck dinners. Turkey tastes as good cold as it does hot. Depending on the number of guests you are feeding, you can marinate a couple of whole turkey breasts with different marinades or rubs, smoking woods, and regional condiments. Turkey breast with skin and bone is extremely succulent and can handle high acid marinades and slow roasting times, much like a beef brisket.

Duck and goose are festive and formal. Since the fat content of these birds is naturally high, the moisture (oil) content of the marinade should be lower, and in some cases nonexistent. If you are marinating breasts, remove the bird's skin and fat. To counteract their natural richness, I don't suggest adding more acid, but I do add more sweeteners in the form of dessert liqueurs.

Nowadays, we hunt for game birds such as quail, wild duck, and pheasant in specialty food stores rather than in the wild. With game farms producing domesticated fowl for the American table, we can try a whole group of free-range poultry. Farm-raised game is free of the hormones, steroids, and antibiotics used in a mass-produced, water-filled chicken.

Game fowl is different from domestic poultry and must be handled differently. Game fowl such as quail, wild duck, or wild turkey, commercial or wild, tends to be dry (especially if it has been frozen). The birds require marinades low in acid and high in moisture, and they should be left with skin and bone intact. Pheasant, which has more delicate meat than chicken breasts, shouldn't be marinated for long periods of time. The gamy and fishy flavor of wild game can be tempered by the marinade, but soaking it in whole milk or buttermilk overnight will wash away unpleasant flavors. Discard the milk bath and then use your favorite marinade.

Safety Concerns

One has to assume that poultry is guilty of bacteria contamination until proven innocent. If you are using frozen poultry, begin defrosting in the refrigerator (never at room temperature) before you begin marinating. Rinse the poultry in cold water before adding it to your marinade. Bacteria such as salmonella or campylobacter, which can cause food poisoning, usually live between 45°F and 140°F. Therefore, marinate poultry in the refrigerator, not on a warm kitchen counter top. Marinated poultry should not remain out of the refrigerator any longer than 30 minutes before you begin to cook it. If you are bringing marinated poultry to be grilled at a cookout or outdoor picnic, pack it in ice. Scrupulously clean containers are a must. Avoid soft plastic containers that will absorb odors and interact with the acidic elements of marinades over time. Glass is the material of choice for reusable containers, or plastic zip-lock or roasting bags for disposable alternatives.

Although the acid content in marinades may kill off some of the salmonella in the marinating process, it can take anywhere from several hours to several days to kill them all. Never reuse a marinade after you removed poultry from it. Aside from the fact that the flavor will have diminished, particles of chicken and seepage of blood that can carry bacteria will be present in the uncooked marinade.

When using your marinade to baste on the grill, bring the marinade to a low boil in a nonreactive saucepan, or microwave the marinade for 3 minutes on high. Not only will this kill off any bacteria that may be present, but you will also avoid the fire hose effect, that is, the lowering of your cooking temperature by pouring cold liquid on hot food. Needless to say, smart cooks make sure their basting brushes are thoroughly clean before using.

Finally, if you cooked too much marinated poultry and figure that the leftovers would make a great chicken salad, refrigerate the leftovers. Don't leave them out at room temperature.

The recipes that follow are in two parts. The first part is the marinade and the second part is a particular cooking technique. Feel free to exchange marinades in the recipes. If you would like to use a marinade from Chapter 4 or a paste from Chapter 5, refer to the charts in Appendix II, Marinades at a Glance, for marinating times and recommended cuts.

Smoked Chicken Salad
with Pasta Strips

This salad has just about everything going for it, a mosaic of tropical flavors, crunchy textures, and color. This recipe is really easy to assemble in stages. The lime marinade can be made a few days ahead of time. The chicken can be smoked or grilled up to a day before. Or if your favorite charcuterie happens to have some interesting looking grilled chicken breasts in the case, save time and substitute.

Lime Marinated Chicken

3 whole chicken breasts, boned, halved, skin removed
Lime Marinade (see page 73)

Place the chicken in a nonreactive container or a 1-gallon zip-lock plastic bag, pour the marinade over the chicken, and refrigerate for 4 to 6 hours.

Grill or smoke the chicken breasts until the meat is firm. Cool the chicken to room temperature and cut into small strips.

Salad

1 red bell pepper, julienned
1 yellow or orange bell pepper, julienned
1 fresh ripe mango, peeled and julienned
1 pound jicama, peeled and julienned
2 to 3 carrots, julienned

Toss the bell peppers, mango, carrots, and jicama with the chicken and set aside.

Vinaigrette

Juice and grated peel of 2 limes
2 tablespoons balsamic vinegar
1/4 cup chopped fresh cilantro leaves
1 to 2 tablespoons of chopped fresh herbs (tarragon, lavender, etc.)
1/4 teaspoon ground cumin
1/4 teaspoon ground cardamom
1 garlic clove, minced
6 to 8 tablespoons extra-virgin olive oil

To make the dressing, combine the lime juice and zest, vinegar, herbs, and seasonings in a small bowl. Slowly whisk in the olive oil, then set aside.

Garnish

3 cups peanut oil
1 pound assorted flavors of fresh angel hair pasta (tomato, spinach, garlic, hot pepper, etc.)
Assorted greens (and reds), such as endive, arugula, and radicchio

Heat the peanut oil in a wok to 375°F. Add the pasta a few strands at a time and fry for 20 to 30 seconds (not too long or the pasta will lose its flavor). Remove the pasta with a slotted spoon and drain on paper towels.

To serve, toss the salad ingredients with the vinaigrette. Line the plate with the greens. Form a nest with the fried pasta strips and add the salad.

Yield: 8 to 12 servings

Szechuan Sesame Chicken Salad

Hacked chicken or chicken bonbon is traditionally served as a cold appetizer on noodles but you can expand it into a Szechuan Chicken Salad with some additional ingredients below.

Chicken

3 cups white wine or unsalted chicken broth
1 tablespoon fresh ginger, cut into small slivers
1/4 teaspoon Szechuan (or whole black) peppercorns
Szechuan Sesame Marinade (see page 50)
2 whole chicken breasts (about 2 pounds), halved

In a large nonreactive saucepan, combine the wine or broth, ginger, and peppercorns and bring to a boil. Add the chicken breasts, reduce the heat to low, cover, and poach for 8 to 10 minutes. Remove the pan from the heat, uncover, and let the chicken cool to room temperature. Remove and discard the skin, bones, and stock. Cut the chicken into bite-size pieces and refrigerate until cold.

When cold, place the chicken in a large nonreactive bowl, pour the marinade over the chicken, cover, and refrigerate at least overnight, preferably for 24 hours.

Salad

1 cup snow peas, blanched
2-ounce package bean thread noodles, soaked in boiling water until soft, drained, and cooled
1/4 cup chopped scallions, white part only
1/2 peeled and seeded cucumber, thinly sliced (about 1 cup)
2 tablespoons sesame seeds, toasted until golden brown

To make the salad, toss the snow peas, scallions, and noodles with the chicken and marinade. Line the circumference of the individual serving plates with the cucumber, add the salad, garnish with sesame seeds, and serve.

Yield: 8 appetizer or 4 main-course servings

Jerked Chicken

Buffalo wings have nothing on jerked chicken wings, or whole chicken breasts for that matter. Jerked chicken tastes best roasted over a low charcoal heat for the flavor of the rub to really bite into the chicken. This recipe comes from *Island Cooking* by Dunstan Harris; it is equally good on fish or pork chops.

2 1/2 pounds chicken parts
1/2 cup freshly squeezed lemon or lime juice
Jerk Rub (see page 96)

Toss the chicken in the lemon and/or lime juice and refrigerate for 2 to 3 hours in a deep, nonreactive baking dish. Massage the rub into the chicken and marinate in the refrigerator for at least 3 hours, preferably overnight.

To grill, slowly roast the chicken over hot coals or on a gas barbecue at least 6 inches away from heat source for a minimum of a 1/2 hour, or until the juices run clear when the chicken is pricked with a fork. The coals should be gray ash, the gas barbecue at its lowest setting. Baste with the warm marinade after 15 minutes, turning frequently.

To cook indoors, preheat the oven to 325°F. Arrange the chicken on a foil-lined baking sheet and bake for about 1/2 hours, or until the juices run clear when chicken is pricked with a fork. Baste with the warm marinade after 15 minutes, turning frequently.

Yield: 8 appetizer or 4 main-course servings

Thai Marinated Chicken
with a Cashew Sauce

By substituting cashew butter for peanut butter and adding garam masala, we've given an Indian tang to a Thai peanut sauce. And that's just the beginning. Any nut butters, such as almond or hazelnut, can be substituted and will work well.

Chicken

3 whole boneless chicken breasts, cut into 1-inch-wide strips
Thai Marinade (see page 46)

Combine the chicken breasts with the Thai Marinade in a nonreactive covered container or a 1-gallon zip-lock plastic bag and refrigerate for 4 to 6 hours.

Remove the chicken from the marinade and bring the marinade to a low boil in a nonreactive saucepan. Or microwave the marinade for 3 minutes on high.

To grill, thread the chicken onto 12 presoaked bamboo skewers. Lightly brush the grill with vegetable oil and grill the chicken for 15 to 20 minutes, turning often and basting with the warm marinade.

To cook indoors, thread the chicken onto 12 presoaked bamboo skewers. Arrange the skewers on a foil-lined baking sheet and broil about 6 inches from the flame for about 10 minutes, turning the skewers every few minutes after basting with marinade.

Serve with the Cashew Sauce for dipping.

Yield: 6 to 8 appetizer servings or 12 hors d'oeuvres

Cashew Sauce

1 cup cashew butter (available from health food stores)
12-ounce can Asian coconut milk
1/4 cup chicken stock or low-salt canned chicken broth (see page 210)
1/4 teaspoon Garam Masala (see page 38) or curry powder
1/4 teaspoon ground cardamom
2 tablespoons unsulphured molasses
2 tablespoons low-sodium soy sauce
1/4 cup fresh lime juice
1/4 cup plain yogurt
1 garlic clove, minced or pressed

To make the sauce, combine the cashew butter, coconut milk, chicken stock, garam masala, cardamom, molasses, and soy sauce in a heavy nonreactive saucepan; bring to a boil, reduce the heat, and simmer for 20 minutes. Remove from the heat and stir in the lime juice, yogurt, and garlic. Keep the cashew sauce slightly warm, while you cook the chicken.

Yield: 2 cups

Thai Fried Chicken

The marinade in this recipe does double duty. First and foremost, it flavors the chicken with the wonderful flavor of spicy Thai Peanut sauce (served with satays), and it acts as a batter for a curry peanut coating, which locks in the flavors. Serve as a main course by marinating whole halves of chicken breasts, or as hors d'oeuvres with the chicken breasts cut into strips.

Thai Peanut Marinade

1/2 cup rice wine vinegar
1/4 cup fresh lime juice
2 tablespoons dark brown sugar
1/2 cup Asian or domestic cold-pressed peanut oil
1 tablespoon sesame oil
2 tablespoons chopped fresh lemongrass
2 garlic cloves, minced or pressed (about 1 tablespoon)
2 tablespoons chopped shallots or green onions
1 cup peanut butter
1-inch cube fresh ginger root, diced
1 tablespoon curry powder or Garam Masala (see
   page 38)

To make the marinade, combine the vinegar, lime juice, and brown sugar in a nonreactive mixing bowl. Whisk in each oil a little at a time. Add the lemongrass, garlic, shallots, peanut butter, ginger, and garam masala.

Yield: 2 1/2 cups

Chicken

2 chicken breasts, boned, skinned, and quartered
1 cup all-purpose flour
1 cup coarsely chopped roasted peanuts
1 tablespoon curry
4 to 6 tablespoons peanut oil for pan-frying

Place the chicken in a nonreactive container or a 1-gallon zip-lock plastic bag, pour the marinade over the chicken, and refrigerate for at least 6 hours, preferably overnight.

Combine the flour, peanuts, and garam masala in a brown paper bag. Remove the chicken from the marinade (the marinade will be thick); then place each piece in the bag and gently shake to coat the chicken evenly.

Heat the peanut oil in skillet over medium-high heat to 365°F (a bread cubed dropped into the hot oil will brown in 60 seconds). The oil should measure at least 1/2 inch deep in the skillet. Pan-fry the chicken for about 10 minutes on each side. Drain on a paper towel before serving.

If you want to cut down on oil, coat the bottom of a cast iron or ovenproof frying pan with a little oil. Heat the oven to 500°F and broil the chicken for 8 to 10 minutes per side. The chicken will be as crisp as if it were pan-fried.

Yield: 8 appetizer or 4 main-course servings

Marinated Chicken Wings

Whenever I need quick party food or an appetizer, I like to make a couple of pounds of wings. Chicken wings are like poultry spare ribs. In fact, I'll use some spare rib and chicken wing recipes interchangeably.

Spicy Garlic Oriental Marinade (see page 51) or Sake Marinade (see page 52) or Oriental Plum Sauce Marinade (see page 54) or Hot Chili Lime Marinade (see page 73) or Lemon Ginger Marinade (see page 74) or Hot Chili Rum Marinade (see page 86)
2 to 2 1/2 pounds chicken wings

To trim and separate chicken wings, lay the wing "elbow" (joint between drumstick and wing section) down on a chopping block and with a sharp knife cut away and discard the web-like skin between the drumstick and the wing section. Grasp both the wing and drumstick section and force them apart at the joint by bending them backward. Cutting between the two sections will give you two separate pieces: a drumstick and a wing section.

Place the wings in a nonreactive container or a 1-gallon zip-lock plastic bag. Pour the marinade over the wings and refrigerate for at least 6 hours, preferably overnight.

Remove the wings and bring the marinade to a low boil in a nonreactive saucepan. Or microwave the marinade on high for 3 minutes.

To grill, lightly brush the grill with vegetable oil and grill the wings for about 10 minutes, turning once. Baste with the warm marinade and grill for 5 to 10 minutes more.

To cook indoors, preheat the broiler. Arrange the wings on a foil-lined baking sheet and broil for 10 minutes, turning once basting with the warm marinade. Broil for 5 to 10 minutes more.

Yield: 6 to 8 appetizer servings

Chicken Fajitas

Rolled in a warm tortilla or stuffed into pita bread, the chicken not only tastes wonderful, but it's easy to prepare. The flavor brims with citrus and robust Yucatecan seasonings, a true summertime delight. If you like, make a little extra marinade to dress the lettuce garnish or salad.

Yucatecan Citrus Marinade (see page 68)
2 whole chicken breasts, boned and skinned, cut into 1/2-inch strips
12 flour tortillas (or 4 pita breads, quartered), warmed
1 tablespoon canola oil (if cooking indoors)
1 tablespoon butter, melted (if cooking indoors)
1/2 cup sliced radicchio
1/2 cup sliced red leaf lettuce
2 tablespoons fresh lime juice
1 tablespoon chopped fresh cilantro leaves

Place the chicken in a nonreactive container or a 1-gallon zip-lock plastic bag. Pour the marinade over the chicken and refrigerate for 6 to 8 hours. Remove the chicken and bring the marinade to a low boil in a nonreactive saucepan or microwave the marinade for 3 minutes on high.

To grill, lightly brush the grill with vegetable oil and grill the chicken for 3 to 4 minutes on each side while basting often with the warm marinade.

To cook indoors, oil a heavy (preferably cast iron) skillet and heat over high heat. Place the chicken strips in the hot skillet, and saute for 3 to 4 minutes on each side. Combine 3 tablespoons of the marinade with the melted butter and pour it over the chicken. Cook for 1 to 2 minutes more.

To serve, toss together the radicchio, lettuce, lime juice, and cilantro. Enclose the chicken in the warm tortilla or pita. Add the tossed radicchio-lettuce salad.

Yield: 8 appetizer or 4 main-course servings

Roast Chicken with Creole Mustard Bourbon Marinade

If you're out in the back parishes of southwest Louisiana, the trick for finding real food is to ask the locals for French food, not Cajun. This recipe combines some of the best local ingredients from that region: Zaterain's Creole mustard, Steen's cane vinegar and cane syrup, and a little bourbon. It's perfect for a roast chicken. The ingredients are all available by mail (see Appendix), and I've also included a Dijon Mustard Cognac variation if you find these ingredients more accessible.

Creole Mustard Bourbon Marinade

1/3 cup Steen's cane vinegar (or cider vinegar)
3 tablespoons Steen's cane syrup (or molasses)
1/4 cup Zaterain's Creole mustard (or any brand of dark coarse-grain mustard)
2 to 3 teaspoons Louisiana hot sauce (preferably Trappey's)
2 teaspoons worcestershire
2 tablespoons bourbon
1/3 cup canola oil
4 garlic cloves, pressed
1 teaspoon dried oregano
1/2 teaspoon dried thyme

Combine the vinegar, syrup, mustard, hot sauce, worcestershire, and bourbon in a nonreactive mixing bowl. Whisk in the oil a little at a time. Add the garlic, oregano, and thyme.

Yield: 2 cups

Variation

Dijon Mustard Cognac Marinade. Replace the cane vinegar with raspberry or tarragon vinegar, the Creole mustard with Dijon, the bourbon with cognac, the canola oil with grapeseed oil, and the dried oregano and thyme with an equal amount of Herbes de Provence (see page 37). Omit the hot sauce. Proceed with the recipe as above.

Chicken

4 1/2-pound to 5-pound roasting chicken

Rinse the chicken and pat dry. Place the chicken in a nonreactive container or a plastic oven-roast bag, pour the marinade over the chicken, and refrigerate for at least 6 hours, preferably overnight.

Remove the chicken from the marinade. Bring the marinade to a low boil in a nonreactive saucepan or microwave the marinade for 3 minutes on high.

Preheat the oven to 425°F. Roast the chicken for about 30 minutes. Reduce the heat to 375°F. Baste and roast for 15 to 18 minutes per pound, or until the juices run clear when the meat is pricked with a fork. Let the chicken rest for 10 minutes before carving.

Yield: 4 main-course servings

Lebanese Chicken Kabobs
(Shish Taouk)

Lebanese Chicken Kabobs are very similar to tandoori chicken. The thick homemade yogurt called laban found at Middle East grocery stores is tart and tasty. The spices can be varied to your taste. You can replace the cumin with cayenne, the coriander with cardamom or cinnamon. They all will work in this yogurt-based marinade.

Lebanese Yogurt Marinade

1 cup plain yogurt, or laban
1/4 cup fresh lemon juice
1 tablespoon grated lemon zest
3 tablespoons extra-virgin olive oil
1/4 cup chopped fresh mint leaves
1/2 teaspoon ground cumin
1 teaspoon ground coriander seeds
1 teaspoon dried oregano
1 teaspoon paprika
3 to 4 garlic cloves, pressed
1/4 cup finely chopped onion

Combine the yogurt, lemon juice, and zest in a nonreactive mixing bowl. Whisk in the oil a little at a time. Add the mint, cumin, coriander, oregano, paprika, garlic, and onion.

Yield: 2 1/2 cups

Kabobs

2 boneless and skinless chicken breast halves
4 pita breads
3 to 4 tablespoons olive oil
1 red onion, sliced into 1/4-inch slices
2 to 3 tablespoons toasted pine nuts or sesame
  seeds
Chopped fresh mint leaves, for garnish

Cut each chicken breast into 4 strips, 3 to 4 inches long. Place the chicken in a nonreactive container or a 1-gallon zip-lock plastic bag. Pour the marinade over the chicken and refrigerate for 3 to 4 hours.

Remove the chicken from the marinade. Reserve the marinade and heat gently in a double boiler for sauce. Using presoaked bamboo skewers, thread 2 strips of chicken on each skewer.

To grill, lightly brush the grill with vegetable oil and grill the chicken kabobs for 9 to 10 minutes, turning often and basting with the warm marinade. Brush the onions with the olive oil and grill for 2 to 3 minutes on each side. Warm the pita bread on the grill for about 1 minute on each side.

To cook indoors, preheat the broiler to its highest setting. Arrange the chicken kabobs on a foil-lined baking sheet and broil the kabobs for 12 minutes, turning and basting often after the first 6 minutes.

Pan-fry the onion in the olive oil for a light glaze. Do not overcook; the onion should still be firm. Warm the pita bread in a preheated oven at low heat.

To serve, half fill each pita with chicken, add the grilled or sauteed onion, top with warm marinade, and garnish with pine nuts and mint.

Yield: 4 servings

Tandoori Chicken Breasts

The trick to really succulent tandoori chicken is to sear the meat at high heat to seal in the juices, then reduce the heat and baste with the remaining marinade. The paprika gives the chicken its characteristic red color.

Tandoori Marinade

2 to 3 teaspoons crushed dried red chili peppers
1/2 tablespoons Garam Masala (see page 38)
2 tablespoons paprika
1 teaspoon ground cardamom
1/2 teaspoon ground cumin
2 tablespoons fresh lemon or lime juice
1 cup unflavored yogurt
1/4 cup Asian or domestic cold-pressed peanut oil
4 garlic cloves, pressed

Combine the chili, garam masala, paprika, cardamom, cumin, lemon juice, yogurt, peanut oil and garlic in a food processor or blender and blend to a smooth sauce.

Yield: 1 1/2 cups

Chicken

3 whole chicken breasts, split
Lime wedges, for garnish

Place the chicken in a nonreactive container or a 1-gallon zip-lock plastic bag. Pour the marinade over the chicken and refrigerate overnight.

Remove the chicken from the marinade and prepare the marinade for basting by bringing it to a low boil in a nonreactive saucepan. Or microwave the marinade on high for 3 minutes.

To grill, lightly brush the grill with vegetable oil and grill the chicken for about 10 minutes, baste, turn, and grill for 10 minutes. Continue cooking, turning and basting every 8 to 10 minutes, until the chicken is done. To cut down on grilling time, you can sear the chicken in your oven broiler first and finish the chicken breasts on the grill.

To cook indoors, preheat the oven to 375°F. Arrange the chicken on a foil-lined baking sheet and bake for 45 to 55 minutes until the juices run clear when pricked with a fork. Baste with the warm marinade after 15 minutes.

Garnish with lime wedges and serve with basmati rice and grilled red onion rings.

Yield: 8 appetizer or 4 main-course servings

Grilled Chicken Kabobs with Provençal-Cognac Marinade

Master butcher Marc Pauvert of Charcuterie Pour Vous in Philadelphia operates a French butcher shop that immediately transports you to the Provence region of France. His marinade for chicken kabobs is your port of entry. The meadow-like flavor of Herbes de Provence, piqued by paprika and Dijon mustard, balances the sweetness of cognac. The added savory depth of the marinade comes from the olives and olive oil.

Provençal-Cognac Marinade

1 tablespoon Dijon mustard
1 cup cognac
1 tablespoon red wine vinegar
1 cup olive oil
1 celery stalk, chopped (about 1/2 cup)
1/4 cup chopped fresh parsley
1/2 cup paprika
1/2 cup Herbes de Provence (see page 37), lightly crushed
4 to 6 Niçoise (black) olives, chopped
Salt and pepper, to taste

Combine the mustard, cognac, and vinegar in a nonreactive mixing bowl. Whisk in the olive oil a little at a time. Add the celery, parsley, paprika, Herbes de Provence, olives, and salt and pepper.

Yield: 3 1/2 cups

Kabobs

4 boneless and skinless chicken halves
16 red pearl onions
16 white pearl onions

Cut each chicken breast into 4 strips, 3 to 4 inches long. Place the chicken in a nonreactive container or a 1-gallon zip-lock plastic bag. Pour the marinade over the chicken and refrigerate for 3 to 4 hours.

Blanch the onions in boiling water for 1 minute and plunge into cold water. Trim the tops and root ends and slip off the skins.

Remove the chicken and bring the marinade to a low boil in a nonreactive saucepan or microwave it for 3 minutes on high. Using presoaked bamboo skewers, thread 2 strips of chicken in an S shape, alternating with red and white onions within the loop. Each skewer should contain 2 strips of chicken with 2 red and 2 white onions.

To grill, lightly brush the grill with vegetable oil and grill the chicken kabobs for about 9 to 10 minutes turning often and basting with the warm marinade.

To cook indoors, preheat the broiler to its highest setting. Arrange the chicken kabobs on a foil-lined baking sheet and broil the kabobs for 12 minutes, turning and basting often after the first 6 minutes.

Yield: 4 main-course servings

Five Spice Chicken Stir-Fry

Marinades are perfect for oriental stir-fries. Any of the Asian-style marinades will work on chicken, shrimp, and vegetables. For an all-vegetarian variation of this dish, omit the chicken and marinate the vegetables for 3 to 4 hours.

Five Spice Marinade

1 tablespoon five spice powder
2 tablespoons dry sherry
2 tablespoons soy sauce
1/4 cup dark honey
1/3 cup Asian peanut oil
1 tablespoon sesame oil
1-inch cube fresh ginger root, diced
3 to 4 garlic cloves, pressed

Combine the five spice powder, sherry vinegar, soy sauce, and honey in a nonreactive mixing bowl. Whisk in the oils a little at a time. Add the ginger and garlic.

Yield: 1 cup

Stir-Fry

2 whole skinless and boneless chicken breasts, (about 2/3 to 3/4 pounds), cut lengthwise into 1/2-inch strips
1/2 cup Asian or domestic cold-pressed peanut oil
1 tablespoon sesame oil
2 carrots, julienned
1 red bell pepper, seeded and julienned
1 cup broccoli florets
2 to 2 1/2 cups hot cooked rice
Coarsely crushed toasted peanuts, for garnish

Place the chicken in a nonreactive container or a 1-gallon zip-lock plastic bag. Pour the marinade over the chicken and refrigerate for 4 to 5 hours.

Remove the chicken from the marinade. Bring the marinade to a simmer in a nonreactive saucepan and keep warm. Heat 1/4 cup of the peanut oil in a large skillet or wok. When the oil is hot, add the chicken strips in batches and saute until they're tender. Remove from the heat and keep warm.

Heat the remaining 1/4 cup peanut oil with the sesame oil in the wok. When the oil is hot, add the carrots and stir-fry for 1 minute. Then add the bell pepper and cook for 1 minute more. Add the broccoli and cook for an additional minute. Remove the vegetables with a slotted spoon and keep warm on low heat in a preheated oven.

Return the reserved marinade to the wok and cook for 1 minute over reduced heat.

To serve, place the chicken over rice on dinner plates, top with vegetables and spoon the remaining marinade over all.

Yield: 4 main-course servings

Grilled Turkey Breast with Lemon-Peppercorn Marinade

This zesty recipe full of lemon and peppercorns, makes an excellent marinade for grilling. A chance thunderstorm was responsible for the tasty indoor version. It almost made me wish it would rain more often.

Lemon-Peppercorn Marinade

1/2 cup fresh lemon juice (3 to 4 lemons)
2 tablespoons grated lemon zest
1 cup light olive oil
1/4 cup chopped fresh parsley
3 tablespoons coarsely cracked mixed peppercorns (black, white, green, and pink, etc.)
1/4 teaspoon cayenne pepper, or to taste
1/2 teaspoon kosher salt
1/4 cup chopped red onion

Combine the lemon juice and zest in a nonreactive mixing bowl. Whisk in the oil a little at a time. Add the parsley, peppercorns, cayenne pepper, salt, and onion.

Yield: 1 1/2 cups

Turkey

4 turkey breast cutlets, 4 to 6 ounces each, pounded thin between 2 sheets of waxed paper
2 cups homemade poultry stock (see page 210) or unsalted canned chicken broth (if cooking indoors)
6 tablespoons chilled unsalted butter (if cooking indoors)

Place the turkey fillets in a nonreactive container or a 1-gallon zip-lock plastic bag. Pour the marinade over the turkey and refrigerate for 4 to 6 hours.

To grill, remove the turkey from the marinade. Bring the marinade to a low boil in a nonreactive saucepan or microwave the marinade on high for 3 minutes. Lightly brush the grill with vegetable oil and grill the turkey for 4 to 5 minutes, turning often and basting with the warm marinade.

To cook indoors, remove the turkey from the marinade and strain the marinade, reserving the solids and about 1/2 cup of the liquid. Heat 4 tablespoons of the butter in a saute pan or skillet. Over medium-high heat, saute the turkey for 4 to 5 minutes, turning often. Remove the turkey from the skillet and place in warm 300°F oven. Add the reserved solids to the skillet and saute for 3 to 4 minutes. Deglaze the skillet with the poultry stock and reserved marinade, and reduce by half. Whisk the remaining 2 tablespoons butter into the sauce, incorporating them 1 tablespoon at a time. Spoon the sauce onto 4 dinner plates, add the turkey, and serve.

Yield: 4 main-course servings

Hickory-Smoked Turkey Breast

For elegant holiday buffets or large barbecues or picnics, nothing beats a smoked turkey breast. You can choose your condiments around the flavor of the smoking woods and marinades, and have your guests build their own flavors. This Hickory-Smoked Turkey lends itself to various fruit chutneys, fruit mustards, or relishes. For some really sophisticated condiment possibilities, see Jay Solomon's cookbook *Condiments!*, published by The Crossing Press.

5 1/2 to 8 pound turkey breast, bone in
Presoaked hickory chunks or chips
Plum-Cassis Marinade (see page 77), Cranberry
Marinade (see page 78), or doubled recipe of
Maple Bourbon Marinade (see page 85)

Wash the turkey under cold water. Place the turkey in a plastic roasting bag, pour the marinade over the turkey. Secure the bag with a couple of twist ties, place in a shallow baking pan, and refrigerate for at least 8 hours or preferably overnight. Turn the turkey periodically to coat with the marinade.

Remove the turkey and bring the marinade to a low boil in a nonreactive saucepan, or microwave the marinade for 3 minutes on high.

To smoke the turkey, follow the Smokehouse Method on page 9 if you have a kettle grill and an available wok, or follow the manufacturer's instructions for indirect cooking over a drip pan. Fill the drip pan with either apple cider, orange juice, or wine. The turkey will take about 20 minutes per pound. The internal temperature should read 160°F.

To cook indoors, preheat the oven to 325°F. Roast the turkey at 20 minutes per pound, or until the internal temperature reads 160°F. For added moisture and flavor, place a pan of apple cider, orange juice, or wine on the floor of the oven during roasting. Refill as the liquid evaporates. To serve the turkey, let the turkey stand for 20 minutes before carving. The turkey can be served warm or cold.

Yield: 8 to 12 servings

Mesquite-Smoked Turkey Breast

Serve this smoked turkey with warm tortillas, a mango pico de gallo, black bean salsa, or marinated jicama (see page 112).

5 1/2 to 8 pound turkey breast, bone in
Presoaked mesquite chunks or chips
Yucatecan Rub (see page 93) or Cinnamon-Chili
Rub for Poultry (see page 93)

Wash the turkey under cold water. Place it in a shallow baking pan. Carefully peel back the skin, keeping it in one piece, from the base of the breast to the top, but do not remove it. Rub the seasoning mix into the turkey meat, replace the skin and cover with plastic wrap. Refrigerate for at least 8 hours or preferably overnight.

To smoke the turkey, follow the Smokehouse Method on page 9 if you have a kettle grill and an available wok, or follow the manufacturer's instructions for indirect cooking over a drip pan. Fill the drip pan with either apple cider, orange juice, or wine. The turkey will take about 20 minutes per pound. The internal temperature should read 160°F.

To cook indoors, preheat the oven to 325°F. Roast the turkey at 20 minutes per pound or until the internal temperature reads 160°F. For added moisture and flavor, place a pan of apple cider, orange juice, or wine on the floor of the oven during roasting. Refill as the liquid evaporates. To serve the turkey, let the turkey stand for 20 minutes before carving. The turkey can be served warm or cold.

Yield: 8 to 12 servings

Sauteed Breast of Goose
with Cassis Marinade

When most people think of goose they think of a whole roast. But I think that goose breast is more tender and flavorful than most of the finer cuts of beef (filet mignon included).

A whole breast from a 7- to 9-pound goose will easily feed 4 people. Have your butcher bone the breast, use the remaining bones and meat for stock, and render the fat for cooking.

The sweet Cassis Marinade has two functions. It cuts the natural richness of the goose breast and caramelizes its surface during a high heat saute.

Cassis Marinade (see page 82)
1 whole goose breast, halved, skinned, with all visible fat and gristle removed (about 1 1/2 pounds)
1 quart goose stock (or full-bodied poultry stock, see page 210)
2 tablespoons clarified butter (or rendered goose fat)

Place the goose breast in a nonreactive container or a 1-gallon zip-lock plastic bag. Pour the marinade over the goose breast and refrigerate overnight.

Remove the goose breast from the marinade and reserve the marinade for the sauce. Let the goose breast come to room temperature before sauteing. Meanwhile, make the sauce by bringing the reserved marinade to a low boil in a small nonreactive saucepan. Reduce the heat and simmer, reducing the marinade to about 1/4 cup. In a 2-quart nonreactive saucepan, reduce the goose stock to 1 1/2 cups, combine with the reduced marinade, and keep warm.

Heat the clarified butter over high heat in large nonstick skillet. Add the breasts to the skillet and saute until well browned, about 7 minutes. Turn the breasts over and continue cooking for 6 to 7 minutes.

Do not overcook or the goose will become tough. Remove the goose from the skillet and let it sit for 5 to 7 minutes before slicing. Deglaze the skillet with the cassis sauce.

To serve, cut the breasts crosswise into 1/8-inch slices. Spoon about 1/3 cup of cassis sauce over the surface of a warm plate. Fan out the goose breasts over the sauce and serve immediately. This goes beautifully with oven-roasted new potatoes and steamed white asparagus tips.

Yield: 4 main-course servings

Sauteed Duck Breast with Pomegranate-Cognac Marinade

Sparkling, sweet-tart pomegranate sauce laced with cognac and caramelized shallots is the perfect accent with a rich duck breast. Complement this dish with wild rice or Braised Chanterelles (see page 116) if they're available. Pomegranates are available from September through December, and the juice and seeds freeze well. Muscovy ducks are available from some of the mail order suppliers listed in the Appendix.

Pomegranate-Cognac Marinade

3 to 4 large pomegranates or 6 small ones
3 tablespoons reserved pomegranate seeds
3 tablespoons Cartas pomegranate molasses or substitute 2 tablespoons molasses with 1 tablespoon cassis
1/4 cup cognac
3 to 4 tablespoons chopped shallots
1/4 teaspoon ground cardamom
1/4 teaspoon coarsely cracked black peppercorns

Cut the pomegranates in half and scoop all but 3 tablespoons of the seeds into a food processor fitted with a plastic dough blade. Process the seeds until all the juice is extracted, 3 to 4 minutes. Strain the juice and combine with the reserved seeds and remaining ingredients in a glass bowl.

Yield: 1 1/2 cups

Duck

2 whole Muscovy duck breasts, skinned, with all visible fat and gristle removed
2 tablespoons clarified butter (or rendered duck fat)
1 quart duck stock or full-bodied poultry stock (see page 210)

Place the duck in a nonreactive container or a 1-gallon zip-lock plastic bag; pour the marinade over the duck and refrigerate overnight.

Remove the duck breast from the marinade and reserve the marinade for the sauce. Let the duck breasts come to room temperature before sauteing. Meanwhile, make the sauce by bringing the reserved marinade to a low boil in a small nonreactive saucepan. Reduce the heat and simmer to reduce the marinade to about 1/2 cup. In a 2-quart saucepan, reduce the duck stock to 1 1/2 cups, then combine with the reduced marinade, and keep warm.

Heat the clarified butter over high heat in large nonstick skillet. Add the duck breasts to the skillet and saute until well browned, about 5 minutes. Turn the duck breasts over and continue cooking for 4 to 5 minutes. Do not overcook or the duck will become tough. Remove the duck from the skillet and let sit for 5 to 8 minutes before cutting. Deglaze the skillet with the pomegranate sauce

To serve, cut the duck breasts crosswise into 1/8-inch slices. Spoon about 1/3 cup of pomegranate sauce over the surface of the plate. Fan out the duck breasts over the sauce and serve immediately.

Yield: 4 servings

Tea-Marinated Duck

Chef Jon Jividen's recipe for Tea-Marinated Duck is unbelievable. The marinade glazes the duck with a lacquer of oriental spices, molasses, and Earl Grey Tea. The duck is best when slowly smoked in an outdoor water smoker, but you can also roast it the oven. Either way you will have a surefire winner.

Tea Marinade

1 tablespoon freshly ground black pepper
4 cups water
2 cups teriyaki sauce
1 cup dark molasses
1/2 cup crushed star anise
1/2 cup diced fresh ginger root
5 Earl Grey tea bags or 1/4 ounce loose tea

Combine all the ingredients except the tea in a nonreactive saucepan and bring to a boil. Add the tea. Let mixture sit until completely cool. Strain the marinade. The marinade can be halved for whole chicken breasts if you wish.

Yield: 8 cups

Duck

4- to 5-pound whole duck

In a large plastic roasting bag or deep nonreactive pot, cover the duck with the marinade and refrigerate for a minimum of 24 hours; 2 to 3 days are best.

To smoke outdoors, remove the duck from the marinade. Add the marinade to the water pan in an outdoor smoker (or the wok in the kettle smoker, see page 9) and smoke over charcoal coals for 4 to 6 hours. The duck is done when the joints move freely. The internal temperature should read about 170°F. Remove the duck from the smoker, let it sit for 10 minutes, and cut into thin slices.

To roast indoors, preheat the oven to 325°F. Remove the duck from the marinade and place the duck on a rack in a roasting pan. Add about 1 inch of the remaining marinade to the bottom of the roasting pan. Place the pan in the oven to roast for 1 1/2 hours. Remove the duck from the oven, let it sit for 10 minutes, and cut into thin slices.

Yield: 8 to 10 appetizer or 4 main-course servings

Marinated Quail with Nutmeg Sauce

This dish typifies some of the sweet heat of Malaysia. What the broth-like nutmeg sauce lacks in consistency, it makes up for in intensity. Serve this with a simple rice dish to mop up the sauce.

Quail

Indonesian Honey Chili Marinade (see page 49)
8 quail, boned

To marinate the quail, place it in a nonreactive container or a 1-gallon zip-lock plastic bag. Pour the marinade over the quail and refrigerate for at least 8 hours or preferably overnight.

Remove the quail from the marinade and bring the marinade to a low boil in a nonreactive saucepan. Or microwave the marinade on high for 3 minutes.

To grill, lightly brush the grill with vegetable oil and grill the quail for 3 to 4 minutes each side, turning often and basting with the warm marinade.

To cook indoors, preheat the oven to its hottest setting Arrange the quail on a foiled-lined baking sheet and broil for 3 to 4 minutes each side, basting with the warm marinade. Remove from the heat and spoon the warm Nutmeg Sauce over. Serve with steamed rice.

Yield: 4 main-course servings

Nutmeg Sauce

1 quart of homemade chicken stock (see page 210), or low-salt canned chicken broth
1 stalk lemongrass (outer covering removed), chopped (about 1/2 cup)
1 teaspoon cardamom seeds
1 tablespoon grated fresh ginger root
3 tablespoons chopped shallots
1/4 cup sweet soya sauce (ketjap manis) or 1 tablespoon dark Chinese soy sauce and 2 tablespoons molasses
1 teaspoon freshly grated nutmeg
1 bay leaf, crumbled
2 tablespoons peanuts or hazelnuts, ground to a powder in blender or spice mill

Combine the chicken stock, lemongrass, cardamom, ginger, shallots, soya sauce, nutmeg, and bay leaf in a heavy nonreactive saucepan. Bring to a boil, reduce the heat, and simmer for 40 to 45 minutes. Strain the sauce and blend in the nut powder; keep the sauce warm until serving.

Pheasant with Poire William Marinade

Pheasant, farm-raised or field-raised, can be the sweetest of all game fowl. This light, pear-flavored marinade is fast acting because of the high acid level of the Sauternes. The marinade also finishes the dish as part of the sauce. For added flavor, texture, and garnish, saute pear slices that have been marinated in lemon juice and fruit liqueur before you deglaze the pan with your sauce.

The marinade will be as flavorful over guinea hen or chicken breasts.

Poire William Marinade

1 cup Sauternes
1/4 cup Poire William (or any pear liqueur)
2 ripe bartlett pears, peeled and cored
1/4 cup fresh lemon juice
2 tablespoons chopped shallots
1 tablespoon coarsely cracked black peppercorns

Combine all the marinade ingredients in a blender or food processor and puree until smooth.

Yield: 3 cups

Pheasant

2 whole pheasants, with breasts halved, skinned and boned; drumsticks left intact, with all visible fat removed
2 tablespoons clarified butter (or rendered duck fat)
1 quart pheasant stock or full-bodied poultry stock (see page 210)

Place the pheasant in a nonreactive container or a 1-gallon zip-lock plastic bag. Pour the marinade over the pheasant and refrigerate for 2 to 3 hours.

Remove the pheasant from the marinade and reserve the marinade for the sauce. Let the pheasant sit at room temperature for about 1/2 hour before sauteing.

While the pheasant comes to room temperature, make the sauce by bringing the reserved marinade to a low boil in a small nonreactive saucepan, reduce the heat to a simmer, and continue cooking until the marinade is reduced to about 1/2 cup.

In a 2-quart nonreactive saucepan, reduce the stock to 1 1/2 cups; then combine with the reduced marinade and keep warm.

Heat the clarified butter over high heat in large nonstick skillet. Add the drumsticks to the skillet and saute until well browned, 4 to 5 minutes. Remove and keep warm in a preheated oven.

Add the pheasant breasts to the skillet and saute for 4 to 5 minutes, or until the juices run clear when pierced by a sharp knife. Do not overcook or the pheasant will become tough. Remove the pheasant from the skillet and let sit for about 5 to 8 minutes before cutting. Deglaze the skillet with the pear sauce.

To serve, slice the leg meat off the bone and cut the pheasant breasts crosswise into 1/8-inch slices. Spoon about 1/3 cup of the pear sauce over the surface of each plate. Fan out the breasts over the sauce, with the leg meat in the center and serve immediately.

Yield: 4 main-course servings

Cider-Marinated Rabbit

The combination of freshly pressed cider with hints of mustard and honey makes this marinade perfect for an Indian Summer dinner. The marinade works equally well with chicken and Cornish hen.

Apple Cider Marinade

1 quart apple cider
3 tablespoons cider vinegar
1 tablespoon Dijon mustard
1 tablespoon chopped fresh tarragon
1 tablespoon honey
1/4 cup grapeseed or light olive oil
1 teaspoon coarsely cracked black peppercorns
1 teaspoon coarsely cracked mustard seeds
2 shallots, diced (about 1 1/2 tablespoons)
Kosher salt, to taste

To make the marinade, reduce the apple cider to about 1 1/2 cups in a nonreactive saucepan. Remove from heat and cool. Combine the cider, cider vinegar, mustard, tarragon, and honey in a nonreactive mixing bowl. Whisk in the oil a little at a time. Add the peppercorns, mustard seeds, shallots, and salt.

Yield: 2 cups

Rabbit

2 1/2-pound to 4-pound rabbit, cut into 8 serving pieces

Place the rabbit in a nonreactive container or a 1-gallon zip-lock plastic bag, pour the marinade over, and refrigerate for at least 6 hours, preferably overnight.

Remove the rabbit from the marinade and bring the marinade to a low boil in a nonreactive saucepan. Or microwave the marinade on high for 3 minutes.

To grill, lightly brush the grill with vegetable oil and grill the rabbit for 15 to 20 minutes, turning often and basting with the warm marinade. To check for doneness, pierce the meat close to the bone. The juices should run clear, and the meat should be white like chicken.

To cook indoors, preheat the oven to 375°F. Arrange the rabbit on a foil-lined baking sheet and bake for 45 to 55 minutes. Baste with the warm marinade after 15 minutes. The rabbit is done if the juices run clear when the meat is pricked with a fork.

Yield: 8 appetizer or 4 main-course servings

9. Beef, Lamb, Pork, and Venison

The tenderizing process of marinades is closely linked with meat in the minds of many. But, nowadays commercially processed beef, lamb, pork, and venison are pretty tender by the time they reach the meat counter, so marinating meat simply for the sake of softening it is no longer necessary. Adding flavor still is, however.

Completely covering the meat with the marinade is essential. The greater the coverage, the faster the flavoring process. To speed up this process, you can always slice the meat into 1-inch slices. Marinating overnight in plastic roasting bags is fine, but since citric acid can interact with plastic during longer stays in the fridge; stay with glass or nonaluminum containers.

Even though a marinade can reduce cooking time, it may, depending on the amount of acid used, draw off fluid from the meat and cause some dryness during cooking. To avoid this, check your meat for graying while it's marinating. The change in color usually indicates that the marinade is cooking the meat, much like the process of seviche. At that point, remove the meat from the marinade and place it covered in the refrigerator until you are ready to cook it.

Frozen meat can be defrosted in your marinade, but this will slow down the defrosting process. It's best to defrost first, and marinate after to ensure an even cooking process.

With marinades, not only do you have extra flavor, you can use leaner cuts of beef, because some of the moisture found in the fat that has been trimmed away can be replaced with oil. If the cut of beef that you happen to be using is marbled, such as a fillet, you need not add as much oil to the marinade. This will enable you to deglaze the saute pan with the marinade and not have the oil separate over high heat.

Not all cuts of beef require the same amount of refrigerated marinating times. Naturally soft or well-marbled beef, such as filet mignon or tenderloins, need only a few hours. Aged meat has a slight grayness to it and requires shorter marinating times as well. Cuts of meat from the leg, which has a much denser muscle system, can handle 1 to 2 days. The tougher cuts, such as brisket, loins, and flank steak, can marinate anywhere from 2 to 4 days. Not only do these cuts require longer marinating times; in some cases, they need more acid in the marinade as well.

Place beef in the freezer for 30 minutes to firm it up for easy slicing or cubing before you marinate.

Pork is raised much leaner than it was 20 years ago; in fact, pork tenderloin is almost one-third leaner than beef tenderloin. Not only is pork raised leaner, it's considered to be safer than it used to be. Trichinosis is almost unheard of these days but, to be safe, cook chops, ribs, and tenderloin to an internal temperature of 150°F to 160°F. You can also deep freeze them at 0° for about 3 weeks, then defrost, and marinate some flavor and moisture back in.

There are two cuts of pork that lend themselves particularly well to marinades: the loin and spare ribs. The loin area, I feel, is the most versatile. It's the leanest and sweetest area, and it gives us tenderloin, pork chops, and cutlets. Loin meat should be whitish pink when purchased.

I simply love barbecued spare ribs. Slow cooked or braised, rubbed or marinated, smoked, grilled, or glazed, ribs tie it all together for me when I think of outdoor cooking. Ribs demand patience; cooking them is an all-day affair. Like beef brisket, the longer they cook over low heat, the more tender they become. High heat grilling or broiling makes them tough. I've seen recipes that suggest parboiling ribs and then browning them on the grill. Forget it. You simply can't get the same flavor that you get by taking your time.

Marinate ribs in the refrigerator and bring them to room temperature for about 30 minutes before cooking. Barbecue sauces should not be used as marinades for ribs. Their sugar content (if catsup-based) will caramelize and burn. Serve barbecue sauce on the side or add at the very last minute. Allow about 1/2 to 1 pound of ribs per person, but always cook some extra. Leftover ribs (if there are any) can be reheated the next day.

Farm-raised game sounds like a contradiction of terms, but game farms are putting the culinary wild right into our backyards. Through a network of specialty food stores and mail order firms, we have access to venison, boar, and bison that marry well to the fruitier marinade recipes in this book. Farm-raised game is less gamy than game hunted in the wild.

If you bag your own game, here's a way of removing some of that gamy flavor. Cookbook author Frank Davis recommends a milk bath in which game is soaked in milk overnight to remove some of the gamy flavor. This works up to a point, but it removes a bit of flavor as well. I recommend going back in with a second marinade to put some flavor back.

Venison tends to be dry. The muscle tissue is firmer, meaning less fat and leaner meat. Marinades are especially good for adding moisture.

The recipes that follow are in two parts. The first part is the marinade and the second part is a particular cooking technique. Feel free to exchange marinades in the recipes. If you would like to use a marinade from Chapter 4 or a paste from Chapter 5, refer to the charts in Appendix II, Marinades at a Glance, for marinating times and recommended cuts.

Marinated Beef Brisket, Texas Style

The trick behind a perfectly moist beef brisket is slow, even heat or smoke. If you have a water smoker and access to mesquite chips or hard wood, Texas beef brisket takes on added depth. But you can get nice results indoors with your own oven. The Texas Dry Rub becomes the basis of a smoky, savory paste. Serve the brisket with your favorite barbecue sauce, a side of coleslaw, and a garnish of sliced, grilled red onions.

Texas Dry Rub (see page 94)
1 tablespoon fresh lime juice
1 1/2 tablespoons Madeira wine
3 tablespoons olive oil
1 whole beef brisket (4 to 5 pounds)

Combine the rub, lime juice, Madeira, and olive oil in a blender. Process until it becomes a smooth paste. Or combine the ingredients in a small nonreactive bowl and stir into a paste. Scrape the paste from the blender or bowl.

With your hands lightly oiled, rub the paste into the brisket, coating both sides well. Cover the brisket with clear food wrap and marinate for a minimum of 36 hours in the refrigerator.

Remove the brisket from the refrigerator and let it sit at room temperature (for about 1 hour) before you begin to cook.

To cook outdoors, use a covered kettle grill or water smoker. In a kettle grill, indirectly cook the brisket over a water pan containing a basting liquid of water, orange juice, wine, or something similar for about 2 hours per pound, refreshing the coals with damp smoking chips every couple of hours. The brisket should have a dark crust when finished. If you are using a water smoker, follow the manufacturer's instructions. Remove the brisket from the grill and let it stand for 10 minutes before slicing.

To cook indoors, preheat the oven to 200° F. Put the brisket in a roasting pan and place in the center of the oven. Roast for 2 hours per pound, undisturbed. Remove the brisket from the roasting pan and let stand for 10 minutes before slicing. If you like, combine the pan juices with some warm barbecue sauce for serving.

To serve, slice the brisket across the grain. Place overlapping slices on a large platter, drizzle with barbecue sauce, and garnish with grilled red onion rings.

Yield: 10 to 12 servings

Tenderloins with Wild Mushroom Marinade

The savory aroma of wild forest mushrooms laced with cognac makes beef fillets a sumptuous feast.

Wild Mushroom Marinade

1/4 cup dried wild mushrooms (cèpes, porcinis, or morels)
3 tablespoons cognac
2/3 cup red wine (Côtes-du-Rhône or pinot noir)
1/3 cup Wild Mushroom Oil (see page 35) or canola oil
2 tablespoons chopped shallots
2 garlic cloves, pressed
1 teaspoon Herbes de Provence (see page 37)
1 generous tablespoon orange blossom or wild-flower honey

In a spice grinder or blender, grind the mushrooms fine to make about 2 tablespoons powder. Heat the cognac in a saucepan or microwave on high for 2 minutes. Stir the cognac into the mushroom powder to form a paste.

Combine the mushroom paste and red wine in a nonreactive mixing bowl. Whisk in the oil a little at a time. Stir in the shallots, garlic, Herbes de Provence, and honey.

Yield: 1/2 cups

Beef

4 beef filets, 6 ounces each, cut about 1/2 inch thick

Place the beef in a nonreactive container or a 1-gallon zip-lock plastic bag. Pour the marinade over the beef and refrigerate for 6 to 8 hours.

Remove the container from the refrigerator and let it stand covered for an hour at room temperature. Remove the beef from the marinade.

To grill, lightly brush the grill with vegetable oil and sear the beef for 1 minute on each side. Continue grilling the beef: 5 to 6 minutes for rare or 7 to 8 minutes for medium rare, turning often.

To cook indoors, preheat the broiler to its highest setting. Place the beef on a broiler rack about 3 inches from the heat source and sear the beef for 1 minute each side. Continue broiling for 5 to 6 minutes for rare, or 7 to 8 minutes for medium rare, turning often.

Yield: 4 main-course servings

Grilled Tenderloins with Ancho Chili Sauce

The caramelized combination of orange and smoky chipotle pepper is seared into the crust of the beef tenderloin. Because of the acidic content of the marinade and the natural tenderness of the beef, this recipe has a shorter marinating time. The Orange Chipotle Marinade makes a wonderful basting sauce for beef ribs as well as Muscovy duck breast (not Long Island or Peking duckling).

Orange Chipotle Marinade (see page 68)
4 beef fillets, 6 ounces each, cut about 1/2 inch thick

Place the beef in a nonreactive container or a 1-gallon zip-lock plastic bag. Pour the marinade over the beef and refrigerate for 2 hours.

Remove the container from the refrigerator and let it stand, covered, at room temperature for an hour. Remove the beef from the marinade.

To grill, lightly brush the grill with vegetable oil and sear the beef for 1 minute on each side. Continue grilling the beef, 5 to 6 minutes for rare, 7 to 8 minutes for medium rare, turning often. Remove the beef from the heat and let stand for 10 minutes before serving.

To cook indoors, preheat the broiler to its highest setting. Place the beef on a broiler rack about 3 inches from the heat source and sear the beef for 1 minute each side. Continue broiling the beef, 5 to 6 minutes for rare, or 7 to 8 minutes for medium rare, turning often. Remove the beef from the heat and let stand for 10 minutes before serving

To serve, nap the Ancho Chili Sauce over the surface of 4 serving plates. Place a fillet on each and serve.

Yield: 4 main-course servings

Ancho Chili Sauce

6 ancho chilies, stemmed and seeded
1 tablespoon peanut oil
3 garlic cloves, pressed
1/4 cup chopped white onions
3 tablespoons chopped shallots
1 jalapeño, stemmed and seeded
1 stick cinnamon
1 tablespoon tomato concentrate
2 cups veal demi-glaze (see page 211)
1 tablespoon honey, or to taste

Place the chilies in a bowl and cover with boiling water. Soak for 30 minutes, then drain, reserving about 1/2 cup of the soaking liquid. Puree the chilies in a food processor or blender with the reserved soaking liquid, and the garlic, onion, shallots, and jalapeño.

Heat the peanut oil in a saucepan over medium-high heat, add the puree and cook for 2 to 3 minutes. Reduce the heat and add the cinnamon, tomato concentrate, and demi-glaze and simmer until the sauce is reduced by half. Remove the sauce from the heat and puree in a food processor until smooth. Add the honey to taste.

Yield: 1 1/2 cups

Marinated Flank Steak Sandwich with Southwestern Peanut Sauce

The marinated flank steak combines two parallel yet geographically distant cuisines. The marinade seasoning is definitely Asian, but the peanut sauce is from the American Southwest, and they play off each other wonderfully. You can serve the beef stuffed in a pita with some lightly grilled red onion rings, or rolled in a warm tortilla topped with cilantro and diced avocado.

Asian Marinade (see page 45)
2 1/2-pound flank steak
6 pita breads or 12 flour or corn tortillas, warmed

To marinate the steak, place the steak in a nonreactive container or a 1-gallon zip-lock plastic bag. Pour the marinade over the steak and refrigerate for 12 to 48 hours.

Remove the steak from the marinade. Bring the marinade to a low boil in a nonreactive saucepan and simmer for 10 minutes. Or microwave the marinade on high for 3 minutes.

To grill, lightly brush the grill with vegetable oil and grill the steak for 6 to 7 minutes, turning often and basting with the warm marinade. Remove the steak from the grill and let the steak rest for 3 to 5 minutes before slicing.

To cook indoors, preheat the broiler to its hottest setting. Place the steak on a foil-lined baking sheet and broil for 7 to 8 minutes per side, basting with the warm marinade. Remove the steak from the broiler and let the steak rest for 3 to 5 minutes before slicing.

To serve, slice the steak diagonally across the grain. Spoon the peanut sauce in the middle of the tortillas, add the steak slices, roll the tortilla and garnish with avocado and cilantro; or add the steak slices and onion slices to pita bread, then spoon in the peanut sauce.

Yield: 6 servings

Southwest Peanut Sauce

1/2 cup peanut butter
1/4 cup Tamarind Juice (see page 25)
1 teaspoon ground cinnamon
1/2 teaspoon ground cumin
2 tablespoons New Mexican chili powder
2 tablespoons jalapeño jelly
1/2 cup beef stock or low-salt canned beef broth (see page 210)

To make the sauce, combine the ingredients in a heavy, nonreactive saucepan. Bring to a boil, reduce the heat, and simmer for 20 minutes. Keep the sauce slightly warm while you grill the steak.

To reheat leftover sauce, bring to a simmer for 5 to 10 minutes and thin with additional beef broth, if necessary, to return the sauce to its original consistency.

Yield: 1 1/2 cups

Grilled Western T-Bone Steak with Tumbleweed Onions

I don't know which I like best in this recipe from Executive Chefs Bob Munich and Joe D'Aquila of Kinterra in Wayne, Pennsylvania: the steak or the onions. The chefs replace a typical red wine marinade with lager beer, which works phenomenally well with fresh herbs.

Beer Marinade

2 (12-ounce) bottles or any lager-style beer
1/2 cup finely chopped fresh basil
1/4 cup finely chopped fresh tarragon
2 to 3 tablespoons finely chopped fresh thyme
1/4 cup chopped shallots
6 garlic cloves, pressed
1 tablespoon coarsely cracked black peppercorns
1 teaspoon kosher salt
1 cup olive oil

Combine the beer, herbs, shallots, garlic, peppercorns, and salt in a nonreactive mixing bowl. Whisk in the oil a little at a time.

Yield: 4 cups

Steak

4 T-bone steaks, 12 to 16 ounces each, bone in, top loin

Place the steaks in a nonreactive container or a 1-gallon zip-lock plastic bag. Pour the marinade over the steaks and refrigerate for at least 24 hours.

Remove the steaks from the marinade. Bring the marinade to a low boil in a nonreactive saucepan or microwave the marinade on high for 3 minutes.

To grill, lightly brush the grill with vegetable oil and grill the steak 6 to 8 minutes for rare, or 8 to 9 minutes for medium rare to medium, turning and basting with the warm marinade.

To cook indoors, preheat the broiler to its highest setting. Arrange the steaks on a foil-lined baking sheet and broil 8 to 10 minutes for rare, 9 to 12 minutes for medium rare to medium, turning often and basting with the warm marinade.

Top the steak with the Tumbleweed onions and serve.

Yield: 4 servings

Tumbleweed Onions

Tumbleweed Spice Mix (see page 95)
1 1/2 cups all-purpose flour
1 large Bermuda onion, thinly sliced in rings
1 1/2 cups milk
3 cups peanut oil

Combine the spice mix with the flour in a brown paper bag. Soak the onions in the milk for 10 minutes. Drain and toss in the seasoned flour.

Heat the oil in a wok and deep-fry the onions for 5 minutes (or until golden brown). Remove from the oil and drain for about 2 minutes.

Yield: 4 servings

Thai Curry Beef

The raves I received for these skewered appetizers were due largely to the savory and spicy Thai Curry Marinade. The marinade has great flavor penetration with the small slices of meat. The dipping sauce is light and tart with a little sweetness to contrast with the curried marinade. To take the flavors to a higher level, serve the appetizers around a portion of the Thai Pickled Vegetables (see page 113).

Thai Curry Marinade (see page 47)
2 1/2-pounds flank steak, sliced 1/8 inch thick across the grain

To marinate the meat, place the steak in a nonreactive container or 1-gallon zip-lock plastic bag. Pour the marinade over the steak and refrigerate for at least 12 hours, or up to 48 hours.

Remove the steak from the marinade and skewer the strips onto presoaked bamboo skewers. Bring the marinade to a low boil in a nonreactive saucepan and simmer for 10 minutes. Or microwave the marinade on high for 3 minutes.

To grill, lightly brush the grill with vegetable oil and grill the steak strips for 2 to 3 minutes over a hot fire, turning often and basting with the warm marinade. Serve immediately with the Thai dipping sauce.

To cook indoors, preheat the broiler to its hottest setting. Place the steak on a foil-lined baking sheet and broil for 2 to 3 minutes per side, basting with the warm marinade. Serve immediately with the Thai dipping sauce.

Yield: 8 appetizer or 4-main course servings

Thai Dipping Sauce

3 tablespoons dark brown sugar
1/4 cup rice wine vinegar
1/4 cup nam pla (fish sauce)
3 tablespoons oriental sesame oil
1 tablespoon chopped fresh cilantro leaves
2 tablespoons roasted peanuts, crushed

Combine the above ingredients in a food processor or blender and pulse until mixed, about 30 seconds.

Yield: 1 cup

Japanese Beef Rolls (*Negimaki*)

With this recipe we have two distinctly flavored marinades working independently, resulting in a whole truly greater in flavor than the sum of its parts. Since the beef is rolled, we can incorporate one marinade in the center, and the second marinade on the completed beef roll. Both marinades come together when you take your first of many bites.

Sesame Marinade with Scallions

1/4 cup oriental sesame oil
3 tablespoons soy sauce
4 to 5 garlic cloves, pressed
2 to 3 tablespoons finely chopped shallots
3 tablespoons finely chopped fresh ginger root
1 tablespoon sherry vinegar
1 teaspoon dark brown sugar
8 large scallions

Combine the oriental sesame oil, soy sauce, garlic, shallots, ginger, vinegar, and brown sugar. Place the whole scallions in a nonreactive container or a 1-gallon zip-lock plastic bag. Pour the marinade over the scallions and refrigerate for 6 to 8 hours.

Yield: 1 cup

Mirin-Soy Marinade

1/4 cup sake
1/3 cup mirin
1/3 cup soy sauce

Combine the sake, mirin, and soy sauce.

Yield: About 1 cup

Beef Rolls

1 pound eye round, sliced very thin (1/8-inch slices)

Remove the scallions from the sesame marinade and reserve the marinade. Lay about 1/4 of the meat slices, with edges overlapping slightly, the length of the scallions. Lay 2 scallions along the edge closest to you and brush the meat with 1 to 2 tablespoons of the reserved sesame marinade. Roll the beef up around the scallions and secure each roll with 2 presoaked bamboo skewers. Repeat with rest of the beef slices to form 3 additional beef rolls.

Place the beef rolls in a nonreactive container or a 1-gallon zip-lock plastic bag. Pour the Mirin-Soy Marinade over the beef rolls and refrigerate for 1 hour. Remove the beef from the marinade and cut the rolls in half to give you 2 skewered beef rolls. Reserve the marinade for basting.

To grill, lightly brush the grill with vegetable oil and grill the rolls for 5 to 6 minutes, turning often and basting with the warm marinade.

To cook indoors, preheat the oven to the broiler setting. Arrange the beef rolls on a foil-lined baking sheet and broil for 5 to 6 minutes, turning and basting with the marinade.

Yield: 8 appetizer or 4 main-course servings

Oriental Beef and Broccoli Stir-Fry

Marinades lend themselves to stir-fries. Not only do they coat the meat with flavor, they finish the dish as a sauce as well. Any of the Asian marinades will work in the following recipe, but this is my favorite with beef.

Oriental Marinade for Beef

1/4 cup hoisin sauce
2 tablespoons black bean sauce
2 tablespoons honey
3 tablespoon rice wine vinegar
3 tablespoons soy sauce
1 1/2 teaspoons cornstarch
1 tablespoon oriental sesame oil
1/3 cup Asian or domestic cold-pressed peanut oil
1 tablespoon minced fresh ginger root
4 garlic cloves, pressed
1 teaspoon Szechuan peppercorns

Combine the hoisin, black bean sauce, honey, rice wine vinegar, and soy sauce in a nonreactive mixing bowl. Whisk in the oils a little at a time. Add the ginger, garlic, and peppercorns.

Yield: 2 cups

Stir-Fry

1/2 to 3/4 pound eye round or flank steak, sliced against the grain 1/4 inch thick
1 pound broccoli
4 to 6 tablespoons Asian or domestic cold-pressed peanut oil
2 to 3 teaspoons Hot Chili Oil (see page 35)
2 tablespoons minced fresh ginger root
2 tablespoons minced garlic
1/2 cup chopped scallions, white part only
2 to 2 1/2 cups cooked rice
Toasted sesame seeds, for garnish

Place the beef in a nonreactive container or a 1-gallon zip-lock plastic bag, pour the marinade over the beef, and refrigerate for at least 6 hours, preferably overnight.

Cut the broccoli florets from the main stem and split the florets in half. With a vegetable peeler, remove the rough outer husk from the stems, and slice the stems lengthwise in 1/4-inch slices.

Heat 2 tablespoons of the peanut oil along with the chili oil in the wok. When the oil is hot, add the ginger and garlic and cook briefly. Add the broccoli and stir-fry for 1 minute. Then add the scallions and stir-fry for 1 additional minute. Add 1/4 cup water, cover the wok, and let the broccoli steam for 3 to 4 minutes. Remove the vegetables with a slotted spoon and keep warm in a preheated oven at a low temperature. Reduce the wok liquid to a glaze over high heat. Add the remaining 2 to 4 tablespoons peanut oil.

Remove the meat from the marinade and add the meat to the wok, reserving 1/4 cup of the marinade. Stir-fry until slightly firm. Add the vegetables and 1/4 cup reserved marinade. Toss with the meat.

To serve, place the beef and broccoli over rice on dinner plates. Garnish with sesame seeds.

Yield: 4 main-course servings

Braised Beef with Provençal Red Wine Marinade

This elegant one-pot meal is perfect for Sunday dinner in winter. The house is filled with the aromas of herbs and vegetables. This is the kind of cooking I like. I can easily put together the ingredients, walk away from it for a while, and then come back to an incredibly tasty dinner.

Provençal Red Wine Marinade

3 to 4 dried cèpes, morels, or shitakes
4 to 5 cups dry red wine (preferably a Côtes-du-Rhône)
2 teaspoons Herbes de Provence (see page 37)
4 to 5 garlic cloves, pressed
1/4 cup chopped fresh rosemary
1/4 cup chopped fresh sage
1 tablespoon cracked black peppercorns

Grind the dried mushrooms in a blender or spice mill. Whisk together the mushroom powder, wine, Herbes de Provence, garlic, rosemary, sage, and peppercorns in a nonreactive bowl.

Yield: 5 to 6 cups

Beef

6 whole cloves
4 to 5 bay leaves
3-pound eye roast
1/2 cup chopped carrots
1/4 cup chopped parsnips
1/2 cup chopped celery
1/2 cup chopped onions or leeks
1/4 cup chopped shallots
4 tablespoons olive oil
Flour, for dusting

Wrap the cloves and bay leaves in a cheesecloth. Combine the cheesecloth, beef, carrots, parsnips, celery, onions, and shallots with the marinade in a large ovenproof roasting bag or deep ceramic casserole. Marinate in the refrigerator for 12 to 24 hours. Drain the meat and strain the vegetables and herbs from the marinade liquid

In a heavy nonreactive saucepan, reduce the marinade by a third and reserve.

In a large, heavy casserole or Dutch oven, heat the olive oil over high heat. Dust the meat with flour. Brown the meat on all sides over high heat. Then remove. Add the vegetables and herbs and continue to brown until the vegetables are caramelized. Add the wine marinade to deglaze, scraping the bottom of the pot. Add the cheesecloth sack and beef. The marinade should come no more than halfway up the beef. Cover the meat with an inverted sheet of aluminum foil. Cover the pot, place in a preheated 325°F oven, and braise for 3 to 4 hours.

To serve, remove the meat and the cheesecloth. Puree the liquid with the vegetables in a food processor and strain through a fine sieve. Return the puree to the pot and reduce slightly for a rich sauce. Let the beef stand for 15 minutes before carving.

Place 2 slices of beef on each plate with a generous helping of the red wine sauce. Steamed carrots are an excellent accompaniment.

Yield: 6 to 8 main-course servings

Cold Fillet of Beef with Fresh Herb Paste

This spectacular picnic dish is made by my friend Donna West, who uses a dry marinade of fresh herbs to season her roast tenderloin. The beef is then sliced thin and served with a cold mustard sauce. Donna also suggests serving the beef with a red cole slaw.

Beef

3 to 4 pound fillet of beef, trimmed of all visible fat

Fresh Herb Paste

12 three-inch sprigs of thyme (or lemon thyme)
12 sage leaves
6 three-inch sprigs rosemary
6 garlic cloves, quartered
1 to 2 tablespoons cracked peppercorns (or to taste)

Place enough plastic wrap or parchment paper to tightly wrap the tenderloin on a flat surface. Place the tenderloin on the front edge of the wrap and rub the fresh herbs and garlic into the meat on all sides. Roll the meat tightly and place in the refrigerator for at least 6 hours.

Preheat the oven to 550°F. Place the meat in the oven and reduce the heat to 225°F. Roast the tenderloin for 1 to 1 1/4 hours, or until an internal thermometer registers 140°F.

Remove the meat from the oven and let it come to room temperature before slicing, or refrigerate to serve the next day.

To serve, slice the meat 1/8 inch thick. Serve with mustard sauce and red coleslaw.

Yield: 8 to 10 main-course servings

Mustard-Horseradish Sauce

1/4 cup Dijon-style mustard
1/2 cup sour cream or low-calorie mayonnaise
2 tablespoons prepared horseradish
2 tablespoons fresh lemon juice
Cracked black peppercorns, to taste

Combine the ingredients in a food processor or blender. Refrigerate until you are ready to use it. This will keep refrigerated for 2 to 3 days.

Yield: 1 cup

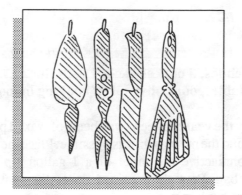

Cognac-Marinated Veal Chops

The Cognac Marinade, with its hints of mustard, pairs nicely with the subtle flavors of veal. Serve the dish with some crusty French bread, garlic-roasted potatoes, and a bottle of Côtes du Rhône.

Cognac Marinade

1/4 cup cognac
1/4 cup fresh orange juice
1 teaspoon Dijon mustard
1/4 cup olive oil
1 tablespoon green peppercorns, drained
1 teaspoon Herbes de Provence (see page 37)

Combine the cognac, orange juice, and mustard in a nonreactive mixing bowl. Whisk in the oil a little at a time. Add the peppercorns and Herbes de Provence.

Yield: 1 1/2 cups

Veal

4 veal chops, 8 ounces each, 1 inch thick
2 to 3 tablespoons olive oil (if cooking indoors)

Lay the veal between two sheets of waxed paper and pound the meat as thin as possible. Place the veal in a nonreactive container or a 1-gallon zip-lock plastic bag. Pour the marinade over the veal and refrigerate overnight.

Remove the veal from the marinade and bring the marinade to a low boil in a nonreactive saucepan or microwave the marinade for 3 minutes on high.

To grill, lightly brush the grill with vegetable oil and grill the veal chops for 8 to 10 minutes per side over a medium-high fire, basting often with the warm marinade.

To cook indoors, heat the oil in a saute pan and saute the veal chops over medium-high heat for about 10 minutes per side. Deglaze the pan with the remaining marinade and cook over high heat until the volume is reduced by about one-third.

To serve, let the chops stand for about 5 minutes before serving. Spoon the sauce from the saute pan over 4 heated serving plates, top with a veal chop.

Yield: 4 main-course servings

Beef or Lamb Kabobs

Grilling skewered meat is one of the world's oldest and most popular cooking methods. The technique goes back to the dawn of time when early chefs held a pointed stick with a piece of that day's hunt over an open fire. Today we may be wrestling with rush hour traffic instead of a saber-toothed tiger, but kabobs are still one of the best ways of preparing a fresh kill from the supermarket.

While nothing looks prettier than skewers of cherry tomatoes interspersed with pearl onions, garlic, and glistening nuggets of marinated beef or lamb, nothing is more demanding for the cook. Not one of these ingredients cooks the same way, or in the same amount of time. The answer is to use separate skewers for separate ingredients. Another hint is to thread kabobs with 2 skewers to avoid having the food roll when it is turning. As for the bamboo skewers, they need not be soaked in plain water. They can be soaked in white or red wine, apple cider, or fruit juice for extra penetrating flavor.

The following is a simple and flavorful Middle Eastern-style marinade for either beef or lamb.

Beef or Lamb Marinade for Kabobs

1 large onion
1/3 cup fresh lemon juice
3/4 cup olive oil
2 teaspoons cinnamon
1 teaspoon ground cumin
1 tablespoon paprika
1 tablespoon freshly cracked peppercorns
1/4 cup chopped fresh parsley leaves

In a food processor, puree the onion until you have a smooth paste. Empty the pureed onion into a fine sieve over a nonreactive mixing bowl and press the solids with the back of a spoon to extract the juice. Discard the solids, add the lemon to the onion juice, and mix in the olive oil a little at a time. Stir in the cinnamon, cumin, paprika, peppercorns, and parsley.

Yield: 1 1/2 cups

Meat

2 pounds beef, from the eye round or 2 pounds lean lamb, from the leg, cut into 1-inch chunks
6 pieces pita bread, warmed

Place the meat in a nonreactive container or a 1-gallon zip-lock plastic bag. Pour the marinade over the meat, toss, and refrigerate for at least 4 hours, preferably overnight.

To grill, lightly brush the grill with vegetable oil. Remove the meat from the marinade and thread on presoaked bamboo skewers. Grill the meat for 3 to 4 minutes per side.

To cook indoors, preheat the broiler to its hottest setting. Remove the meat from the marinade and thread it on presoaked bamboo skewers. Arrange the skewers on a foil-lined baking sheet and grill for 3 to 4 minutes per side.

Slide the meat from the skewers into warm pita bread and serve.

Yield: 6 servings

Shashlik
(Moroccan Lamb Kabobs)

At sidewalk stands on the street of Morocco, vendors slide tangy seasoned lamb kabobs from skewers into warm pita. Chef Jon Jividen suggests serving these kabobs in mini pitas for hors d'oeuvres. The marinading paste can also be used on cubes of chicken breast and jumbo shrimp. If you like, you can alternate various firm vegetables, such as mushrooms, pearl onions, or even whole garlic cloves, on the skewers with the lamb. Or use different skewers for grilling the lamb and vegetables, so that the vegetables don't overcook before the meat is done.

Moroccan Shashlik Paste

2 to 3 tablespoons lime juice
1/4 cup light olive oil
1/4 cup finely chopped fresh parsley
1 small onion, finely chopped (1/3 to 1/2 cup)
2 garlic cloves, pressed
1 tablespoon kosher salt
1 tablespoon fresh ground pepper
1 tablespoon paprika
1 tablespoon ground cumin
1 tablespoon ground coriander seeds

Make the marinade by combining all the ingredients in a nonreactive mixing bowl.

Yield: About 3/4 cup

Lamb

2 pounds lean lamb cubes, from leg or shoulder, cut in 1-inch cubes
6 pita breads, warmed

Place the lamb in a nonreactive container or a 1-gallon zip-lock plastic bag. Pour the marinade over the lamb, toss, and refrigerate for at least 4 hours, preferably overnight.

To grill, lightly brush the grill with vegetable oil. Remove the lamb from the marinade, and thread the lamb onto presoaked bamboo skewers. Grill for 3 to 4 minutes per side.

To cook indoors, preheat the broiler to its hottest setting. Remove the lamb from the marinade, and thread the lamb, onto presoaked bamboo skewers. Arrange the skewers on a foil-lined baking sheet and grill for 3 to 4 minutes per side.

Slide the meat from the skewers into some warm pita breads and serve.

Yield: 6 servings

Grilled Marinated Lamb Salad

Chef Bruce Cooper of Jake's in Philadelphia orchestrates a variety of simple seasoning themes in a salad that bursts with flavor. The flavors of rosemary-marinated grilled lamb with hints of apricot from the chanterelles are enhanced by a sweet sauce containing caramelized shallots, cassis, and balsamic vinegar. The salad of tossed fresh herbs and greens provides a perfect contrast.

Marinated Lamb

4 lamb tenderloins, 4 ounces each, about 1 1/2 inches thick
1/2 cup olive oil
1 tablespoon fresh rosemary, chopped
1 garlic clove, minced
1 tablespoon freshly cracked black pepper

Combine the olive oil, rosemary, garlic, and pepper in a nonreactive container or zip-lock plastic bag Add the lamb, toss, and refrigerate for 24 hours.

Remove the lamb from the marinade and grill for about for 5 minutes, turning often. Remove the lamb from the grill and let it rest for 10 minutes before slicing each piece into 4 thin sections.

Berry Sauce

1 cup balsamic vinegar
1 tablespoon minced shallots
4 tablespoons Mûre (Alsatian berry liqueur) or crème de cassis

In a nonreactive saucepan, combine the vinegar and shallots, bring to a simmer, and cook to reduce by half. Add the liqueur and reduce to a syrup consistency.

Salad

1 tablespoon white wine vinegar
1 cup extra-virgin olive oil
2 tablespoons mixed fresh herbs (such as basil, chervil, tarragon, and chives)
Kosher salt and freshly ground white pepper, to taste
6 cups mixed greens (mizuna, arugula, red mustard, or any fresh salad greens)
8 chanterelles, halved (about 1/4 pound)
2 tablespoons unsalted butter

Whisk together the vinegar, olive oil, herbs, salt and pepper and allow to sit for at least 4 hours.

To serve, saute the chanterelles in the butter. Toss the greens with the dressing. Place some salad in the middle of 4 plates. Place 4 sauteed chanterelle halves around each plate and alternate with thin slices of lamb. Drizzle the warm berry sauce over the lamb and mushrooms and serve immediately.

Yield: 4 main-course servings

Marinated Roast Rack of Lamb

Marinated spring lamb need not wait until spring. This elegant recipe from Marc Pervout of Charcuterie Pour Vous in Philadelphia can be the centerpiece of a dazzling dinner party any time of the year. The preparation is easy, the cooking time is short, and the flavor is magnificent. Serve the lamb with a bottle of merlot or pinot noir.

Red Wine Marinade for Lamb

1 cup fresh lemon juice
1 cup burgundy
1 cup red wine vinegar
3 tablespoons brandy or cognac
3/4 cup Dijon mustard
3/4 cup olive oil
1 1/2 tablespoons minced garlic
1 tablespoon fresh thyme
1 tablespoon dried oregano
2 tablespoons chopped fresh rosemary
1 tablespoon kosher salt
1 tablespoon freshly cracked black pepper

Combine the lemon juice, burgundy, vinegar, cognac, and mustard in a nonreactive mixing bowl. Whisk in the oil a little at a time. Add the garlic, thyme, oregano, rosemary, salt, and pepper.

Yield: 4 1/2 cups

Lamb

2 racks, 7 to 8 ribs, 1 1/2 to 1 3/4 pound each

Trim the fat from between the ribs and trim the excess covering of fat from the meat. Place the lamb in a nonreactive container or a large plastic roasting bag, pour the marinade over the lamb, and refrigerate overnight.

Remove the lamb from the marinade and let it sit for 30 minutes at room temperature before roasting. Bring the marinade to a low boil in a nonreactive saucepan, or microwave it for 3 minutes on high.

Preheat the oven to 450°F. In heavy saute pan over high heat, sear the lamb for 1 to 2 minutes on both sides. Place the lamb on a rack in a roasting pan and then place in the oven, reduce the temperature to 400° F, and roast for 20 minutes to an internal temperature of 120°F for medium-rare. Remove the lamb from the oven and let it rest for 10 minutes before slicing.

Serve with steamed asparagus drizzled with Sherry-Hazelnut Marinade (see page 107).

Yield: 4 servings

Indonesian Grilled Lamb with Cashew-Ginger Chutney

I remember the traditional Sunday night roast lamb dinners of my youth, but Jon Jividen's roast given here is anything but traditional. The marinated lamb and chutney make up a medley of sweet heat tastes. Your palate spins around the combination of sherry and chili with the surprise match of ginger and cashews.

Indonesian Marinade for Lamb

3/4 cup good-quality teriyaki sauce
1/4 cup fresh orange juice
2 tablespoons honey
2 tablespoons dry sherry
2 teaspoons finely chopped garlic
2 teaspoons Garam Masala (see page 38) or curry
  powder
1/4 teaspoon crumbled dry red pepper

To make the marinade, combine all the marinade ingredients in a nonreactive bowl.

Yield: 1 1/2 cups

Lamb

3 to 4 pounds loin of lamb, boned
Cashew-Ginger Chutney (see page 207)

Place the lamb in a shallow glass baking dish, fat side up. Pour the marinade over the lamb, cover, and refrigerate overnight. Remove the lamb, bring the marinade to a low boil in a nonreactive saucepan, and simmer for about 5 minutes, or microwave on high for 3 minutes. Roll the lamb and tie with presoaked butcher's twine.

To grill, place the loin about 6 inches above the heat source, baste with the remaining marinade while turning frequently. Cooking time for medium rare should be at least 30 minutes.

To cook indoors, preheat the oven to 425°F. Place the lamb in a shallow baking dish and roast in the top portion of the oven for 30 to 40 minutes. Baste the lamb frequently with the remaining marinade and pan juices.

Remove the lamb from the grill or oven and let the roast rest for 10 minutes before slicing. Slice the lamb loin in 1/4-inch slices and serve with 1/3 to 1/2 cup Cashew-Ginger Chutney.

Yield: 6 to 8 main-course servings

Roast Lamb Loin with Herb Pesto Rub

What's particularly nice about Jon Jividen's recipe is that the herb pesto infuses the lamb throughout. I serve this dish with brandy-braised baby carrots.

You can even serve this loin cold at a picnic with a Smoked Pepper Sauce (see page 208).

Herb Pesto Rub (see page 99)
2 to 3 pounds lamb loin, boned

Lay the lamb loin flat, fat side down. Rub 1/4 of the herb pesto into the lamb. Roll the loin and tie securely. Rub the remaining pesto over the surface of the lamb loin. Place the lamb in a heavy-duty roasting bag and marinate in the refrigerator for up to 8 hours.

Remove the lamb from the roasting bag and place in a shallow roasting pan. Roast the lamb at 425°F for 30 minutes (rare) to 40 minutes (medium rare). Remove the lamb from the oven and let it sit for 10 minutes before carving.

Yield: 6 main-course servings

Barbecued Lamb Ribs

This recipe comes from Chef Jack McDavid of Philadelphia's Down-Home Diner and Jack's Firehouse. Inexpensive lamb ribs are usually shunned by most cooks because of their fat content. Through a slow braise, the fat is melted off, leaving tender succulent ribs that are more flavorful than beef ribs. Jack allows the lamb ribs to sit for an hour in the barbecue sauce so that the flavor really bites into the ribs.

Firehouse Mustard Barbecue Sauce

1 to 2 tablespoons olive oil
1 jalapeño, stemmed and diced (seeding is optional)
1/3 cup chopped onions
4 to 5 garlic cloves, chopped
2 cups ketchup
1/2 cup yellow mustard
2 tablespoons cider vinegar
2 tablespoons molasses
1 teaspoon chopped fresh rosemary
1 teaspoon fresh thyme
3 to 4 bay leaves

In a large saucepan, heat the oil. Add the jalapeño, onions, and garlic, and saute for 3 to 4 minutes, or until the onions become translucent. Add the ketchup, mustard, cider vinegar, molasses, rosemary, thyme, and bay leaves. Simmer over moderate heat for about 60 minutes.

Yield: 3 cups

Lamb Ribs

1 cup apple cider vinegar
5 tablespoons dry mustard
1 tablespoon cracked black peppercorns
1 teaspoon kosher salt
6 racks of lamb ribs (about 6 pounds)

Combine the vinegar, mustard, peppercorns, and salt and rub generously over the 6 lamb racks. Place the racks in a plastic roasting bag or nonreactive covered container and marinate in the refrigerator overnight.

Remove the racks from the marinade and brown the lamb ribs on both sides under a broiler set to high. Place the ribs on a rack in a Dutch oven. Cover and roast in a 400°F oven for 1 1/2 hours.

Remove the lamb ribs from the heat and brush each rack with about 1/2 cup of the barbecue sauce. Let the ribs stand for at least an hour.

To serve, heat the ribs in a 400°F oven for 10 minutes.

Yield: 6 servings

Barbecued Pork

Mama Rosa's, operated by Rosa and Walter Ritter, is one of the oldest running barbecue pits in North Philadelphia. The marinade is as good as it gets north of the Carolinas. It is used as a baste and then added to the barbecue sauce. For extra hot barbecue sauce, the Ritters suggest substituting Mombasa Pepper Sauce for the cayenne. The dish keeps well on low heat, and the longer it sits, the better it gets.

Mama Rosa's Pork Marinade

1/4 cup unsalted butter
1 cup finely chopped onion
2 to 3 garlic cloves, pressed or minced
1 cup cider vinegar
1 cup worcestershire
2 tablespoons dry mustard
2 tablespoons dark brown sugar
2 tablespoons paprika
2 teaspoons kosher salt (optional)
2 teaspoons cayenne pepper

In a nonreactive saucepan, melt the butter. Add the onion and garlic and saute until translucent, but not browned. Stir in the vinegar, worcestershire, mustard, sugar, paprika, salt, and cayenne pepper. Bring to a boil; then remove from the heat and cool to room temperature. You can also use this marinade as a baste for spare ribs.

Yield: 3 cups

Pork

6 center cut boneless pork chops, cut 3/4 inch
  thick, or 4- to 5- pound shoulder (or Boston)
  butt, cut into 1-inch slices
14-ounce bottle ketchup

Place the pork chops in a nonreactive container or a 1-gallon zip-lock plastic bag, pour the marinade over the chops, and refrigerate for 3 to 4 hours.

Remove the pork chops from the marinade, reserving 3/4 for the barbecue sauce. Bring the remaining marinade to a low boil in a nonreactive saucepan or microwave for 3 minutes on high.

To smoke outdoors in a kettle grill with a drip pan or a smoker, cook the pork over low heat with a combination of hickory and mesquite wood chunks, turning often and basting with the warm marinade. When done, the meat should still be moist.

To cook indoors, preheat the oven to 375°F. Arrange the pork on a rack over a foil-lined baking pan or pyrex dish and roast for 45 to 55 minutes. Baste with the warm marinade every 10 to 15 minutes, turning often.

Remove the pork from the heat, let it rest for 10 minutes, then chop it finely.

Stir together the reserved marinade and ketchup in a nonreactive saucepan over low heat. Combine the pork and the pan juices with the warm sauce and cook for at least 15 minutes over low heat.

Remove the pork from the sauce and serve the pork in a hard roll with coleslaw and barbecue sauce on the side. This dish is great the next day.

Yield: 8 servings

Marinated Pork Spare Ribs

I suggest you use presoaked hickory wood for firing the grill with the barbecue rub; but if you are using the chipotle paste, I recommend burning mesquite.

Chipotle Rub (see page 92) or Southern Barbecue Rub (see page 95)
2 1/2 pounds spare ribs

Apply the rub or paste to the ribs and refrigerate overnight. Bring them to room temperature for 30 minutes before cooking.

To cook outdoors, follow the manufacturer's instructions for using a water smoker or covered grill. Depending on the heat of the coals, outdoor temperature, and wind, the ribs will take anywhere from 4 to 6 hours by the Smokehouse Method on page 9. To cover yourself, it wouldn't hurt to finish the ribs in a 300°F preheated oven for 30 minutes. Let the ribs stand for 10 minutes before serving.

To cook indoors, preheat the oven to 450°F and brown the ribs for 20 to 30 minutes. Reduce the heat to 300°F and roast the ribs for about 90 minutes. Let the ribs stand for 10 minutes before serving.

Note: Anything that is put into an airtight oven for an hour or more will start to dry it out. Place a water pan on the floor of the oven, filled with either orange juice, apple cider, wine or, according to one southern cook, root beer. The liquid will simultaneously steam, moisturize, and flavor the ribs.

Yield: 4 servings

Marinated Baby Back Ribs
2 1/2 pounds baby back ribs
Honey-Hoisin Marinade (see page 54) or Adobe Red Chili Marinade (see page 67)

Separate the ribs and marinate in the refrigerator for at least 8 hours, preferably overnight. Bring them to room temperature for 30 minutes before cooking.

To cook outdoors, follow the manufacturer's directions for cooking in a covered grill over indirect heat, without using a water pan. Add fresh coals every 30 minutes or so and turn the ribs and brush with the marinade. The ribs will be done in 2 hours.

To cook indoors, preheat the oven to 300°F. Remove the ribs from the marinade and arrange the ribs on a rack in a roasting pan. Roast for 3 to 4 hours.

Yield: 4 servings

Glazed Ribs with Dr. Pepper Marinade

One of my biggest surprises came when a southern pit boss told me that his secret marinade for ribs was Dr. Pepper and vinegar. I thought he was pulling my leg, but I'll try anything once. This recipe works.

2 cups Dr. Pepper, root beer, or water
1 cup cider vinegar
1 to 2 tablespoons kosher salt
2 1/2 pounds spare ribs or baby back ribs
Apricot Marinade, for the glaze (see page 77)

Combine the Dr. Pepper, vinegar, and salt. Pour over the ribs and marinate in the refrigerator for 8 hours, preferably overnight.

Bring the marinade to a simmer in a nonreactive saucepan. Or microwave on high for 3 minutes.

To cook outdoors, follow the manufacturer's instructions for using a water smoker or covered grill. Depending on the heat of the coals, outdoor temperature, and wind, the ribs will take anywhere from 4 to 6 hours by the Smokehouse Method on page 9. Baste every hour. Glaze with the Apricot Marinade and place in a preheated 300°F oven for 30 minutes.

To cook indoors, preheat the oven to 450°F and brown the ribs for 20 to 30 minutes. Baste and reduce the heat to 300°F and roast the ribs for about 90 minutes, basting once or twice. Glaze with the Apricot Marinade and return to the oven for 15 minutes more.

Yield: 4 servings

Marinated Beef or Lamb Ribs

This is done as a braise on top of the stove.

Amber Beer Marinade (see page 81)
2 1/2 pounds beef or lamb ribs
Canola oil

Cut the ribs into 2-inch to 3-inch pieces. Remove all visible fat and gristle. Marinate the ribs for 8 hours or preferably overnight. Remove the ribs from the marinade, reserving the marinade.

Heat about 1/4 inch of canola oil in a large deep-sided skillet or Dutch oven, add the ribs in batches, and brown on all sides. Remove the ribs from the skillet and deglaze with the reserved marinade. Lower the heat and return the ribs to the skillet, cover, and simmer for 90 minutes.

To serve, remove the ribs from the skillet and place them in a warm preheated oven while you reduce the marinade by half. Spoon the marinade over the ribs and serve.

Yield: 4 servings

Marinated Pork Canapés

Jon Jividen's Mediterranean recipe is a garlic lover's delight. You can go one of two ways with this recipe: elegant or earthy depending on how you slice the bread. For elegant Spanish canapés or tapas of marinated pork tenderloins, place on thin rounds of crusty bread. Or make one heck of a grilled tenderloin and roasted pepper sandwich by slicing the bread right down the middle and stuffing the pork and peppers inside.

Mediterranean Marinade

2 tablespoons fresh lemon juice
1/3 cup Spanish olive oil
6 to 8 garlic cloves, pressed
2 tablespoons Spanish paprika
1 teaspoon fresh thyme
1 teaspoon dried oregano
1 bay leaf crushed
Kosher salt and freshly ground black pepper, to taste

To make the marinade, combine all the ingredients in a nonreactive mixing bowl. (If you want to double this recipe for larger cuts of meat, increase the herbs by half and double the remaining ingredients.)

Yield: 1/2 cup marinade

Pork Tenderloin

3/4 pound boneless pork tenderloin, cut into 1/4-inch slices
Oil
1 long crusty loaf of bread
Pimento pieces or Roasted Tri-Color Sweet Peppers (see page 119), for garnish

Arrange the pork slices in a shallow glass baking dish and pour on the marinade, coating each slice well. Cover and refrigerate for at least 4 hours, preferably overnight.

Coat a skillet lightly with oil and heat until it's very hot. Drain the pork slices slightly and saute very quickly until just done. Do not overcook.

To serve, place the slices on thin pieces of crusty bread and garnish with a slice of roasted pepper.

Yield: 8 to 10 canapés

Hickory-Smoked Pork Tenderloin with Plum-Rosemary Marinade

This is one of the recipes that makes me keep the grill out all winter. Roast pork tenderloin can take the same flavorings that one would use on denser white meat like turkey breast. I like it better in some cases because pork tenderloin is sweeter. The Plum-Rosemary Marinade works wonderfully well with this dish, especially against the hickory flavor from the grill. This dish can also be cooked indoors (without the hickory).

Plum-Cassis Marinade (see page 77)
2 to 3 tablespoons chopped fresh rosemary leaves
2 to 3 pounds lean boneless pork loin
Presoaked hickory wood chunks
Apple cider, apple juice, or orange juice

Combine the marinade and rosemary. Place the pork in a nonreactive container or a 1-gallon zip-lock plastic bag. Pour the marinade over the tenderloin and refrigerate overnight.

Remove the tenderloin from the marinade. Bring the marinade to a low boil in a nonreactive saucepan, or microwave the marinade for 3 minutes on high.

To cook outdoors, build a charcoal fire in a kettle grill with a water pan, and add the hickory chunks to the coals (see the Smokehouse Method on page 9). Add apple cider or apple juice to the water pan. Lightly brush the top grill with vegetable oil. Place the tenderloin on the grill and smoke it for 1 1/2 to 2 hours, or until the tenderloin reaches an internal temperature of 140°F. Baste with the warm marinade every 20 to 30 minutes. Remove the tenderloin from the grill and let it rest for 10 minutes before slicing.

To cook indoors, preheat the oven to 375°F. Pour a cup or two of apple cider or orange juice into a nonreactive baking pan and place on the floor of the oven for flavorful steam. Place the tenderloin on a rack in a roasting pan and roast in the center of the oven for 45 to 50 minutes or until the tenderloin reaches an internal temperature of 140°F. Remove it from the oven and let it rest for 10 minutes before slicing.

Serve some red cabbage cole slaw as an accompaniment.

Yield: 6 to 8 servings

Grilled Pork Tenderloin with Adobo Red Chili Marinade

The marinade in this recipe does double duty as a rich adobo sauce. The tenderloin is marinated with the flavors of orange and chilies. You can also substitute tenderloin of kid, equal weights of Muscovy duck breasts, or even flank steak. The marinade has a flavor that can work with practically anything.

2-pound to 3-pound lean boneless pork loin
2 tablespoons of clarified butter or peanut oil (for sauteing indoors)
Adobo Red Chili Marinade (see page 67)
Presoaked mesquite chunks
1 cup fresh orange juice or poultry stock
(see page 210)

Leave the pork whole if you are grilling or roasting, but slice it 3/4 inch thick if you are planning to saute the meat. Place the tenderloin in a nonreactive container or a 1-gallon zip-lock plastic bag, pour the marinade over the tenderloin, and refrigerate overnight. Remove the tenderloin from the marinade.

To cook outdoors, bring the marinade to a low boil in a nonreactive saucepan, or microwave the marinade for 3 minutes on high. Thin it with either orange juice or chicken stock to use as a sauce. Build a charcoal fire in a kettle grill with a water pan, and add the mesquite chunks to the coals (see the Smokehouse Method on page 9). Add 2 to 3 cups of orange juice to the water pan. Lightly brush the top grill with vegetable oil. Place the tenderloin on the grill and smoke the tenderloin for 1 1/2 to 2 hours or until it reaches an internal temperature of 150°F. Remove it from the grill and let it rest for 10 minutes before slicing.

To cook indoors, you can saute or roast the meat. **To saute**, heat the peanut oil or clarified butter in a large skillet over medium-high heat. Add the slices and saute for 2 to 3 minute per side. Place the slices in a preheated warm oven (250° F) and deglaze the pan with the orange juice or stock. Add the remaining marinade and bring to a simmer. Reduce for a sauce.

To roast, preheat the oven to 375°F. Place a nonreactive baking pan with a cup or two of apple cider or orange juice on the floor of the oven for flavorful steam. Place the tenderloin on a rack in a roasting pan and roast in the center of the oven for 45 to 50 minutes, or until it reaches an internal temperature of 150°F. Remove it from the oven and let it rest for 10 minutes before slicing.

To serve, spoon 3 to 4 tablespoons of the adobo sauce onto a serving plate. Slice the tenderloin in 1/4-inch slices and overlap 3 to 4 slices on top of the sauce. Serve with a rice pilaf.

Yield: 6 main-course servings

Juniper and Orange-Cured Venison with Herb Salad

With this recipe, Philadelphia food consultant Aliza Green takes advantage of the farm-raised venison that's been finding its way into specialty food markets. She combines fresh herbs and citrus to make a salad that's an instant success for an elegant wintertime buffet or sit-down dinner.

Orange and Juniper Cure

2 tablespoons kosher salt
1 tablespoon crushed coriander seeds
1/4 cup juniper berries
2 tablespoons crushed black peppercorns
1 tablespoon crumbled bay leaves
1/4 cup grated orange zest (about 3 to 4 medium oranges)
2 tablespoons chopped fresh thyme leaves
2 tablespoons chopped savory leaves

Combine the above ingredients in a food processor and blend, then puree to a fine paste.

Yield: 2 cups

Venison

2 pounds venison loin (preferably fresh), trimmed of fat

Spread the paste on the venison and let cure in the refrigerator for 3 days, turning each day so that the spices penetrate evenly. The venison should feel firm when fully cured.

By cutting the salt to 1 teaspoon, the cure becomes a wonderful rub for a roast loin of venison. Marinate the venison in the refrigerator overnight. Roast in a preheated 450°F oven for 15 to 18 minutes, turning occasionally. Once cooked, the venison should be slightly pink inside.

Herb Salad

1/4 cup fresh lemon juice
1/4 cup fresh orange juice
1/2 cup extra-virgin olive oil
Kosher salt and freshly ground black pepper, to taste
1/2 cup packed flat-leaf parsley, chopped
1/4 cup chervil sprigs
1/4 cup tarragon sprigs

Combine the lemon and orange juice in a nonreactive mixing bowl. Whisk in the oil a little at a time. Add the salt and pepper. Toss together the herbs, add the dressing, and toss again.

Shallot-Buttered Toasts

4 tablespoons unsalted butter
2 to 3 slices rye bread, crusts removed
4 to 5 tablespoons chopped shallots

Butter the rye bread, top with chopped shallots, and toast until golden brown. To serve, slice the venison in thin (1/8-inch) slices. Sprinkle with the herb salad. Top with Shallot-Buttered Toasts.

Yield: 8 to 10 main-course servings

Medallions of Venison with Beaujolais-Raspberry Marinade

Dr. Anne Pearl and I developed this recipe on a late night phone call when she asked me what to do with a loin of venison. Now this recipe has become part of the repertoire in both kitchens. The trick behind the recipe is that when you cut the venison loin into medallions you have better surface penetration of the marinade—and more of that wonderful raspberry flavor.

Beaujolais-Raspberry Marinade (see page 79)
1 1/2 pounds loin of venison, cut into 12 medallions
2 tablespoons canola oil
Cracked black peppercorns, to taste
1 quart veal or game stock (see page 210)

Place the venison in a nonreactive container or a 1-gallon zip-lock plastic bag, pour the marinade over the venison and refrigerate for at least 12 hours, or up to 1 day.

Remove the venison from the marinade. Reserve 2 cups of the marinade for the sauce. Let the venison come to room temperature before sauteing.

Meanwhile make the sauce. Bring the reserved marinade to a low boil in a small nonreactive saucepan, reduce the heat, and simmer to reduce the marinade to about 1/2 cup. In a 2-quart nonreactive saucepan, reduce the stock to 1 1/2 cups. Combine with the reduced marinade and keep warm.

To saute, heat the canola oil in a large nonstick skillet over high heat. Lightly season the venison medallions with the pepper, place meat on the skillet, and sear on all sides. Reduce the heat and gently saute for about 4 minutes each side. Remove the venison from the pan, keep warm in an oven preheated to 250°F while you deglaze the skillet with the raspberry-Beaujolais sauce.

To serve, spoon about 1/2 cup of raspberry-Beaujolais sauce over the surface of each plate. Place 3 medallions on each plate and serve with orange-glazed carrots.

Yield: 4 main-course servings

10. Dipping
Sauces, Salsas,
and Chutneys

*D*ipping sauces are a marinade's encore. Here's where you can spotlight some of the flavors you've used in your marinade. With a couple of ramekins of dipping sauces centered on serving plates with skewered cuts of grilled meat, seafood, and vegetables, you can entertain with a potpourri of flavor, combining cuisines and tastes.

Dipping sauces can be anything from Thai peanut sauces to barbecue sauces. I often use leftover marinade ingredients as a base for a dipping sauce. The sauces need not be as intense as the marinade you've used.

Chances are you may come across a marinade recipe that you feel would make a marvelous dipping sauce. Go right ahead and use it—with one note of caution: Don't use leftover marinades as dipping sauces after they have been in contact with raw food. In all likelihood they will have bacteria present. Keep a little marinade off to the side for dipping before you begin marinating the food.

If you want to go with a contrasting flavor or texture to accompany your grilled food, then consider salsas and chutneys. Salsas and chutneys perform the role of smoke cutters. They can be sweet, tart, or piquant enough to pull your palate in directions other than where the grilled flavors were taking you. That flavorful push-pull experience is for me what grilling is about. You'll find in this chapter a few of my favorite zings.

Japanese Dipping Sauce

This is one of the most simple to prepare but intensely flavored dipping sauces.

1/2 cup light soy sauce
2 tablespoons rice vinegar
2 tablespoons mirin
3 tablespoons tamari sauce (available in Asian grocery stores)
1 tablespoon chopped pickled ginger (available in Asian grocery stores)

Combine the ingredients in a blender or food processor. Pour into a glass jar and refrigerate until ready to use. This will keep for 2 to 3 weeks in the refrigerator.

Yield: 1 cup

Recommended recipe accompaniments: *Negimaki* (see page 182) and in combination with these marinades: Sake Marinade (see page 52), Sesame-Rice Wine Marinade (see page 53), and Miso Marinade (see page 53)

Spicy Thai Dipping Sauce

There are as many Thai dipping sauces as there are Thai marinades. Any of the Thai marinade recipes in the book can double as a dipping sauce. Here's a simple one that's infallible with almost all variations of Thai grilled meat and fish. Feel free to add diced ginger or chopped lemongrass for flavor variations.

1/4 cup soy sauce
3 tablespoons rice wine vinegar
1 tablespoon sweet soya sauce (ketjap manis) or 1 teaspoon dark Chinese soy sauce and 2 teaspoons molasses
3 garlic cloves, crushed
2 to 3 tablespoons chopped fresh basil
2 Thai bird chilies, seeded and chopped

Combine the ingredients in a blender or food processor. Pour into a glass jar and refrigerate until ready to use. This will keep for 2 to 3 weeks in the refrigerator.

Yield: 1/2 cup

Recommended recipe accompaniments: Thai Marinated Chicken with a Cashew Sauce (see page 156), Thai Curry Beef (see page 181), and in combination with these marinades: Thai Marinade (see page 46), Thai Basil Marinade (see page 47), and Thai Curry Marinade (see page 47)

Sesame-Ginger Dipping Sauce

The perfect accompaniment for chicken wings or spare ribs.

1/4 cup light soy sauce
1 tablespoon Asian or domestic cold-pressed peanut oil
1 tablespoon oriental sesame oil
2 tablespoons dry sherry
2 tablespoons diced ginger root

Combine the ingredients in a blender or food processor. Pour into a glass jar and refrigerate until ready to use. This will keep for 1 to 2 weeks in the refrigerator.

Yield: 1/2 cup

Recommended recipe accompaniments: Szechuan Sesame Marinade (see page 50), Spicy Garlic Oriental Marinade (see page 51), Orange-Sesame Marinade (see page 51), Ginger Marinade (see page 52), Oriental Plum Sauce Marinade (see page 54), Honey-Hoisin Marinade (see page 54)

Vietnamese Mint Dipping Sauce

This lively dipping sauce, flavored with mint and serrano chilies, picks up its signature from nuoc mam, Vietnamese fish sauce.

1/4 cup mint leaves
1 serrano chili, seeded and diced
2 garlic cloves pressed
1/4 cup fresh lime juice
1 tablespoon grated lime zest
2 tablespoons nuoc mam (Vietnamese fish sauce) or nam pla

Combine the ingredients in a blender or food processor. Pour into a glass jar and refrigerate until ready to use. This will keep for 2 to 3 weeks in the refrigerator.

Yield: 1/2 cup

Recommended recipe accompaniments: Indonesian Shrimp (see page 130), and in combination with these marinades: Vietnamese Peanut Marinade (see page 48), Cilantro Marinade (see page 49), Asian Tamarind Marinade (see page 49), Indonesian Honey Chili Marinade (see page 49), Malaysian Marinade (see page 50)

Smoked Pepper Sauce

Because of its pronounced flavor, people swear that there's more to this recipe than the few ingredients. You can use either red or yellow peppers or streak a combination of the two pepper sauces in a plate for color.

1 to 2 whole yellow or red sweet peppers
1/2 cup homemade or good-quality mayonnaise
1 jalapeño pepper, seeded and chopped

In a covered grill with a water pan or water smoker, smoke the sweet pepper for no longer than 30 minutes. Do not let it burn. Seed and devein the pepper. Combine the smoked sweet pepper, mayonnaise, and jalapeño in a blender or food processor and process until smooth. Strain the sauce and pour into a glass jar and refrigerate until ready to use. This will keep for 2 to 3 weeks in the refrigerator.

Yield: 1/2 cup

Recommended recipe accompaniments: Lime-Cilantro Gravlax (see page 134), and in combination with these marinades on chicken: Honey Ancho Marinade (see page 66), Adobo Red Chili Marinade (see page 67), Chipotle Marinade (see page 69), New Mexican Pineapple Marinade (see page 70)

Cold Mustard Sauce

1/4 cup Dijon-style mustard
2 tablespoons fresh lemon juice
1/2 cup sour cream
2 to 3 tablespoons finely chopped tarragon, dill,
    or flat-leaf parsley
1 to 2 tablespoons prepared horseradish
    (optional)
Kosher salt and fresh cracked pepper, to taste

Combine all the ingredients in a blender or food processor. Pour into a glass jar and refrigerate until ready to use. This will keep for 2 to 3 weeks in the refrigerator.

Yield: 1 cup

Recommended recipe accompaniments: Juniper Gin-Cured Gravlax (see page 134), Lemon Mint Cured Brook Trout (see page 134), Lime-Cilantro Gravlax (see page 134), Marinated Pork Canapés (see page 196), Cold Fillet of Beef with Fresh Herb Paste (see page 185)

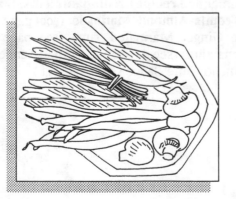

Middle East Dipping Sauce

This lemon-scented yogurt sauce is perfect spooned over kabobs of marinated lamb or chicken. For a quick, light dinner I like combining grilled vegetables and marinated lamb in a toasted pita bread topped with salad greens.

1 cup plain yogurt or laban
2 garlic cloves, pressed
1 to 2 tablespoons chopped fresh mint
3 tablespoons fresh lemon juice
1 tablespoon grated lemon zest
1/2 teaspoon cumin
Kosher salt and fresh cracked pepper, to taste

Combine the ingredients in a blender or food processor. Pour into a glass jar and refrigerate until ready to use. This will keep for 1 to 2 weeks in the refrigerator.

Yield: 1 cup

Recommended recipe accompaniments: Beef or Lamb Kabobs (see page 187), Shashlik (see page 188), and in combination with these marinades on chicken: Lemon Mint Marinade (see page 60), Tahini Marinade (see page 57), Lemon Sesame Seed Marinade (see page 57)

Pineapple-Jalapeño Salsa

Chef Jon Jividen's Pineapple-Jalapeño Salsa combines the sweet with the piquant. But what piques my interest is the saffron, which gives the salsa a nice neon yellow color and a simple savory accent to match the grilled marinated fish and shrimp.

1 cup chopped fresh pineapple
2 cups unsweetened pineapple juice
1/2 cup white wine vinegar
1/2 cup dark brown sugar
1 generous pinch saffron threads
1 fresh jalapeño, seeded and diced

To make the salsa, combine all the ingredients in a nonreactive saucepan and simmer, reducing by half. Serve the sauce warm as a main-course accompaniment. Or serve it cold with grilled swordfish kabobs. The salsa will last 1 to 2 weeks in the refrigerator.

Yield: 1 1/2 cups

Recommended recipe accompaniments: Grilled Vegetable Kabobs (see page 118), Lemon-Soy Swordfish Steaks (see page 143), Grilled Mahi-Mahi with Chardonnay Marinade (see page 141)

Sweet Corn Salsa

One of my favorite ways to prepare this salsa is to rub shucked corn with a little corn oil and grill outdoors for a nice smoky flavor. Freshly picked corn is essential because you want to contrast its sweetness with the tart lime and tangy serrano. This makes a nice accompaniment to the Orange Ginger Marinated Tuna.

3 ears fresh corn (cooked and then cooled)
1/2 cup diced red onion
1 tablespoon diced serrano chili
2 tablespoons avocado oil
2 to 3 tablespoons chopped fresh cilantro leaves
1/4 cup fresh lime juice
1 tablespoon grated lime zest
1 tablespoon maple syrup (optional, use if corn is not freshly picked)

Cut the corn kernels from the cobs and toss the kernels with remaining ingredients in a nonreactive bowl. Refrigerate the salsa until serving. This will last 1 to 2 weeks in the refrigerator.

Yield: 2 cups

Recommended recipe accompaniments: Scallops with Tequila-Almond Marinade (see page 131), Orange Ginger Marinated Tuna (see page 145), Chicken Fajitas (see page 158), Grilled Tenderloins with Ancho Chile Sauce (see page 178)

Peach Salsa

I like salsas that accompany grilled food with flavor as well as color. This salsa does both. This, the sweetest of the salsas, is contrasted with a slight flush of heat from the chilies. Its variety of flavors makes this one of the most flexible accompaniments in the book. It can go with practically any grilled dish. (In the cooler months, you may substitute pears for the peaches.)

1 1/2 pounds fresh peaches (5 to 6 small or 3 to 4 large peaches)
2 tablespoons dried currants
1 tablespoon dark rum
1/4 cup finely diced red sweet pepper
1/4 cup chopped red onion
1/4 cup peach vinegar (see page 31) or white wine vinegar
2 tablespoons grapeseed oil
1 to 2 tablespoons diced jalapeño pepper
3 to 4 tablespoons chopped fresh basil
3 garlic cloves, minced or pressed

Bring 3 quarts of water to a rolling boil and blanch the peaches for 2 to 3 minutes. Immediately plunge the peaches into a bowl of ice water to stop the cooking process. Peel and pit the peaches and coarsely chop. Soak the currants in the rum for about 1 hour. Combine the peaches and currants with the rest of the ingredients in a nonreactive bowl and refrigerate for 4 to 6 hours before serving. This will last 1 to 2 weeks in the refrigerator.

Yield: 3 to 4 cups

Recommended recipe accompaniments: Tuna with Beaujolais Marinade (see page 146), Grilled Chicken Kabobs with Provençal-Cognac Marinade (see page 162), Hickory-Smoked Pork Tenderloin with Plum-Rosemary Marinade (see page 197)

Cashew-Ginger Chutney

I use Chef Jon Jividen's Cashew-Ginger Chutney with grilled marinated lamb and pork tenderloins. But I confess I use it with a bowl of tortilla chips to satisfy my high-end snack food cravings. With this recipe you can distinctly taste each flavor in a single bite.

1 cup raw cashews
2 jalapeños, seeded and diced
1/4 cup chopped fresh ginger
1/2 cup fresh cilantro or mint leaves (or a mix of the two)
1 tablespoon kosher salt

Finely chop the nuts in a food processor; then add the remaining ingredients and process again until the chutney is well blended. (Note: You may want to thin it with water or yogurt to use it on pasta or as a dressing.)

Yield: 1 1/2 cups

Recommended recipe accompaniments: Indonesian Shrimp (see page 130), Marinated Quail with Nutmeg Sauce (see page 169), Thai Curry Beef (see page 181), Indonesian Grilled Lamb (see page 191)

Appendices:
Stock Options, Charts,
Mail Order Sources

*I*f there's one ingredient that can bring you to a grinding halt after you've started a recipe, it's stock. You can't run out and buy it or make it quickly in a microwave; either you have it on hand or you can't do that recipe. Not to worry, there are options.

Stock is a balance between the savory flavor of caramelized bones or meat, tempered by natural sweetness of the vegetables. Stock should never be too sweet (from too many vegetables) or too robust like a stew.

Making stock is easy. The technique for making seafood, poultry or brown (beef or veal) stock is almost the same and the payoff is great—added depth to your sauces. I'm going to give you some personal tricks of the trade to help you make clear, flavorful stock. They are browned bones, ice, and an oven.

1. Brown your bones. Heat releases flavor. You can extract more flavor by browning bones in a 400 degree oven than you can by simmering the bones in a stock pot.

2. Ice it down. I add a combination of ice and water (1/3 ice to 2/3 water) to my stock pot after I've added the brown bones and vegetables. The chemistry works something like this. Warm water on browned bones release tiny fat particles that cloud the stock. Cold water on browned bones releases the same particles, except they're bigger; they float to top and therefore are easier to skim.

3. Use your oven. Stock should never boil. Once a stock begins to boil a churning process begins and particles of fat, like an oil in a marinade, become emulsified. The stock becomes cloudy. Most 20-gallon stock pots will fit into a conventional oven. Remove all but the bottom rack. Preheat the oven to 400°F. Place the stock pot in the oven for 45 minutes, then reduce the heat to 250°F and let it simmer for the appropriate time.

When making stock on the stove top, there is a split second when the stock will break into a rapid boil. If you're around to catch it—great. If not, you will have cloudy stock. The oven technique gives you an even heat like the steam jackets or stock cauldrons found in large commercial kitchens. This technique is infallible.

I like to use a combination of bones and meat. If I'm marinating duck breasts, every piece of fat-trimmed meat is browned along with the bones and placed in the stock pot. Butchers may also sell you additional parts.

If you're using stock for duck or game birds, you can easily halve the proportions.

If you're making chicken stock, make as much as you can. It will make a great soup base.

Poultry or Game Bird Stock

12 to 14 pounds poultry carcasses, trimmings, or stewing hens (for chicken stock)
2 to 3 coarsely chopped onions
1 cup coarsely chopped carrots
1/2 cup coarsely chopped celery
9 to 10 quarts cold water (with some additional ice)
1 cup dry white wine
1 bouquet garni (1 bay leaf, a few celery tops, parsley, thyme)
4 to 5 juniper berries

Preheat the oven to 400°F. Place the bones and trimmings in a roasting pan and brown them in the oven until they turn golden brown (about 45 minutes to an hour). Do not burn. Remove the bones from the pan and add them to a 20-gallon stock pot.

Add the onions, carrots and celery to the roasting pan and roast until the vegetables are slightly browned (about 20 minutes). Add the vegetables to the stock pot, deglaze the roasting pan with the wine, and empty the contents into the stock pot.

Pour sufficient cold water and ice into the stock pot to barely cover the bones and vegetables. Return the pot to the oven for about 45 minutes, then reduce the heat to 250°F and simmer for 3 to 4 hours. Skim the stock periodically. Strain the stock, discard the solids, and cool the stock uncovered in the refrigerator or freezer.

When the stock is chilled, you can remove the remaining fat on top with a large spoon. The stock will keep for 3 to 4 days refrigerated, about 4 to 6 months frozen.

Yield: 8 quarts

Variations

Veal or Brown Stock. Replace the poultry with an equal amount of beef shanks and knuckle bones. Proceed with the above recipe but simmer the stock in the oven for 6 to 8 hours.

Glace de Viande. Glace de Viande is reduced poultry, beef, or game stock that provides sauces with a good foundation. It's basically a 4 to 1 stove-top reduction of any stock to a syrupy viscosity. It freezes well and is truly worth your time. One quart of chilled stock will yield about 1 cup of Glace de Viande when reduced.

Marinades at a Glance

Need a recipe for marinated salmon? How about a marinade for some chicken wings for a potluck. This chart will tell you at a glance what marinade to use on different cuts of meat or fish.

You'll find all the recipes listed in the chart in the order as they appear in Chapters 4 and 5. The recipes are grouped by regions and ingredients. Across the top of the chart you'll find different cuts of food divided into three main sections: seafood, poultry and meat. Match the marinade with the suggested cut of food by the marinating times in the boxes. For cooking techniques see Chapters 7, 8, and 9.

	Seafood		Poultry					Beef		Lamb	Pork			
	Shrimp	Fish—Fillets/Steaks	Chicken Breasts	Chicken Wings	Turkey	Duck	Game Birds	Steaks/Kabobs	Roasts, Briskets, Flanks Steaks	Kabobs	Tenderloins	Chops	Spare Ribs	Venison
Basic Marinades														
Basic Fish Marinade (pg. 43)	2-4 hrs	2-4 hrs												
Basic Chicken Marinade (pg. 44)			3-4 hrs	4-6 hrs										
Basic Beef Marinade (pg. 44)								6-8 hrs	12 hrs					6-8 hrs
Port Marinade for Game Fowl (p. 45)						8 hrs	4-6 hrs							
Asian-Style Marinades														
Asian Marinade (p. 45)			3-4 hrs					6-8 hrs	12 hrs					
Korean Beef Marinade (p. 46)			3-4 hrs					6-8 hrs			6-8 hrs			
Thai Marinade (p. 46)	2-3 hrs		3-4 hrs					6-8 hrs			6-8 hrs			
Thai Basil Marinade (p. 47)	2-4 hrs		4-6 hrs											
Thai Curry Marinade (p. 47)	2-4 hrs		4-6 hrs	6-8 hrs					Over-night					
Vietnamese Peanut Marinade (p. 48)	3-4 hrs		4-6 hrs											
Cilantro Marinade (p. 48)	2-4 hrs	2-4 hrs	4-6 hrs											
Asian Tamarind Marinade (p. 49)	2-4 hrs	3-4 hrs												
Indonesian Honey Chili Marinade (p. 49)			6-8 hrs			6-8 hrs	8 hrs						8 hrs	

	Seafood		Poultry					Beef		Lamb	Pork			
	Shrimp	Fish—Fillets/Steaks	Chicken Breasts	Chicken Wings	Turkey	Duck	Game Birds	Steaks/Kabobs	Roasts, Briskets, Flanks Steaks	Kabobs	Tenderloins	Chops	Spare Ribs	Venison
Malaysian Marinade *(pg. 50)*	3-4 hrs		4-6 hrs								3-4 hrs			
Szechuan Sesame Marinade *(pg. 50)*	3-4 hrs		4-6 hrs								4-6 hrs			
Spicy Garlic Oriental Marinade *(pg. 51)*				8 hrs									Over-night	
Orange-Sesame Marinade *(pg. 51)*	3-4 hrs		4-6 hrs			6-8 hrs								
Ginger Marinade *(pg. 52)*	3-4 hrs		4-6 hrs			6-8 hrs				3-4 hrs				
Sake Marinade *(pg. 52)*	1-2 hrs		1-2 hrs	6-8 hrs									6-8 hrs	
Sesame-Rice Wine Marinade *(pg. 53)*		2-3 hrs	4-6 hrs					4-6 hrs						
Miso Marinade *(pg. 53)*		1-2 hrs												
Oriental Plum Sauce Marinade *(pg. 54)*			4-6 hrs	6-8 hrs									Over-night	
Honey-Hoisin Marinade *(pg. 54)*				6-8 hrs									Over-night	
Teriaki/Yakitori *(pg. 55)*	3-4 hrs		4-6 hrs					3-4 hrs						
Curry Marinade *(pg. 55)*	2-3 hrs			6-8 hrs									Over-night	
Sake-Mustard Marinade *(pg. 56)*	2-4 hrs		4-6 hrs	6-8 hrs										
Lemongrass Marinade *(pg. 56)*	2-3 hrs													
Mediterranean-Style Marinades														
Tahini Marinade *(pg. 57)*		2-4 hrs												
Lemon Sesame Seed Marinade *(pg. 57)*	1-2 hrs	1-2 hrs												
Herbes de Provence Marinade *(pg. 58)*		2-3 hrs												

	Seafood		Poultry					Beef		Lamb	Pork			
	Shrimp	Fish—Fillets/Steaks	Chicken Breasts	Chicken Wings	Turkey	Duck	Game Birds	Steaks/Kabobs	Roasts, Briskets, Flanks Steaks	Kabobs	Tenderloins	Chops	Spare Ribs	Venison
Basic Italian Marinade *(pg. 58)*	2-4 hrs	2-4 hrs	2-4 hrs											
Basil Marinade *(pg. 59)*		3-4 hrs												
Lemon-Sorrel Marinade *(pg. 59)*		2-3 hrs												
Lemon-Caper Marinade *(pg. 60)*		2-3 hrs												
Lemon Mint Marinade *(pg. 60)*		2-4 hrs	2-4 hrs					4-6 hrs		4-6 hrs				
Tapenade Marinade *(pg. 61)*		2-4 hrs												
Balsamic-Herbal Marinade *(pg. 61)*	1-3 hrs	1-3 hrs	2-4 hrs											
Tomato-Basil Marinade *(pg. 62)*		2-4 hrs												
Spicy Tomato Marinade *(pg. 62)*		2-4 hrs												
Laurel and Lemon Marinade *(pg. 63)*	1-2 hrs	2-3 hrs												
Marinating Mustards														
Mustard-Dill Marinade *(pg. 63)*		2-4 hrs												
South Carolina Mustard Mustard *(pg. 64)*			4-6 hrs	6-8 hrs										
Mustard-Soy Marinade *(pg. 64)*	1-3 hrs	1-3 hrs	2-4 hrs	6-8 hrs								3-4 hrs	Over-night	
Mustard-Ginger Marinade *(pg. 65)*		2-3 hrs	4-6 hrs	6-8 hrs						4-6 hrs		4-6 hrs	Over-night	
"New World" Marinades														
Southwest Chili Corn Marinade *(pg. 65)*		2-4 hrs	2-4 hrs									3-4 hrs	Over-night	
Honey Ancho Marinade *(pg. 66)*			2-4 hrs	6-8 hrs		6-8 hrs						3-4 hrs	Over-night	

	Seafood		Poultry					Beef		Lamb	Pork			
	Shrimp	Fish—Fillets/Steaks	Chicken Breasts	Chicken Wings	Turkey	Duck	Game Birds	Steaks/Kabobs	Roasts, Briskets, Flanks Steaks	Kabobs	Tenderloins	Chops	Spare Ribs	Venison
Smoked Pepper Marinade for Seafood (*pg. 66*)	1-3 hrs	◆												
Adobo Red Chili Marinade (*pg. 67*)			2-4 hrs	6-8 hrs								3-4 hrs	Overnight	
Orange Chipotle Marinade (*pg. 68*)						6-8 hrs					4-6 hrs	4-6 hrs		
Yucatecan Citrus Marinade (*pg. 68*)	2-3 hrs	2-3 hrs	2-4 hrs											
Yucatecan Achiote Marinade (*pg. 69*)	2-3 hrs	2-3 hrs	2-4 hrs							4-6 hrs		3-4 hrs		
Chipotle Marinade (*pg. 69*)				6-8 hrs									Overnight	
Pineapple-Chili Marinade (*pg. 70*)	2-3 hrs	2-3 hrs	2-4 hrs						4-6 hrs			3-4 hrs	6-8 hrs	
Sofrito Marinade (*pg. 70*)			2-4 hrs						4-6 hrs		3-4 hrs		6-8 hrs	
Passion Fruit Marinade (*pg. 71*)	2-3 hrs		2-4 hrs										6-8 hrs	
Yellow Hell (Mango Marinade) (*pg. 71*)	2-3 hrs		2-4 hrs	6-8 hrs								6-8 hrs		
The Dreaded Red Menace (*pg. 72*)	2-3 hrs		2-4 hrs											
Zesty Fruit Marinades														
Lemon Marinade (*pg. 72*)			2-4 hrs	6-8 hrs			4-6 hrs							
Lime Marinade (*pg. 73*)		2-3 hrs	2-4 hrs				4-6 hrs							
Hot Chili Lime Marinade (*pg. 73*)				6-8 hrs									6-8 hrs	
Lemon Ginger Marinade (*pg. 74*)			2-4 hrs	6-8 hrs			4-6 hrs				4-6 hrs	4-6 hrs	Overnight	
Espresso Lemon Marinade (*pg. 74*)			2-4 hrs	6-8 hrs							4-6 hrs	4-6 hrs	Overnight	
Orange Ginger Marinade (*pg. 75*)		2-3 hrs	2-4 hrs	6-8 hrs		6-8 hrs					4-6 hrs	4-6 hrs	Overnight	

◆ Fillets: 1-3 hrs, Steaks: 2-4 hrs

	Seafood		Poultry					Beef		Lamb	Pork			
	Shrimp	Fish—Fillets/Steaks	Chicken Breasts	Chicken Wings	Turkey	Duck	Game Birds	Steaks/Kabobs	Roasts, Briskets, Flanks Steaks	Kabobs	Tenderloins	Chops	Spare Ribs	Venison
Orange Tarragon Marinade (pg. 75)			6-8** hrs				4-6 hrs							
Bitter Orange Marinade (pg. 76)											Over-night*	6-8 hrs		
Orange Saffron Marinade (pg. 76)	2-4 hrs	2-3 hrs												
Apricot Marinade (pg. 77)			4-6 hrs	6-8 hrs		6-8 hrs						3-4 hrs		
Plum Cassis Marinade (pg. 77)			4-6** hrs		Over-night	4-6 hrs	4-6 hrs				6-8 hrs	6-8 hrs	6-8 hrs	
Cranberry Marinade (pg. 78)			6-8** hrs	6-8 hrs	Over-night	6-8 hrs					8 hrs-Ov.			
Blueberry Marinade (pg. 78)			3-4 hrs				4-6 hrs							
Raspberry Marinade (pg. 79)			4-6 hrs		8-10 hrs	8-10 hrs	8-10 hrs							
Spirited Marinades														
Beaujolais-Raspberry Marinade (pg. 79)			3-4 hrs			6-8 hrs	6-8 hrs							8 hrs-Ov.
Sage-Port Wine Marinade (pg. 80)						6-8 hrs		6-8 hrs						8 hrs-Ov.
Madeira Marinade (pg. 80)								6-8 hrs						8 hrs-Ov.
Asian Sauternes Marinade (pg. 81)	2-3 hrs		4-6 hrs											
Amber Beer Marinade for Braised Ribs (pg. 81)				6-8 hrs									8 hrs-Ov.	
Spicy Beer Marinade (pg. 82)								3-4 hrs			6-8 hrs	6-8 hrs	8 hrs-Ov.	
Cassis Marinade (pg. 82)			2-4 hrs		8-10 hrs	6-8 hrs	8-10 hrs				6-8 hrs	6-8 hrs	8 hrs-Ov.	
Cointreau-Orange Marinade (pg. 83)			2-4 hrs		8-10 hrs	6-8 hrs	8-10 hrs							
Hazelnut Galliano Marinade (pg. 83)		2-4 hrs												

*Whole pork roast **Whole chicken

	Seafood		Poultry					Beef		Lamb	Pork			
	Shrimp	Fish—Fillets/Steaks	Chicken Breasts	Chicken Wings	Turkey	Duck	Game Birds	Steaks/Kabobs	Roasts, Briskets, Flanks Steaks	Kabobs	Tenderloins	Chops	Spare Ribs	Venison
Vodka Dill Marinade *(pg. 84)*		2-4 hrs												
Juniper-Lemon Marinade *(pg. 84)*		2-4 hrs												
Scotch Whiskey Marinade *(pg. 85)*		2-3 hrs	4-6 hrs											
Maple Bourbon Marinade *(pg.85)*			2-3 hrs	6-8 hrs							3-4 hrs	4-6 hrs	6-8 hrs	
Rum-Rosemary Marinade *(pg. 86)*	2-3 hrs		2-3 hrs	6-8 hrs										
Hot Chili Rum Marinade *(pg. 86)*				6-8 hrs									6-8 hrs	
Yogurt Marinades														
Spicy Yogurt Marinade *(pg. 87)*			3-4 hrs							3-4 hrs				
Yogurt Dill Marinade *(pg. 87)*		2-4 hrs												
Rubs and Pastes														
Rosemary Seasoning Rub *(pg. 91)*		2-4 hrs	4-6 hrs							3-6 hrs				
Mixed Peppercorn for Beef *(pg. 91)*								3-6 hrs	3-6 hrs					
Chipotle Rub *(pg. 92)*								6-8 hrs						
Achiote Chipotle Rub *(pg. 92)*			4-6 hrs	6-8 hrs				4-6 hrs		4-6 hrs			8 hrs-Ov.	
Yucatecan Rub *(pg. 93)*			4-6 hrs					6-8 hrs				3-4 hrs		
Cinnamon-Chili Rub for Poultry *(pg. 93)*			4-6 hrs	6-8 hrs	8 hrs-Ov.									
Cumin Spice Rub *(pg. 94)*	2-4 hrs		4-6 hrs		8 hrs-Ov.					4-6 hrs				
Texas Dry Rub *(pg. 94)*				6-8 hrs					8 hrs-Ov.				8 hrs-Ov.	

	Seafood		Poultry					Beef		Lamb	Pork			
	Shrimp	Fish—Fillets/Steaks	Chicken Breasts	Chicken Wings	Turkey	Duck	Game Birds	Steaks/Kabobs	Roasts, Briskets, Flanks Steaks	Kabobs	Tenderloins	Chops	Spare Ribs	Venison
Tumbleweed Spice Rub (*pg. 95*)				6-8 hrs				3-4 hrs	8 hrs-Ov.				6-8 hrs	
Southern Barbecue Rub (*pg. 95*)									8 hrs-Ov.				8 hrs-Ov.	
Sour Mash Pink Peppercorn Rub (*pg. 96*)		2-4 hrs						6-8 hrs						
Jerk Rub (*pg. 96*)	2-4 hrs		4-6 hrs	6-8 hrs				4-6 hrs		4-6 hrs		3-4 hrs	8 hrs-Ov.	
Cajun Rub (*pg. 97*)			4-6 hrs						6-8 hrs				8 hrs-Ov.	
Sambal Mint Paste (*pg. 97*)	2-4 hrs		4-6 hrs										8 hrs-Ov.	
Wasabi Rub (*pg. 98*)								6-8 hrs	8 hrs-Ov.					
Hoisin Sesame Paste (*pg. 98*)	2-3 hrs		4-6 hrs							3-4 hrs	8 hrs-Ov.			
Herb Pesto Rub (*pg. 99*)		3-4 hrs	4-6 hrs							3-4 hrs				
Charmoula (*pg. 99*)	2-3 hrs	2-3 hrs	4-6 hrs				4-6 hrs							
Roasted Garlic and Jalapeño Paste (*pg. 100*)	2-4 hrs	2-4 hrs												
Tamarind Chipotle Paste (*pg. 100*)	2-4 hrs	2-4 hrs								3-6 hrs				
New Mexican Red Pepper Paste (*pg. 101*)			4-6 hrs	6-8 hrs					8 hrs-Ov.				8 hrs-Ov.	
Cilantro Ginger Pesto (*pg. 101*)	2-4 hrs		3-4 hrs											
Lemon Cumin Paste (*pg. 102*)	2-4 hrs		4-6 hrs	6-8 hrs				4-6 hrs		4-6 hrs				
Indian Spice Paste (*pg. 102*)	2-4 hrs		4-6 hrs							4-6 hrs				

I am the first to admit it—I'm a catalog junkie. Nothing gives me greater pleasure than to circle the little numbers on those reader response cards that keep falling out of my cooking magazines. For specialty condiments, imported seasonings, and hard-to-get ethnic staples, the mail is often the best source.

Here's a list of a few places where you can get some of the esoteric ingredients in the recipes that I feel you couldn't possibly live without. Where possible, I listed toll-free numbers. In fact, I called them and let them know that a few of you would be calling. They all said fine.

Asian Staples

De Wildt Imports, Inc.
20 Compton Way
Hamilton Square, NJ 08969
800-338-3433
Huge selection of Asian staples, great for one-stop mail order shopping. Catalog available.

Kam Man Food Products
200 Canal St.
New York, NY 10013
212-571-0330
One of the best sources for Chinese ingredients.

Katagiri & Co.
224 E. 59th St.
New York, NY 10022
212-755-3566
Catalog available, specializes in Japanese ingredients.

Indian Spices

House of Spices
76-17 Broadway
Jackson Heights
Queens, NY 11373
718-476-1577
One of the best collection of Indian and Pakistani ingredients under one roof.

Louisiana Hot Sauces and Southern Ingredients

New Orleans School of Cooking
620 Decatur St.
New Orleans, LA 70130
800-237-4841
Catalog available. Great source for hot sauces, Zatarain's Fish Fry, Creole mustards, Steen's vinegars and syrups. Nice catalog.

Cane Syrup and Cane Vinegar

C. S. Steen Mill, Inc.
Abbeville, LA 70510
318-893-1654
Cane syrup is less musky than molasses; the cane vinegar is a wonderful substitute for cider vinegar. Worth writing for their recipe booklet.

Chilies

La Cantina
6140 Brocton Rd.
Hatboro, PA 19040
215-925-8085
My local source for dried chipotle and dried habañeros as well as anchos, guadjillos, and Scotch bonnet chilies. They will mail order.

Old Southwest Trading Company
P.O. Box 7545
Albuquerque, NM 87194
800-747-2861
Catalog available. Nice collection of Southwest ingredients.

Casados Farms
P.O. Box 852
San Juan Pueblo, NM 87566
505-852-2692
Catalog available. Excellent source for fresh and dried chilies including habañeros (Scotch bonnet) chilies.

Dried Herbs and Spices

Penn Herbs
603 North 2nd St.
Philadelphia, PA 19123
800-523-9971
Catalog available. Penn Herbs is basically a medicinal herb house that has one of the freshest and largest collection of dried herbs and spices (and even flower petals) you can find. Perfect place for hard-to-get culinary herbs and spices. This is a source for making Herbes de Provence.

Spice House
1048 N. Old World 3rd St.
Milwaukee, WI
414-272-0977
Catalog available. Nice collection of international spice blends as well as individual herbs and spices. Great catalog.

Flavored Vinegars

Assouline & Ting
324 Brown St.
Philadelphia, PA 19123
800-521-4491
Catalog available. Joel Assouline makes all his flavored vinegars on premises. He could probably write a cookbook himself. This is a good ingredient source for oils and dried wild mushrooms as well.

Hot Sauces, Mustards, and Condiments

Spectacular Sauces
P.O. Box 30010
Alexandria, VA 22310
800-999-4949
Nice catalog with good running commentary on sauces; lots of esoteric flavors here. One of the best collection of hot sauces by mail.

Olive Oils, Vinegars, Mustards, etc.

Just about all of the marinating ingredients you'll ever need can be had at these established sources. All have catalogs and will mail order in a hurry.

Balducci's
424 Sixth Ave.
New York, NY 10011
800-247-2450

Dean & Deluca
560 Broadway
New York, NY 10012
800-221-7714

G. B. Ratto, International Grocers
821 Washington St.
Oakland, CA 94607
800-325-3483

Rafal Spice Co.
2521 Russell St.
Detroit, MI 48207
800-228-4276

Mail Order Game

If it's wild, they have it. They will ship by overnight delivery. These game sources are cheaper, quicker, and safer, and above all, much gentler than hunting trips. Catalogs available.

D'Artagnon, Inc.
399 St. Paul Ave.
Jersey City, NJ 07306
800-327-8246

The Game Exchange
107 Quint St.
San Francisco, CA 94188
800-GAME USA

Seasoned Smoke

Smoking Woods Char Broil
1037 Front St.
P.O. Box 1300
Columbus, GA 31993
800-241-8981
I've listed this source for smoking woods such as fruitwoods, pecan, vine clippings, as well as hickory and mesquite chunks and chips. Great source for grilling accessories.

INDEX

The Crossing Press
publishes many cookbooks.
For a free catalog, call toll-free
800-777-1048